Taming the Revolution in Nineteenth-Century Spain

Andrea Acle-Kreysing graduated from El Colegio de México, and obtained her master and PhD degrees from the University of Cambridge, UK. She has been awarded with a fellowship from the Humboldt Foundation for her Habilitation project at the universities of Munich and Leipzig.

Andrea Acle-Kreysing

Taming the Revolution in Nineteenth-Century Spain

Jaime Balmes and Juan Donoso Cortés

Campus Verlag
Frankfurt/New York

ISBN 978-3-593-51598-4 Print
ISBN 978-3-593-45123-7 E-Book (PDF)
ISBN 978-3-593-45124-4 E-Book (EPUB)

All rights reserved. No part of this book may be reproduced or transmitted in any form or by any means, electronic or mechanical, including photocopying, recording, or by any information storage and retrieval system, without permission in writing from the publishers.
Despite careful control of the content Campus Verlag GmbH cannot be held liable for the content of external links. The content of the linked pages is the sole responsibility of their operators.
Copyright © 2022 Campus Verlag GmbH, Frankfurt am Main
Cover design: Campus Verlag GmbH, Frankfurt am Main
Cover illustration: Juan Donoso Cortés (standing) and Jaime Balmes (seated), oil on canvas by Luis Brochetón y Muguruza (1848) © Wikimedia Commons, Real Academia de la Historia, Madrid
Typesetting: le-tex xerif
Printed in the United States of America

www.campus.de
www.press.uchicago.edu

The lives of most men are a web of contradictions that are simply impossible to explain; if one were to give any importance to this fact, nothing less would follow than that we would need to demand that all men should adjust their conduct to their ideas, and that whoever held a conviction should always act in accordance with it. But when and where has this ever been a common practice?

Jaime Balmes, Letters to a Sceptic in Religious Matters (1846).

Contents

Acknowledgements 9

Introduction 11

    I.   Historical and biographical overview 13

    II. Catholic Spain: myths and realities 21

Chapter 1: Spain belongs to Europe 35

    I.   Donoso: man of letters with a European outlook 37

    II. Donoso: a politician with a European outlook 43

    III. Balmes & European civilisation 56

    IV. Balmes: Spain as a Catholic nation 64

Chapter 2: Varieties of Spanish Liberalism 73

    I.   The ambiguities of the *moderados* 74

    II. A marriage of convenience 83

    III. Donoso & the Constitution of 1845 92

    IV. Balmes & the people of Spain 99

Chapter 3: The Politics of Spanish Catholicism 111

    I.   Old and new trends in Church-State relations 113

    II. Balmes *versus* Donoso (1844–1845) 120

    III. Balmes: updating Spanish Catholicism 130

    IV. The impact of conversion on Donoso's thought 139

Chapter 4: Spain and Catholic Europe 153
 I. Balmes, Donoso and a liberal Pope 155
 II. A turning point: 1848 164
 III. An essay on pessimism 175
 IV. The return to order & authority 188
 V. Afterlives 197

Conclusions 203

Bibliography 209
 Primary / Nineteenth-century sources 209
 Secondary sources 214

Index 227

Acknowledgements

This book is the revised version of my PhD dissertation, completed at the University of Cambridge (2012). While incorporating the most recent publications in the field, I have at the same time sought to preserve the youthful tone of the original. The art of finding one's own voice amidst a vast sea of scholarship remains the most valuable lesson I learned from Alison Sinclair, my PhD supervisor at the Department of Spanish & Portuguese in the Faculty of Modern & Medieval Languages. Ten years later, she continues to be an unwavering source of help, inspiration and encouragement. During my years as a graduate student from 2006 to 2011, I profited immensely from meeting leading experts in both European and intellectual history. I would thus like to express my profound gratitude to Christopher Clark, David Brading, Gareth Stedman Jones, Javier Herrero, Javier Fernández Sebastián, Josep Fradera, María del Carmen Sáenz, Michael Costeloe, Emile Perreau-Saussine † and, last but not least, Gregorio Alonso – to whom I owe the title of this book. Furthermore, I would like to thank my PhD thesis examiners, Andrew Ginger and Guy Thomson, whose comments proved invaluable when drafting this book. Additionally, I am indebted to Xosé Manoel Núñez Seixas for helping me to make the transition from British to German academia.

Even if taking the road less travelled has presented its challenges, it has also brought a reward: the ability to feel at home in several countries and their respective scholarly traditions. The seeds of intellectual curiosity sown by my former professors at El Colegio de México (Francisco Gil Villegas, Anne Staples, Andrés Lira, Ilán Bizberg and Rafael Segovia †) have gone on to bear fruit.

In navigating the unexpected, I have unfailingly found solace and wisdom in Alfredo and Lourdes, my parents, *mi patria*. After completing a research project in Dresden that was born in Cambridge, I wish to honour cherished memories of friendships and conversation with Hannah Mowat, Julieta Falcón, Clara Panozzo, Stefanie Gänger, Fabián Rosales, Carrie Gibson and Mariama Ifode. Finally, my heartfelt thanks go to Clara, Jakob and Moritz Kreysing for being my joy, *meine Heimat*.

Introduction[1]

Writing a book about the political thought of Jaime Balmes and Juan Donoso Cortés is an ideal opportunity to reflect upon the uses and abuses of intellectual history. Regarded as the two major Catholic thinkers in Spain between the 1830s and 1850s, Balmes and Donoso have continued to be influential on subsequent generations of conservative and right-wing thinkers. Adapted to new scenarios, their ideas have often been simplified and subjected to misappropriations, in order either to suit them to the needs of a given political agenda, or to affirm the belonging of Balmes and Donoso to an allegedly timeless Catholic tradition. For example, in the context of Francoist Spain (1939–1975), Balmes and Donoso became incorporated into the narrative of the Two Spains, the liberal and the conservative, whose allegedly irreconcilable differences were seen as leading to the outbreak of the Spanish Civil War (1936–1939). Seen from outside Spain, Balmes and Donoso possess a steady reputation as traditionalists who, seeking to reverse the revolutionary tide that swept through both Spain and Europe, raised what sympathetic commentators referred to as the timely banners of order and authority. To put it shortly, it is in their guise as conservatives, traditionalists, Catholic apologists and even as counter-revolutionaries that Balmes and Donoso persist in the historical imagination. It might be added that, in the twentieth century, the thought of Donoso experienced a revival, as the anti-liberal views of his later years were (in)famously revived by the German political theorist and Nazi sympathiser Carl Schmitt (1888–1985).

The problem is that, when deployed in the actual historical period in which Balmes and Donoso lived and wrote, these categories are ill-fitting and inaccurate. Instead of the clear-cut conflict between a liberal and a

---

[1] All translations from Spanish, German and French sources are, otherwise indicated, mine.

conservative Spain, what then existed was an heterogeneous liberal party divided – at least – into two main branches, as well as a relatively diverse traditionalist and monarchic opinion, deeply affected by the division of the royal family into two competing branches. Moreover, when entering into biographical details, the idea that Balmes and Donoso struggled for an identical cause does not wholly match reality. Whereas the worldly lawyer Donoso remained close to the *moderados* (moderate liberals) for most of his life, the secular priest Balmes eschewed political labels altogether. Despite sharing a similar goal, that of maintaining the centrality of Spain's traditional institutions, the Church and the monarchy, they applied dissimilar means to its attainment. Last but not least, while the writings of Balmes prefigured a relatively open-minded and socially-oriented Catholicism, Donoso ended up positing Christianity as the highest social good, yet one incompatible with both liberalism and socialism. Nevertheless, despite the many differences between them, the trajectories of Balmes and Donoso did run parallel to each other, so that it is possible to see their works as variations on a same theme (Koch 1993: 108–109). However, if an accurate sense of the actual (i.e. historical, contextual and even comparative) significance of Balmes and Donoso in mid-nineteenth century Spain is to be gained, it makes sense to focus upon their lives, rather than just in their afterlives as Catholic or conservative icons.

My intention in this book is thus twofold: first, to reconstruct the trajectories of Balmes and Donoso, highlighting the nuances and unresolved tensions within their work. Therefore, instead of presenting them as brothers-in-arms (who, it might be added, avoided any personal acquaintance during their lives), my aim is to show the complexity of contemporary Spanish political thought. This aim matches the latest developments in the study of nineteenth-century Spanish political and intellectual history. A deliberate effort has been made to escape dualistic interpretations of this period, that is, seen as torn between extremes: tradition *versus* modernity, reaction *versus* revolution, etc. In this sense, what the study of thinkers such as Balmes and Donoso shows, is that the very act of defending tradition was an essentially modern endeavour. It also becomes clear that tradition is not perennial but contingent upon time and place, and thus often tailored (i.e. modernised) to suit a variety of political agendas. Hence the need to insist upon how Balmes and Donoso engaged in a political as well as a semantic struggle, as they sought to endow key concepts – such as revolution, civilisation or people – with a specific content, that is, one among many other competing ones. In doing

INTRODUCTION   13

so, they were well aware of wider European developments, and sought actively to discredit the stereotypical view of Spain as a backward and isolated country.

The title of this book – *Taming the Revolution in Spain* – serves as an apt description of the leitmotiv behind the ideas of Balmes and Donoso. They saw themselves not as merely as thinkers but rather as actors capable of channelling and tempering Spain's social and political development. In doing so, they followed a key imperative: that of keeping revolution at bay. In the writings of Balmes and Donoso, revolution acquired a variety of meanings. At the most basic level, it conjured up the spectre of anarchy, that is, a situation in which consecrated rights and properties would no longer be respected. Due to its sudden and disruptive character, a revolution was also seen as antithetic to the gradual and orderly development that, it was claimed, could only be achieved by long-standing institutions. However, for Balmes and Donoso, the revolution was much more than an imminent threat, deployed either to chastise political opponents or to cast predictions upon future developments. Ascertaining the meaning of revolution also meant looking back to past events, such as the French Revolution (1789), but mostly to Spain's own revolution – what historians mostly refer to as the liberal revolution – at the turn of the nineteenth century. This had hailed the advent of a new institutional framework in Spain, as well as novel discourses of justifying and exercising political power. In this book, I deliberately focus upon the character of Balmes and Donoso as conservative (re)interpreters of *this* revolution, yet without assuming that such outlook would inexorably lead to a negation of Spain's basic liberal (i.e. constitutional) order. The actual story, as I hope to show, was much more complicated.

I. Historical and biographical overview

When Balmes and Donoso were born, Spain was largely occupied by Napoleonic troops. The so-called War of Independence (1808–1814) against France was driven by an incipient nationalism which brought together, albeit temporarily, a series of divergent visions on the future of Spain. On the one hand, there was a conservative majority of the clergy who identified the French invader with the 'impious' ideas of the Enlightenment and the French Revolution, as these threatened the values of the *ancien régime* and the privileged position of the Church. On the other, there were the *liberales* who sought not only to set Spain free from French rule, but also to endow it with new institutions. This group effectively continued the reforming spirit of the eighteenth-century Bourbon monarchs of Spain, while heralding the emergence of a new way of thinking and doing politics. The Cortes assembled at Cádiz elaborated a liberal-inspired constitution (1812) which created a constitutional monarchy that derived its legitimacy from the sovereignty of the nation. Though willing to uphold the traditional values of Spain (i.e. Catholicism was established as the official religion), the new constitution inaugurated a new era of Church-State relations, as the right to interfere in ecclesiastical matters, previously a prerogative of the monarch, came now under the control of the nation's representatives.

When Fernando VII was restored to the throne in 1814, Spain returned to absolutism and the liberal legislation was declared null and void. Except for the brief parenthesis of the Liberal Triennium (1821–1823), in which the Constitution of Cádiz was restored and a bolder legislation related to the Church put into practice, Fernando VII was the ruler of Spain until 1833. The last years of his reign were marked by conflicts among court factions: María Cristina, queen consort, managed to secure the succession to the throne for her daughter Isabel. In 1830, Fernando issued a Pragmatic Sanction which, by allowing female succession to the crown, implicitly excluded his brother Don Carlos from power (Canal 2000: 52–3). Following the king's death in 1833, the Bourbon family split into two branches which contended for the succession to the throne in what became known as the First Carlist War (1833–1840), allegedly 'the bloodiest civil war in nineteenth-century Europe' (Lawrence 2014: 20). Don Carlos resorted to war in order to oppose Isabel's right to succession. Carlism, as his movement came to be known, upheld a traditionalist and reactionary view of Catholicism, along with a patriarchal and hierarchical view of society. Although she was far from being a radical in politics, the threat represented by Carlism forced María Cristina – queen regent until the majority of age of Isabel II – to enter into an alliance of convenience with liberal political groups, ranging from *moderados* (moderates) to *progresistas* (radicals). In this context of turmoil and civil war, Balmes and Donoso made their first incursions into their country's political life.

Jaime Balmes, a secular priest, came from a fairly modest background. After finishing his studies at the University of Cervera, he returned to his native Vic in Catalonia, where he devoted himself to ambitious intellectual endeavours. Balmes emerged from this relative obscurity and acquired a national reputation with his *Observaciones sociales, políticas y económicas sobre*

INTRODUCTION 15

los bienes del clero [Social, Political, and Economic Observations on Clerical Property] (1840). In this book, he expressed a deep concern about the standing of the Church as, under the rule of the *progresistas* (1835–1837), a massive disentailment and sale of ecclesiastical properties had taken place. During the 1840s, the Spanish Church was in a vulnerable position: it had lost a considerable amount of its riches and had to renegotiate its privileged position with the State. This situation of fragility brought about, as an unintended consequence, a significant degree of ideological flexibility among distinguished clergymen, with Balmes heading the list (Fradera 2003: 305). This flexibility would eventually disappear once the Church reassured its pre-eminence with the Concordat of 1851. In *El protestantismo comparado con el catolicismo en sus relaciones con la civilización europea [Protestantism compared to Catholicism in its Relation to European Civilisation]* (1842–1844), Balmes vindicated Catholicism as capable of promoting both intellectual enquiry and political liberty. By holding firm to the Catholic faith, Balmes argued, Spain was the European country which remained closest to what he believed was the essence of Europe, its 'Catholic civilisation'. Balmes' book, originally intended as a scholarly diatribe against the French Protestant writer François Guizot, had a long-lasting impact among successive generations of Catholic thinkers. By positing Spain as an essentially Catholic nation, Balmes consummated a symbolic marriage between traditional Catholicism and the liberal idea of the nation (Álvarez Junco 2007: 417; Villalonga 2012: 59–60).

The last years of his brief life – Balmes died at thirty-eight years of age – showed a growth in importance that was truly meteoric. He increasingly moved towards the epicentre of Spanish politics: in Barcelona, he edited the journals *La Civilización [The Civilisation]* (1841–1843) and *La Sociedad [The Society]* (1843–1844), reflecting a willingness to defend a Catholic stance and nevertheless engage with intellectual debates then taking place in Europe. Yet Balmes' most important project was *El Pensamiento de la Nación [The Thought of the Nation]*, published in Madrid from 1844 to 1846. In its pages, Balmes expressed his disaffection towards the prevalent political situation and presented his own ideas on how Spain could reach a long-desired stability. On the conclusion of the civil war, and after several years of arbitrary rule by the *progresista* strongman Baldomero Espartero (1840–1843), Spain began a period dominated by the moderate liberals: the *década moderada* (moderate decade) (1843–1854). Balmes criticised the elitist and oligarchic nature of the *moderado* regime, which he thought was based upon the consistent exclusion of what were the two extremes in Spanish politics: traditionalist Carlism and revolutionary liberalism. He resented the exclusion of the Carlists, whose conservative views he believed were representative of the majority of Spain's – still rural – population. In addition, Balmes stated that this 'ancient Spain' had been unjustly neglected by the 'new Spain' which, despite being a minority, was active in the most important cities and controlled the government.

Between 1844 and 1846, precisely the years in which *El Pensamiento de la Nación* was published, the marriage of Isabel II occupied the centre of Spanish politics. It was a step taken by the *moderado* party rather than by the queen herself, under the assumption that the election of a king consort would influence the course of Spanish politics. On that occasion, Balmes put forward the project of marrying Isabel to Count Montemolín, the son of Don Carlos, in an effort to quell not only the divisions within the Spanish dynastic family but to bring together the traditional spirit of the 'ancient Spain' with the modern spirit of the 'new Spain'. What is interesting about Balmes' position is not only that he made full use of modern means (i.e. the periodical press) in order to pursuit conservative goals, but that he was able to maintain a relative independence from the political groups that could sympathise with his views – from the right-wing of the *moderados* to the Carlists. For a variety of reasons, Balmes failed in achieving what he called a marriage of conciliation, setting the basis for a truly national government (Balmes 1845 f, *OC* VII: 252). Nonetheless, Balmes' plea for the rapprochement between tradition and the 'modern spirit' would be revived on a more ambitious and significant way: it became a statement on the path that European Catholicism should take.

The papacy of Pius IX began with a note of hope and excitement, produced by his inclination towards political reform in the Papal States, along with his favourable views on Italian unification. The Pope thus raised a wave of expectations across Catholic Europe as regards the relation between Catholicism and modern ideas such as popular sovereignty and nationalism. In *Pío IX* (1847), Balmes welcomed the Pope's measures and stressed that Catholicism was not bound to absolutist and monarchical regimes, but could actually flourish in regimes that fostered higher degrees of political liberty. Yet the Pope's alleged liberalism was cut short by the European Revolutions of 1848, and was soon replaced by an intransigent stance. These were developments that Balmes did not have time to appreciate fully: he died in July 1848, and left a series of unfinished sketches on the revolutionary events which had just taken place in Paris. Though he was far from being a friend of both revolution and socialist doctrines, Balmes insisted upon the need to

INTRODUCTION 17

address the social and economic roots of these upheavals: from an unequal distribution of wealth to the current organization of labour.

This emphasis upon the social questions was a distinctive feature of Balmes as a Catholic thinker – and a rather unique one (Koch 1993: 113). He had previously referred to the consequences of disentailment in rural Spain: once the Church properties passed into the hands of a small number of rich landlords, the situation of landless peasants would be worsened. Balmes also called attention to the incipient proletariat that was appearing in the industrial centres of Catalonia. Significantly, Balmes thus signalled the emergence of social Catholicism, which made a qualitative jump from the idea that social problems were the result of either a lack of morality or a deficient religiosity, to the conviction that institutional reform – and not only charity – was needed in order to address them. Yet Catholic social doctrine would only acquire a more definite shape during the pontificate of Leo XIII (1878–1903). It might be added that Balmes was also the author of several philosophical works. Many of the epistemological concerns that he had raised in *El criterio [On Discernment]* (1845), including the ability of human reason to discern truth, as well as the relationship between science and religion, were significantly expanded in *Filosofía fundamental [Fundamental Philosophy]* (1846) and *Filosofía elemental [Elemental Philosophy]* (1847).

Juan Donoso Cortés came from a well-to-do family from Extremadura, and completed his legal studies at the University of Seville. After a brief experience as lecturer in the Colegio de Humanidades of Cáceres, he moved to Madrid in 1832, where he joined a variety of literary and political *tertulias* (salons). Circumstances were about to change dramatically in Spain, and this was a moment in which the succession of Fernando VII was being hotly debated. Donoso made his first political move with a *Memoria sobre la situación actual de la monarquía [Statement on the current Situation of the Monarchy]* (1832), declaring himself to be a moderate and a supporter of Isabel's right to the throne. It is worth stressing that Donoso's allegiance to Isabel remained unaltered throughout his life, regardless of any variation in his political thought. At this point, however, Donoso's defence of the legitimate monarchy was underpinned by *doctrinaire* liberalism, as reflected in his first serious political writing, *Consideraciones sobre la diplomacia [Considerations on Diplomacy]* (1834), and in a series of *Lecciones sobre derecho político [Lectures on Constitutional Political Law]* (1836–1837) delivered in the Ateneo of Madrid.

Doctrinaire liberalism was a theory on government, devised in order to establish 'an eclectic synthesis between revolution and tradition' (Fernández

Sebastián 1997: 132). Its origins were in the French *doctrinaires* whose middle-of-the-ground position, conceived of as an alternative to the extremes represented by the ultra-royalists and the republicans, were particularly influential during the reign of Louis Philippe (1830–1848). Their ideas were echoed in Spain, where the moderate liberals (*moderados*) aimed at overcoming the divisions that had led to civil war (1833–1838), presenting themselves as a *juste milieu* between Carlists and radical liberals. In the case of Donoso, the influence of the doctrinaires was most felt in his views on the 'sovereignty of reason', in which there was no democratic intent but rather a justification of the upper middle classes' right to rule. Despite this attempt to escape from the Scylla and Charybdis of the Carlists' divine right of kings and the radical liberals' defence of national sovereignty, Donoso was an imperfect *doctrinaire*. The key preoccupation in his political thought was not conciliation but expediency, understood as the government's ability to overcome the political stalemate and to guarantee social order – especially in times of crisis. As he affirmed in his *Lecciones*, in exceptional moments, what would ensure the maintenance of order were not the *doctrinaires'* carefully crafted theories but rather the 'social omnipotence' as embodied in a dictator.

Donoso's career followed the vicissitudes of the *moderado* party. At the beginning of the 1840s, when Espartero was in power, Donoso joined in Paris the circle of *moderado* émigrés who followed the Queen Mother María Cristina into exile. On his return to Spain, Donoso joined the Cortes as deputy for Extremadura. However, during the *década moderada* (1843–1854), Donoso's influence in Spanish politics would be mostly exercised in a far less institutional way, following his appointment in 1844 as private secretary to Isabel II. As shown in a recent biography of Isabel II (Burdiel 2010), this allowed Donoso to mediate the relationship between the thirteen-year old queen and her mother. His manoeuvres within the Spanish royal family were crucial for the *moderados'* objective of controlling the institution of the monarchy according to their own interests. Moreover, as a secretary of the committee on constitutional reform, Donoso was a key figure in drafting the *moderado*-inspired Constitution of 1845. Sovereignty was then declared to rest with both Crown and Cortes, in an attempt to reach a 'conservative compromise' between the strong affirmation of royal authority put forward by the Estatuto Real of 1834, and the principle of full popular sovereignty consecrated by the *progresista* Constitution of 1837 (Payne 1984: 772). So, apart from establishing the basis of the *moderados'* instrumental relationship

INTRODUCTION 19

with the Crown, the Constitution of 1845 consolidated a new aristocracy composed of upper middle class interests.

Donoso also played an important role in what became a marriage of convenience between the Church and the *moderados*. Desirous of using the Church as bulwark of stability and order, the *moderado* regime was willing to make concessions: the sales of ecclesiastical property were suspended and the first steps were taken to re-establish relations with the Papacy. Yet the *moderados* staunchly refused to regard the previous sales of ecclesiastical properties as anything other than a *fait accompli*; after all, many of those who had benefited by these sales were now supporters of the regime. From now onwards, the relations between Church and State would be reorganized on a completely new basis: deprived of a substantial part of its riches, the Church was no longer self-sufficient and would depend upon the State for its maintenance. Speaking in the Cortes in early 1845, Donoso referred to the sales of ecclesiastical property as an irreversible fact and affirmed the State's right to intervene in the Church's temporal affairs – that is, matters of governance and internal administration. Donoso's arguments were contested by Balmes who, writing in *El Pensamiento de la Nación*, regretted what he believed was not only a significant loss of independence for the Church but represented its subordination to the State. Interestingly, the marriage of Isabel II constituted another instance of disagreement between Balmes and Donoso. As a reward for his involvement in bringing about the marriage between Isabel and her cousin Francisco de Asís in 1846, Donoso was raised to the nobility with the title of Marquis of Valdegamas. Yet Donoso's support of someone who was a relatively uninteresting husband for Isabel ought to be interpreted taking into account both the heavy diplomatic pressure from Britain and France, and the relatively strong position of the *moderados*, which meant they did not have to seek the support of the Carlists – as Balmes proposed – in order to prevail.

1847 was a crucial year in Donoso's life: he underwent a religious conversion to a more committed and deeply-felt Catholicism. This had the effect of exacerbating, rather than producing *ex novo*, an already strong conservative strand in his thought. This had been reflected in a constant affirmation of order and authority over radical change (i.e. revolution), along with a definition of Spanish identity that rested on traditional institutions (i.e. Church and Crown). Nevertheless, following his conversion, Donoso would assert with increasing conviction what he thought to be the superiority of Catholicism as a guide in all areas of life: what he called the 'Catholic solution' in a series of articles on Pius IX, and 'Catholic civilisation' in the early 1850s. The Revolutions of 1848 further radicalised Donoso's position, as reflected in a 'Discurso sobre la dictadura [Speech on dictatorship]' (1849) which made him famous across Europe. Speaking in the Cortes, Donoso defended the need to combat revolution and to maintain order at all costs – including that of resorting to a dictatorship. He predicted the advent of a socialist revolution in Europe, thus gaining the reputation among favourable commentators of being a prophet, and warned about the shortcomings of liberalism, beginning with its supposed inability to prevent the eventual outbreak of revolution.

This was the topic of his best-known work, *Ensayo sobre el catolicismo, el liberalismo y el socialismo [Essay on Catholicism, Liberalism and Socialism]*, published in 1851. It is important to mention that the European projection of Donoso's ideas was partly facilitated by his appointments as ambassador in Berlin (1849) and Paris (1851–1853). At the end of his (also) brief life – he died at forty-three years of age –, he gradually moved towards the conviction that the only real alternative to either revolution or dictatorship was a religious reawakening among the peoples of Europe. Yet his tone became apocalyptic, and his stress upon Catholicism as the *only* solution excluded the possibility of reaching an understanding with any aspect of modern life or culture that diverged from the Church's teachings, including the liberalism that he professed in his youth.

This overview, however brief, justifies the need to study Balmes and Donoso *in parallel*, highlighting similarities but especially the differences among them. The latter include, in the first and most obvious place that, despite sharing the conviction that Catholicism ought to be the pillar of Spanish identity, their political projects diverged in several key aspects, including Church-State relations. Second, and most significantly, they did not share an identical religious ideal, given that they envisaged dissimilar ways of guaranteeing the pre-eminence of religion in society. It could be added that the differences go well beyond their contrasting literary styles, and are mainly philosophical, as illustrated by their contrasting epistemological stance. For example, Balmes affirmed that 'simplicity is the character of truth' (Balmes 1841, *OC* V: 465), whereas Donoso maintained that 'absolute clarity is always a symptom of error' (Donoso 1837, *OC* I: 382).

Yet emphasising the differences between Balmes and Donoso, however important, is just one first step in the direction of a critical reappraisal of their works. The question remains: are they nevertheless to be inscribed within a larger – and relatively coherent – category, that is, as belonging

INTRODUCTION   21

to a larger tradition of conservative, Catholic or traditionalist thinkers? Starting from the assumption that their political thought was rooted in a given historical experience, how is one to account for their views on how Spain *should* be, as this seemingly reduced their field of vision – and maybe ours too – to what was normative and desirable, to the exclusion of what was deemed as 'foreign' or 'heterodox'? And how are we to avoid seeing Balmes and Donoso through the lens of myths that they contributed to create (i.e. the former as the true representative of Spain's necessarily Catholic spirit, the latter as a cogent proof of the alleged incompatibility between Catholicism and modern, secular values)? Answering these complex questions involves reflecting not only upon their lives, but their afterlives: that is, the reception of their works. In the next section, I will go on to give an overview of the most significant twentieth-century scholarship produced on Balmes and Donoso, highlighting the recent scholarship on Hispanic political thought. By revisiting fundamental research questions, as well as larger debates on nineteenth-century Spain, it is possible to critically rethink cult figures such as Balmes and Donoso and, more significantly, to show that Spanish political thought was a variation on – rather than an aberration of – contemporary European debates.

II. Catholic Spain: myths and realities

The debate about two or more Spains is *passé*. Yet it is worth analysing its core arguments, so as to better understand the claims of current scholarship. The passion elicited by the topos of the *two Spains*, the liberal and the conservative, can be explained by its being a crossroads between political conviction and religious belief. Broadly speaking, liberal Spain drew its arguments from the Black Legend, blaming the intolerance of the Catholic Church for having hindered in Spain those intellectual and scientific achievements which constituted the prosperity of more advanced countries. In turn, conservative Spain created its own White Legend, one of a traditional Spain in which Catholicism was both a sign of identity and the inspiration behind the country's greatest deeds (Menéndez Pidal 1991: 229–30; Carr 2001: 2; García Cárcel 2013: 357–358). Underlying the *two Spains*, was a process of 'rhetorical inflation' at work, one in which the 'enemy' was increasingly defined as the negation of one's own values, eventually leading to the creation of a 'virtual reality' (Clark 2003: 36–42).

This explains why, during the Franco years (1939–1975), many of the ideas of Balmes and Donoso were applied retrospectively in order to give a historical justification to the polarisation of Spanish society during and after the Civil War (1936–1939). Quite predictably, Donoso's prophecies about the dangers of socialism were then recalled, while stressing the superiority of his own Catholic doctrine (Larraz 1948: 20; Suárez Verdeguer 1964: 272–3). Balmes was invoked with the aim of demonstrating that the Spanish people had always been naturally religious, peace-loving and politically passive. The counterpart of this argument was that, in consequence, revolutionary or left-wing elements had always been a small fraction of society, so that their numerical inferiority prevented them from being truly representative of the Spanish people (Larraz 1948: 17; Martín Artajo 1962: 9–10). Significantly, José María García Escudero claimed that the failure of Balmes' attempt at reconciling the warring factions in Spanish society proved that there could be no 'third Spains' (1950: 86–7). According to García Escudero, the Spanish Civil War had been not only the culmination of the nineteenth-century struggle between the *two Spains*, but also an 'anachronistic reenactment' of the sixteenth-century European wars of religion (García Escudero 1980: 4–5).

Nowadays, however, the findings of recent scholarship have contributed to blur the lines between the *two Spains*, especially in relation to the liberal side of the equation. Many paradigms have been called into question, beginning with the idea that the end of the *ancien régime* in Spain – and the subsequent rise of liberalism as a political ideology – was the result of a bourgeois revolution, one that pitted the rising middle classes against a feudal oligarchy. As Cruz has demonstrated, liberalism did not advance the interests of a single social class, but those of a broad coalition composed of diverse social classes and interests (Cruz 2000: 12–13). It did have a radical impact in Spain's political institutions, but its effects reached only slowly the social and economic sphere, where the norm was much less revolution than adaptation and renovation (Cruz 2000: 259–260). In addition, the relationship between Spanish liberalism and the Church has been the subject of new studies that cast doubt on the claim that contemporary attempts at reducing the secular power of the Church were necessarily conducive to the eventual 'dechristianisation' of Spain (Escrig 2018: 146–7). It becomes clear that, in nineteenth-century Spain, the fundamental question to be asked was *not* if the nation should or should not be informed by religious values. The question to ask was, rather, whether the powerful and influential Spanish Catholic Church could hamper – or not – the construction of the new liberal State. After all,

INTRODUCTION

even if they repeatedly entered into alliances of convenience, both the Church and the State constantly renegotiated their respective spheres of influence.

This, in turn, leads to one of the most heated debates in Spanish historiography: to what extent was the strong presence of the Church in Spain's political life compatible, in the long run, with the State's objective of creating Spaniards rather than just Catholics. In the 1980s and 1990s, as historians came to terms with the decades-long legacy of Franco, the so-called theory of 'nineteenth-century weak nationalization' prevailed. This was an attempt at explaining the alleged failure of the Spanish State in creating a 'nation of citizens', viewed as being synonymous of a modern, democratic and pluralist society (Molina & Cabo 2012: 65). In particular, it was argued that the enthusiastic promotion of Spain's religious identity had been an obstacle to the emergence of a strong national feeling embodied in the State (Shubert 1990: 205). This paradigm has been increasingly called into question by the most recent historiography, on the assumption that its measure of success was not only anachronistic but, to a certain extent, prescriptive too – for example, uncritically identifying 'modern' with 'secular'. In addition, historiography no longer focuses exclusively upon the State as the main protagonist in processes of nation-building, highlighting instead the role played by 'non-State led nationalizing agents'. Among those are agents who, in parallel to the State's nationalising efforts, were capable of creating and fostering a feeling of nationhood too, were waves of migration, regional and local historical agents, colonial wars and, last but not least, the Church (Molina & Cabo 2012: 62; Núñez Seixas 2018a: 38–39).

The idea that Catholicism was an essential component of nation-building processes in nineteenth-century Spain has been cogently articulated by Gregorio Alonso. For the liberals that drafted the Cádiz Constitution in 1812, 'a Catholic and a citizen were meant to be one and the same thing' (Alonso 2017a: 48). Combining religious and revolutionary sources of legitimacy, they ventured a deliberate overlap between the (Catholic) religious community and the sovereign political body (Portillo 2000: 460). The underlying assumption was the Church, just as it had previously disseminated the state directives of the eighteenth-century Bourbon monarchs, would now be in charge of instilling the Spanish population with civic and constitutional values, thus turning *creyentes* (believers) into *patriotas* (patriots) too (Alonso 2017a: 59–60; Alonso 2020: 5). The role played by the Church in strengthening these values remain open to question, considering that it remained *in toto* wedded to an anti-liberal stance – and, as its detractors would add, an anti-rationalist outlook too.

The fact remains that, for Spain's ruling elites, reaching a *modus vivendi* with the Church proved useful in reinforcing the legitimacy of the State, considering the strong support that the ecclesiastical institution still retained in most of small-town and rural Spain (Smith 2014: 48–49). For most of the nineteenth century, Spanish governing elites consistently supported a confessional State, while rejecting religious tolerance. This tolerance was accepted only by the stillborn 1856 constitution, whereas the 1876 Constitution recognised freedom of worship – as long as such freedom was exercised in private (Suárez Cortina 2017: 73). In this scheme of things, as the trajectories of Balmes and Donoso illustrate, Church-State relations might have been based on the principle of mutual advantage but were much less a harmonic collaboration than a contentious *quid pro quo* negotiated on a regular basis.

A related debate concerns not only nationalization but nationalism. A first question to be asked is whether nationalism (i.e. loyalty to the national State) and Catholicism (i.e. loyalty to a supranational Church) are compatible. The most recent scholarship distinguishes the nation – seen as the locus of national identity, as well as the subject matter of nationalism – from the State, identified with political and administrative institutions (Romeo 2021: 22). Regarding nationalism, two main paradigms prevail: the 'constructivist' approach, that claims that nations are built through myths and traditions that are reworked and reformulated according to perceived needs and goals, and the 'essentialist' one, under the assumption that a nation is nothing but the expression of a timeless and unchanging spirit, seen as a given both culturally and even ethnically (Nuñez Seixas 2018b: 9). As Colom rightly asserts, the differences between these two paradigms are more apparent than real, as both perspectives tend to combine fact with fiction (2011: 184). The tensions between these two paradigms will be illustrated with Balmes who, as 'the first and most important [European] Catholic thinker to build a consistent Catholic nationalistic theory', sought to portray Spain as an essentially Catholic nation (Villalonga 2012: 52 & 2014: 311). This confirms Louzao's argument that the very idea of nation in nineteenth-century Spain, rather than acquiring a modern (i.e understood as secular and non-religious) connotation, actually underwent a process of sacralization (2013: 65–66).

At this point, however, the discussion of nineteenth-century portrayals of Spain as a (necessarily) Catholic nation serve to call attention to current debates on this country's alleged *exceptionalism*. As María Cruz Romeo argues,

INTRODUCTION 25

neither the lack of pluralism nor a state of latent civil strife were exclusive to Spain, that is, when seen from a broader European perspective. As she contends, by asking why Spain has not been like France or Britain, one runs the risk of neglecting what it actually *was* (Romeo 2010: 71). Whereas this involves, on part of the researcher, a deliberate effort to avoid deterministic explanations (i.e. based on whatever national essence or exclusive peculiarity), there is nevertheless a need to come to terms with a great degree of cultural anxiety on part of actual historical actors who, indeed, felt compelled to refute the stereotypical image of Spain as a backward and fanatical country. Running through the works of Balmes and Donoso, as it will be seen, there is an idealised vision of Europe, one that encompassing France, Britain and sometimes Germany, served two main purposes. On the one hand, it spurred on a sense of inferiority vis-à-vis countries that were allegedly more sophisticated in both cultural and political matters. On the other, it served as a vehicle for a vehement affirmation of Spain's cultural specificity that, according to Balmes, was to be regarded as synonymous with its *exceptional* Catholic heritage.

This brings us to what, according to González Cuevas, has been the main characteristic of Spanish right-wing thinkers, that is, their strong association with Catholicism, seen as constant source of symbols, as well as the foundation of their concept of national identity (2000: 19). During the nineteenth century, according to González Cuevas, right-wing thought can be classified into two hegemonic traditions: firstly, the 'tradition of liberal conservatism' that, heir to the Enlightenment, sought to combine Catholicism with liberalism, and tended to support a constitutional monarchy. Secondly, the 'theological-political tradition' that viewed Catholicism the *ultima ratio* of politics, and was often wary of liberalism. A liberal stance was often seen as promoting an individualistic rather than a communitarian model of society, as well as with favouring a secular (i.e. non-religious) view on both the origins and goals of political power. Within this tradition, the uncompromising eighteenth-century *reaccionarios* (reactionaries) coexisted with the relative more open-minded nineteenth-century 'traditionalists' or 'authoritarian conservatives' such as Balmes and Donoso (González Cuevas 2000: 44–46). So, it might be asked, who were their predecessors and where do we draw a line between a reactionary and a merely conservative stance?

The Origins of Spanish Reactionary Thought was a pioneering work by Javier Herrero (1971) who traced the emergence, in the late eighteenth century, of what he called a 'foundational myth': a pervasive interpretation of Spanish history as a conflict between national tradition and foreign ideas (Herrero 1971: 15). The Spanish Enlightenment, understood as the reforming ideal of a minority, did not call into question the country's Catholic character (Herr 1958: 84; Carr 1966: 71). Yet the urge to reform the workings of the Church, along with the influence of the French *philosophes*, was nevertheless perceived to be a potential threat to traditional values, such as the respect for the authority for both kings and popes. Moreover, any attack on the preponderance of the Church – i.e. its riches or political privileges – was interpreted as involving a desire to banish God from society. These were many of the topics developed in *La falsa filosofía [The False Philosophy]* (1774–1776) by fray Fernando de Zevallos, who thus set the foundations of future Spanish reactionary thought. He called attention to the disastrous consequences that religious doubt and an eventual loss of faith might have within the political body, arguing that this revolt of the intellect led necessarily to the rebellion of human appetites or 'unleashing of the passions' (Acle Aguirre 2012: 61). According to Zevallos, the followers of the *falsa filosofía* – that is, French philosophy – were inexorably bound to become atheists, libertines and enemies of the State.

The French Revolution gave an unprecedented boost to the production of reactionary literature across Europe (i.e. counterparts of Zevallos were Luigi Mozzi in Italy and Claude Nonotte in France), which had already been preaching against the disruptive potential of the ideas of the Enlightenment. The crudest expression of this was a tendency towards conspiracy theory, laying the blame on freemasons, philosophers, Jews, Protestants, etc. for recent revolutionary upheavals. The classic example was the widely-read *Memoirs Illustrating the History of Jacobinism* (1797) by the Abbé Augustin Barruel. He described the French Revolution as 'the first step towards the universal dissolution', plotted by a sect of Jacobins whose 'Anti-Christian conspiracy' united the adepts of impiety, rebellion and anarchy (Barruel 1799: xvxvi). In Spain, such views were echoed in the *Causas de la Revolución de Francia en el año 1789 [Causes of the Revolution in France in the Year 1789]* by Lorenzo Hervás y Panduro who argued that the revolution aimed at the destruction of Christianity and of every political authority, as these were the only safe barriers against the natural freedom of men, conceived of as the unrestrained exercise of instincts and passions (Herrero 1971: 157–60).

The war between Spain and France (1793–1795), sparked off by Spain's protests against the execution of Louis XVI, foreshadowed the religious exaltation which would characterise the struggle against the Napoleonic

INTRODUCTION

invasion in 1808. The regular clergy[2] played a crucial role in winning support for the war effort, as the *frailes* preached vengeance against (French) atheism and the murderers of the Bourbon king. The classic example of this attitude was *El soldado católico en guerra de religión [The Catholic Soldier in War of Religion]* (1794) by the Capuchin friar Diego José de Cádiz. In this book, he assured his followers that if fallen in battle, they would receive the crown of martyrdom in heaven: 'because the cause of your death is your enemy's hatred of the faith you defend' (Cádiz 1812: 62). During the War of Independence (1808–1814), the call to arms was once again expressed in religious terms. Martínez Albiach has referred to the 'theologisation of Spanish history' taking place during this period, illustrated with the belief that the French invasion had come to Spain as a (rightly deserved) divine punishment or that the Spanish people – chosen by God – was waging a 'holy war' against Napoleon (1969: 21, 34). The glorification of the Spanish king, the 'sighed-for and adored Ferdinand', went hand-in-hand with xenophobic evocations of the apostle Santiago who, according to tradition, had aided the Spaniards in their battle against the Moors during the *Reconquista*. Such a rhetoric identified *patria* with religion, *españolidad* with Catholicism (Álvarez Junco 2007: 339–41).

The emergence of a liberal discourse within Spain made things far more complicated. The epithets that until then had been reserved to the foreign invader/philosopher were now addressed to the *liberales*, whose interference in ecclesiastical matters was deeply resented – for example, the Cortes assembled at Cádiz abolished the Inquisition in 1813. The rejection of the liberal reforms was personified in Francisco de Alvarado, a Dominican also known as 'Filósofo Rancio' (Archaic Philosopher), whose writings exemplified the conviction that the ideas which went against Spanish traditional values were necessarily of foreign origin. For example, Alvarado praised the Inquisition for having guaranteed the survival of the kingdom, on the assumption that 'there is hardly any enemy of the motherland that does not end up as enemy of religion'; additionally, in order to eradicate the dangerous influence of what he called 'philosophism', he recommended the issuing edicts against philosophers in the same way as had been done against Jews (Alvarado 1846: 11–2). A similar stance can be found in the writings of the Capuchin friar

---

2 Regulars are clerics who follow the rule of life of a religious institute (from the Latin *regula* or rule), such as an order or a congregation, and live in community. In contrast, the secular clergy lives in the world or 'century' (from the Latin *saeculum* or century), engaging in pastoral work within the administrative units of the Catholic Church, from parishes to dioceses.

Rafael de Vélez. In *Preservativo contra la irreligión: o los planes de la falsa filosofía contra la religión y el Estado [Preservative against impiety: Or Plans of the False Philosophy Against Religion and State]* (1812), Vélez lamented the liberty of the press decreed by the Cortes in November 1810, accusing journalists and pamphleteers of entertaining the aim of 'to enlighten us in the French way, that is, to pervert us' (1814: 12–14).

Vélez attacked the *liberales* on grounds of their lack of authenticity, of their rejection of the 'Spanish tradition'. In his *Apología del altar y del trono*, a justification of the absolutist return of Fernando VII, Vélez referred to the reforms carried out by the Cortes of Cádiz as having been the workings of a radical and illegitimate minority who did not count with the assent of the people (1818: I, 32). Summarising the views of the conservative opinion, known as the *partido servil* (servile party), Vélez thought of the *liberales* as being the enemies of the *fatherland*, the enemies of religion and the enemies of the king (1818: I, 72). They had no right to belong; if anything, they were Spain's illegitimate children. Such were the pro-Catholic, pro-absolutist *views* professed by Vélez (1818: I, 475):

> If our Spain needs reform, let our legislation be reformed. ...] Why, then, if Spain needs reform, do we have to resort to foreigners, to their plans, their books, their maxims, their doctrines? How can our nation be denigrated with the insults that many of our reformers have uttered against us? Who can suffer, that some Spaniards have given to the mother who bore them the insulting remarks of being a century behind other nations, superstitious, ignorant, fanatical... [...] Spain, always Catholic, always religious, and always faithful to her sovereign, will look on these seduced ones, as spurious children, to whom, if she gave them life, certainly did not give them any instruction, just because they refused to receive it.

I have mentioned men like Zevallos, Cádiz and Vélez in order to illustrate the tendency, especially among the clergy, to give the labels of heretical, anti-national or unauthentic to any idea that questioned Catholic orthodoxy (González Cuevas 2000: 40). This tendency is shared by the pervasive interpretation of Spanish political thought as a conflict between the Spanish tradition and disruptive foreign ideas. These ideas had been uncritically imported from foreign contexts that differed markedly from the Spanish one, so the argument ran, and were thus unable to reflect local traits and circumstances. Hence we have the portrayal of Balmes and Donoso as mere variations on a perennial theme, that of the Spanish tradition: 'in a foreign-inclined and decadent century, [Balmes and Donoso] form the nerve of the national tradition and serve as models of the creative originality of the

Hispanic race' (Martín Artajo 1962: 19). So, one might ask, is it possible to study Balmes and Donoso without resorting to a comprehensive framework such as the Spanish tradition? What are the differences – and similarities – between them and their (alleged) forerunners?

Authors such as Javier López Alós and Josep Escrig have recently sought to go beyond what Santos Juliá once referred to as 'meta-historical accounts' that have reduced nineteenth-century Spanish history to a 'clear-cut conflict between antagonists' (Juliá 2004: 148). In this sense, the most recent scholarship is less interested in portraying men as Vélez or Alvarado as being the mere antithesis of the *liberales*, but rather as their counterparts – both sides bound, as Escrig insists, within a dialectic relationship (Escrig 2018: 154). Even if the *reaccionarios* were prone to singing the praises of the former and allegedly unproblematic unity between the Throne and Altar, they did not inhabit a nostalgic, bygone world. As López Alós insists, they used the past mainly as a means of legitimation with a very clear objective: to exercise an influence upon present and future Spanish politics (2011b: 23). This projection to the future, while claiming to restore an idealized past, is what Pedro Rújula and Juan Ramón Solans have called 'the paradox of reaction' (2017: 2–3). More significantly, as Escrig boldly suggests, the political stance of reactionary and anti-liberal thinkers could be summed up as 'fake Catholic absolutism'. This is because their aim was not to restore the *ancien régime*, but to herald a new era in which the Church would reign supreme over *both* the liberal State and the monarch (Escrig 2018: 150–151).

In this sense, the 1830s marked an decisive break in Spanish politics (Mücke 2008: 425). The marriage of convenience between *cristinos* and *liberales*, namely as the legitimate monarchy joined forces with liberalism against the supporters of Don Carlos, put an end to whatever dreams might be entertained of ever returning to the *ancien régime*. The choice was no longer to be made between either revolution or the restoration of absolutism. In what contemporaries increasingly viewed as a post-revolutionary society, the priority was to restore order and stability. Therefore, liberalism – in Spain and elsewhere – would acquire a distinctively moderate and even conservative outlook. The conservative liberals of the 1830s would stand, as Mücke shrewdly argues, 'against the Revolution but in favour of preserving the gains of previous revolutions' (2008: 43). Once in power, they would establish an alliance with the Church hierarchy and local elites, underpinning their position with both the symbolic and practical prerogatives of the monarch, who enjoyed the power to appoint and dismiss governments

(Smith & Garner 2017: 14). Due to these historical circumstances, as well as to their own intellectual background, Balmes and Donoso decisively steered away from the *reaccionarios'* staunch anti-liberal rhetoric. Yet the role of the Church as well as the relationship between the Church, the monarchy and the liberal State, continued to be under debate. In the works of Balmes, for example, a significant tension remains as whether where to put the Church within the liberal edifice: hand-in-hand with the State, but certainly not subordinated to it.

Ultimately, what really makes Balmes and Donoso different from their predecessors is that they consciously acted as *Europeans*, that is, as conservatives operating in a European climate: actively seeking contact with similar-minded thinkers abroad, thus breaking the stereotype of Spain as being necessarily retrograde and isolated. Balmes visited France, Britain and Belgium, while Donoso not only travelled through France and Germany, but became one of the few Spanish thinkers who, during the first half of the century, earned a European reputation. In addition, they actively sought an audience outside Spain, and therefore both printed their most important works simultaneously in Madrid and Paris. Balmes and Donoso carried out a defence of religion from a truly European perspective, that is, they upheld Catholicism as a remedy for a whole civilisation rather than as an *ad hoc* solution to the political ills and social maladies of just Spain. In this sense, what has been overlooked is how conservatism also quenched the Spanish intellectuals' century-old thirst for acknowledgement; in other words, it became a vehicle for affirming Spain's full belonging to Europe.

The main objective of this book, a study of how Balmes and Donoso responded to the social and political changes of their age, is to restore the *historicity* of their thought. This involves a departure from teleological accounts that, starting from the assumption that the advent of modernity (mostly understood as secular, pluralistic and rational outlook) was inevitable, portray Balmes and Donoso as clinging to 'an unswervingly orthodox appraisal of the past' (Flitter 2006: 59–60). But if Balmes and Donoso cannot be reduced to the status of relics of a bygone past, they cannot be uncritically turned either into anti-modern prophets. It is true that, towards the end of his life, Donoso thundered against what he saw as imminent dangers, from a forthcoming socialist revolution in Europe to a rapidly-developing technology that would enable States to exercise an absolute control of their citizens. Yet I am not interested in writing 'desde (from)' Donoso', thus proving *ex post facto* how accurate his prophecies were, but mainly 'sobre (about) Donoso' – and Balmes (cf. Gallego 2013: 13). Moreover, this work certainly aims at undoing the historic merger of Balmes and Donoso into an allegedly continuous body of National Catholicism. However, it does not aim at proving them either wrong (or right) in view to what happened in late-nineteenth or twentieth-century Spain. In other words, there is a need to view Balmes and Donoso less as cult figures and timeless sources of inspiration, than as thinkers constrained by their time and place.

For previous generations of researchers, it had been central to prove that, rather than being merely 'derivative', Spanish thinkers had actually achieved a certain degree of originality vis-à-vis their European counterparts. Nowadays, instead of distinguishing the 'original' from its 'copies', emphasis is laid upon reconstructing the historicity of political thought. In this sense, this book draws significant inspiration from the work of Elías José Palti, as it offers valuable insights on how to deal – from a hermeneutic perspective – with a central motif in the writings of Balmes and Donoso: the need to justify Spain's belonging to (an idealized) Europe. This anxiety often led them to distinguish between what was authentically 'Spanish' and what was merely an importation – or bad copy – of allegedly foreign models. As Palti insists, these kind of judgements constitute everything but a rarity in the study of intellectual history in both Spain and the Spanish-speaking world. In this sense, there is an overarching idea that has not lost its appeal: that the political instability that marked the nineteenth century in Spain and the Hispanic world was a direct consequence of having imported (from abroad) a set of (liberal) ideas that ran against local cultural and political mores (Palti 2007: 24–25). In contrast to this, Palti reminds us of impossibility of defining a national essence, as well as of finding perfect 'models' – of, say, liberalism – outside a purely ideal world.

Amid heated debates, Palti has sought to combine the contributions made by the three most representative currents in the field of intellectual history: conceptual history (*Begriffsgeschichte* in German), the so-called Cambridge School of Ideas and French politico-conceptual history – as all strive to ascertain not *what* was said in a given text, but *how* and *why* it was said (Palti 2014; Breña 2021). Palti differentiates political ideas, seen as the subjective representations of individuals, from actual 'political languages' that are objective and social in nature – as well as essentially contestable, and thus everything but logical and coherent ideal types (Palti 2017: 404). Writing a history of political languages involves, in the first place, reconstructing the 'contexts of debate' in which they emerged, highlighting the 'contending views' on especially divisive questions (Palti 2017: 402–404). These constitute the 'problematic junctions' that reveal the crucial shifts made during the development of political languages, as classically illustrated by nineteenth-century debates on sovereignty (Palti 2006: 255). As Javier Fernández Sebastián concludes, albeit from the perspective of conceptual history, political concepts constitute 'conceptual constellations' of an essentially polemic character (Freeden & Fernández Sebastián 2019: 2).

Consequently, this work seeks to match new developments within intellectual history, written mostly in Spanish, with the relative lack of recent studies on Balmes and Donoso within the English-speaking scholarship. Although both continue to routinely appear in volumes devoted to European or Spanish Catholic thinkers (Menczer 1951; Wilson 2004; Beneyto 2018), the fact remains that biographical studies in English centred exclusively upon Donoso are relatively outdated (Herrera 1995 & Graham 1974) – or, in the case of Balmes, almost non-existent. Significantly, this is practically the first study in decades that analyses, from a comparative perspective, the *whole* lives and the *complete* works of Balmes and Donoso (see also Koch 1993). My aim is to put forward a portrait of Balmes and Donoso that, highlighting the complexity of contemporary debates, does not shy away from pointing at ambiguities and tensions within their thought. This involves a careful re-reading of their prolific works: the two volumes of Donoso's *Obras completas* edited by Valverde (1970) and the eight volumes of Balmes' *Obras completas* edited by Casanovas (1948–1950), both part of the Biblioteca de Autores Cristianos (Madrid, Editorial Católica). Given that my focus is upon the religious and political thought of Balmes and Donoso, the philosophical or literary aspects of their works are given secondary attention. Nonetheless, the reconstruction of their eventful lives, set against an equally hectic background, will serve the point of showing how Balmes and Donoso can be labelled as political thinkers only in retrospective. In fact, they participated in Spanish affairs under various guises: clergyman, journalist and philosopher, in the case of Balmes; lawyer, civil servant and lay theologian, in that of Donoso.

I have chosen a chronological approach in order to explain how the thought of Balmes and Donoso was not only crafted in response to a series of historical circumstances but embedded within ever-changing 'contexts of debate' – to use Palti's expression. My approach is also comparative, as the contrast between Balmes and Donoso is constantly brought forward in order to emphasize how they experienced contemporary affairs from a very different position – and even perspective. Chapter 1 shows how contact with European intellectual movements enabled Balmes and Donoso to contribute to the political debates taking place in Spain, and which were exacerbated by civil war (1833–1839). This awareness of Europe was also crucial to the way in which Balmes and Donoso gained a sense of Spain's identity, seen as resting on Catholicism. Chapters 2 and 3 have a special relevance, covering the least known period in the lives of Balmes and Donoso, and giving a detailed analysis of both the political scenario and Church-State relations during the *década moderada* (1843–1854). Balmes and Donoso shared a similar ideal, that of Spain resting on the twin pillars of the monarchy and the Church, and yet diverged when it came to realising it. Chapter 2 explores their different approaches to political struggle, according to their standpoint: on the sidelines of power, Balmes tried to broaden the scope of Spanish politics; in a central position within the ruling *moderado* party, Donoso furthered his career. Chapter 3 analyses the differences between Balmes and Donoso at an additional level: their views on Church-State relations, especially as they involved dissimilar practical consequences. This is illustrated with reference to the debates on how to maintain the Church that took place in the Spanish Cortes (1844–1845), pitting Balmes against Donoso. Chapter 4 further illustrates their dissimilar approach to the understanding and practice of Catholicism in reference to a couple of exceptional circumstances: the short-lived liberalism of Pope Pius IX and the European Revolutions of 1848. In the conclusions, I will give a final overview of the key concepts developed by Balmes and Donoso throughout their lives, as well as an account of the differences between them, with the objective of dismantling the historical merger of these thinkers into an allegedly coherent body of Spanish Catholic thought.

Did they manage to tame the revolution? The answer given here will avoid, first and foremost, anachronisms and *ex post facto* arguments. It will thus not hold Balmes and Donoso personally responsible for the sustained influence wielded by Spain's traditional institutions, the Church and the monarchy, throughout the nineteenth and even up to the twentieth century. Consequently, neither will their lives be judged against their afterlives, nor will their writings be ranked according to their ability to anticipate and even propitiate future developments. A more accurate, if less straightforward, answer to this question of taming involves reconstructing the way in which Balmes and Donoso came to terms with the legacy of a true revolution, as Spain passed from being an absolutist monarchy to turning into a constitutional, liberal State. As will be seen, however revolutionary, this passage was translated only with difficulty into a living reality after decades of adaptation, experimentation and renewal. For Balmes and Donoso, taming the revolution assumed a slightly paradoxical character. Despite their conservative outlook, one that decried individualism and highlighted instead the role of tradition and providence in shaping human destinies, they nevertheless saw themselves as personal representatives of these forces. In so doing, they actively sought to steer social and political change, that is, to avert the "revolution", either by tempering what was already a *fait accompli* and by preventing what they saw as further damage, through vantage positions in both the government and the Church. Conveying these intricate developments with clarity, rather than reducing their complexity to a simple "take away" message to be applied to present times – that is the aim pursued by this book.

Chapter 1: Spain belongs to Europe

The use of authenticity as a criterion to determine the validity of political thought possesses a particular appeal. At a first glance, it seems to confirm the long-standing views of writers with a more or less conservative opinion: the idea that a given society's legal and political framework should be an accurate reflection, not of abstract universal principles, but of local circumstances and developments. However, authenticity might also be related to a more complex assumption, namely that is possible to establish a clear distinction between ideas which are national and ideas which are foreign. When it comes to Spanish nineteenth-century political thought, describing ideas which run against the status quo as dangerous foreign importations was, essentially, an act of self-defence. It must be stressed, however, that 'one can never determine which ideas are out of place, and which are not, except from within a given, particular conceptual framework' (Palti 2006: 158). In the case of Jaime Balmes, such a framework was Catholicism; consequently, he regarded ideas which questioned his own image of Catholic Spain as being "misplaced", ill-suited to his country's needs and innermost beliefs. As I show throughout this chapter, a certain defensiveness characterised Balmes' relation to European intellectual movements. He accepted them insofar they did not oppose either his own idea of Spain as a Catholic nation or his strict adherence to Catholic dogma. Though limited by ideological constraints and religious commitments, Balmes nevertheless provided a path towards new ideas and re-shaped Spain's relationship with Catholicism by taking current developments into consideration. In this sense, the role of Balmes as leader of a veritable Catholic 'revival' in mid-century Spain, in this being 'the first and most important [European] Catholic thinker to build a consistent Catholic nationalistic theory', has been confirmed by recent scholarship (Villalonga 2012: 52 & 2014: 311).

When it comes to analysing the relationship of Juan Donoso Cortés with "foreign" ideas, mainly French political thought, the question of authenticity takes a different shape. It reflects the anxieties engendered by cultural influences from abroad, and here the question usually asked by critics is how authentic (i.e. original, fresh, innovative) Donoso's political ideas were, taking into account the fact that during his early years he was heavily dependent upon French sources. It is useful to remember that the exchange of ideas between different cultures never consists solely of passive reception, but rather implies a process of assimilation in which ideas are made legible by the culture that is going to incorporate them (Palti 2006: 173). Attaining such legibility involved, in the case of the young Donoso, a far more accommodating spirit than that of Balmes. Both worked within a Catholic framework, and yet Donoso was far more flexible when it came to positioning Spain within a European intellectual setting.

Authenticity in nineteenth-century Spain can be regarded as a preoccupation with both coherence and originality. During this period, political ideas were often assessed in terms of their being *locally produced* and *applicable to local realities*. The acute preoccupation with authenticity, rather than being a sign of cultural isolation, was an indicative of Spain's intense involvement with debates taking place in Europe. Selective readings and a spirit of creative appropriation characterised the process of intellectual exchange between Spain and other European countries. Reconstructing this process can be seen as tantamount to 'intellectual archaeology', to use the happy expression of Fernández Sebastián, as this involves unearthing the logic that governed the beliefs, institutions and practices of contemporary historical actors (2014a: 70). Therefore, instead of searching for 'ideological innovation', the emphasis ought to be placed in restoring the multiple and often controversial meanings behind political concepts (Fernández Sebastián 2014a: 65). In the case of Balmes and Donoso, as I contend, this involves highlighting the fact that they conscientiously operated within a European – and not merely a Spanish – framework, so that tracing their links to their non-Spanish contemporaries serves the purpose of underlining the living and polemic nature of their thought.

In the case of Juan Donoso, the political ideas of the French *doctrinaires* served to consolidate his profile as an aspiring political figure within the context of the *partido moderado*. Following and re-creating the example of his French counterparts, Donoso aimed at turning his party into a middle ground between the reactionary Carlists and the progressive liberals. He used the *doctrinaire* ideas on sovereignty and intelligence in order to justify the superiority and right to rule of the upper middle class in Spain. In doing so, he echoed the doctrinaires' understanding of liberalism, that is, as a 'centrist doctrine that opposed the revolutionary spirit in all its forms and promoted gradual political reform' (Craitu 2003: 8–9). Moreover, the first works of Donoso as a political writer, dwelling insistently upon matters of foreign policy, are an eloquent of expression of his desire to reinstate Spain within the European international order. The story of how Donoso became both a man of letters and a politician with a European outlook is the subject of the first two sections of this chapter.

In contrast to Donoso, the response of Balmes to French political thought was carried out at a more fundamental level. For Balmes, there was a crucial issue to take into account when "importing" the ideas of the *doctrinaire* and Protestant historian François Guizot, whose historical works were highly influential in the Spain during the 1830s and 1840s. Balmes found Guizot's definition of civilisation to be deeply distressing, as it was grounded upon a profound critique of the Catholic Church, portrayed as having been a hindrance to the modern freedom to think and to dissent. Balmes devoted several works to challenging such idea. With tremendous consequences for the next generations of conservative thinkers, Balmes united the cause of Spain with that of Catholicism. Balmes was eager to emphasise that Spain, not despite of its Catholicism but thanks to it, fully belonged to the civilised order of Europe. In sum, by vindicating the superiority of Catholicism as a faith, Balmes intended to demonstrate the validity of Spain as a civilisation. The last two sections of this chapter will analyse the contributions of Balmes to the both the concept of civilisation and the idea of Spain as a Catholic nation.

I. Donoso: man of letters with a European outlook

The ascent of Juan Donoso Cortés to the centre stage of Spanish culture and politics was heralded by a conscious desire to participate in intellectual movements taking place at home and abroad. As shown in his correspondence and first serious writings, Donoso aimed at constructing his own profile from both recent developments in Spain's intellectual life (i.e. the liberal experiences of 1810–14 and 1820–3) and from a deep awareness of European political thought. Donoso's ascent to the epicentre of Spain's public life had several stages: enlightened youthful readings in his native Extremadura, an early friendship with the liberal patriarch Manuel José Quintana, legal studies at the University of Seville, participation in provincial cultural enterprises, the writing of tracts with obvious political intentions and – by the early 1830s – an incorporation into both the bureaucracy and literary circles of Madrid.

Juan Francisco Manuel María de la Salud Donoso Cortés was born on the 6th of May 1809 in the Valle de la Serena, in the province of Extremadura (Dardé 2015: 5). Just before he was born, his family had left their native Don Benito, escaping from the approach of the invading French army, and was on its way to their estate in the nearby Valdegamas. His father, Pedro Donoso, was a successful lawyer and important landowner, as well as a member of the progressive Sociedad Económica de la Provincia de Cáceres; he was married to María Elena Fernández Canedo whose genealogical tree supposedly went back to Hernán Cortés, the conqueror of Mexico. In 1820, the eleven-year-old Donoso was sent by his father to the University of Salamanca. It is open to speculation how strongly Salamanca could have influenced the young Donoso who only stayed there for a year (Garrorena 1974: 84–86).

Yet the choice of Salamanca was a significant one: its university had been characterised by its openness to new ideas, from the works of Jansenist theologians, to the sensualist philosophy of Destutt de Tracy and the utilitarian approach of Jeremy Bentham (Schramm 1936: 19–25; Garrorena 1974: 84). Moreover, Salamanca had been the *alma mater* of several of the leading figures of the Cortes of Cádiz, including the politician and man of letters Manuel José Quintana, with whom Donoso spent the summer of 1823. Taking into account the fact that the Liberal Triennium (1820–1823) had just concluded, Quintana was busy writing his *Cartas a Lord Holland [Letters to Lord Holland]*, an attempt at explaining why the liberal regime had failed, prompting the return of the absolutist Fernando VII in 1823. A passage taken from these letters shows Quintana's strong belief that both Spanish politics and political ideas happened within a larger European framework:

Spain, without colonies, without navy, without commerce, without influence, should be indifferent to Europe, and be dispensed with in the political combinations of the cabinets, as happens with Berber regencies or the empire of Morocco. Might the heavens grant us what has so often been said in derision, and that Africa should begin at the Pyrenees! We would no doubt be rough, coarse, barbarous, ferocious; but we would not be driven by our alliances and connections to debasement, servitude and misery. [...] The worst of it is that even this desire, expressed less by reflection than by anger, cannot be satisfied among us.

The cause of the King of Spain is linked with that of the other kings of Europe, and that of our liberals with that of all the liberals of the world (Quintana 1853: 299–300).

Donoso's experience as a student in the University of Seville (1824–1828) came close to that of his mentor Quintana insofar as the two of them combined political and literary pursuits. In his university years, Donoso developed an interest in poetry. According to Sánchez León, Donoso was directly following on the steps of Quintana, for whom poets were 'moral representatives' of the people and, as such, entrusted with the task of enlightening and channelling popular enthusiasm (2006: 85–87). In both the neoclassical lines of eighteenth century poetry and the new Romantic style, Donoso and friends such as Juan Bravo Murillo and Joaquín Francisco Pacheco wrote under the cover of bucolic pen-names and calling themselves Sons of Apollo (Graham 1974: 23). Yet literature was also a way of making a political statement: as liberal figures such as Quintana or Francisco Martínez de la Rosa had done before him, Donoso decided to write a literary piece on Juan de Padilla, the leader of the revolt of the Castilian *comuneros* (1520–22) against Carlos I (Schramm 1936: 33–4). The liberals, seeking to portray constitutional rights as the modern version of idealized medieval freedoms, often presented Padilla, seen a martyr of despotic absolutism, as their forerunner (Labanyi 2005: 67).

On the conclusion of his legal studies, Donoso spent a year in Madrid (furnished with a recommendation letter by Quintana) polishing and augmenting the knowledge gained at Seville. During the period between 1829 and 1831, Donoso returned to Don Benito and joined his father's law firm. These were years of intensive reading, covering the following authors: Rousseau, Machiavelli, Voltaire, Madame de Staël, de Pauw, Helvétius, Montaigne, Montesquieu, Ferguson, Chateaubriand, Byron and Calderón de la Barca (Schramm 1936: 40–3). The impact of such readings on Donoso can be measured in the erudite letters which he wrote to his university friends, letters containing authoritative judgements on European philosophy. Interestingly, Donoso found the sensualist philosophy followed by Locke, Condillac and Destutt de Tracy to be wanting (Donoso 1829a, *OC* I: 174–6). Sensualist philosophy was constructed upon the basic tenet that man's knowledge came only from his sense perceptions. It ran against those who were convinced that divine revelation could be a valid source of certainty (i.e. not directly verified by the senses) or that men possessed certain innate ideas such as God's existence (Herr 1958: 69).

Yet Donoso's reaction against sensualism symbolised, above all, his emancipation from the ideas which had fascinated previous generations of Spanish intellectuals (i.e. the eighteenth-century *ilustrados*); as Graham put it, by re-educating himself according to his age's needs and viewpoints, Donoso was implicitly proclaiming 'his intellectual independence as a Romantic' (1974: 26). Whereas ascertaining the full significance of Romanticism in Spain is outside the scope of this work, it is nonetheless important to refer to the main debates in the scholarship. As Ginger wittingly argues, Spanish Romanticism is often viewed as having been a 'brief eruption [in the mid-1830s] of a spirit of aesthetic and intellectual adventure', as in the works of Mariano José de Larra, that was eventually superseded by 'the triumph of kitsch nationalism, orthodox Catholic moralizing [and] hollow cliché', as illustrated by the works of novelist Fernán Caballero and dramatist José Zorrilla (2007: 125). In other words, it is often assumed that the 'defeat of radicalism in literature' gave way to 'a restorative, traditionalist and Catholic Romanticism founded on Schlegelian principles' (Flitter 2006: 60). This argument also points towards the long-lasting and pioneering influence exercised in Spain by Nicolás Böhl de Faber, a German immigrant who, acting as a 'cultural mediator' at the heart of a 'pan-European revaluation of culture', is credited with introducing German Romantic historicism to Spanish readers (Tully 2007: 97). Inspired by the Spanish-themed writings of August Wilhelm and Friedrich Schlegel, Böhl de Faber put forward a view of the Spanish national character as distinctively Christian and chivalric, best exemplified in the religiosity of the Counter-Reformation, as well as in the seventeenth-century baroque theatre of Spain's Golden Age (Álvarez Junco 2006: 55).

The advent of Schlegelian historicism signalled a crucial shift within the European imaginary. Now that the most advanced nations of Northern Europe 'turned to those who Progress had spurned', according to Iarocci, Spain became a quintessentially *romantic* place, one in which the civilized world looked for the 'mystified past of the Middle Ages' (2006: 20). What at first glance appeared as a vindication, one that glorified the country's attachment to the perennial values of religion and tradition, eventually relegated Spain to the 'periphery of the modern' (Iarocci 2006: xii). In other words, "Romantic" Spain was stuck in the past, however gilded and idealized; therefore, it could not be modern, in the sense of being progressive, rational and secular. The importance of this development is not only that it affected the way in which Spain was viewed, especially from a Northern European perspective, but the way in which Spaniards viewed themselves. The trend inaugurated by Böhl, based on the underlying assumption that Spanish national identity was essentially non-modern, was furthered by successive generations of writers, included Agustín Durán, Alberto Lista, Ramón López Soler and – last but not least – Juan Donoso Cortés (Iarocci 2006: 26). Whereas the prevailing view of Spain as impossibly non-modern had led previous scholars to argue that in Spain there had been only 'a dissemination of the detritus of European high Romanticism' (Silver 1997: 71), recent scholarship deliberately rejects the use of adjectives such as 'weak', 'derivative', 'failed' or 'absent' when referring to Hispanic cultural production. Hence, in turn, the need to avoid the uncritical pairing of Romanticism and modernity, including narrow definitions of the latter as being synonymous of secularization and rationalism. Here it is worth highlighting the plea recently made by Ginger, who argues that it is time for nineteenth-century historiography to move beyond a normative category such as 'modernity', as this presupposes searching *mostly* for what was disruptive, innovative and exceptional. If we are to trace the integration of the Spanish-speaking world into the rise of cultural modernity in the 'West', then it makes more sense to identify 'commonalities', that is, what Spain – in this case – had in common with developments elsewhere (Ginger 2020: 2, 5–6).

In the specific case of Donoso, these broader discussions prove helpful in order to avoid what is a common pitfall in the interpretation of his early works. These works are seen as meaningful only insofar as they serve as an anticipation of what was to come: the conservative turn that was fatally – or providentially, depending on the perspective – taken by Donoso and many others, due to Spain's alleged inability either to be modern or to escape its own Catholic essence (cf. Larios Mengiotti 2003). Therefore, instead of searching for the seeds of what was to come, it is more historically productive to trace the 'outpouring of connections throughout time and place' – to use Ginger's expression (2020: 2) – that Donoso orchestrated in his work. This, in turn, leads to Palti's insistence upon reconstructing the 'context of debate' in which political languages emerged, that is, borne out of the interplay between 'contending views' (Palti 2017: 402–404). As it will be seen, the works of the young Donoso are a unique illustration of how Spain's intellectual elite, far from being a passive consumer of broader European debates, actively sought to shape and influence these debates, woven around words charged of meaning: civilisation, revolution, progress and sovereignty.

Donoso's first chance to give a public expression to his ideas – a veritable rite of initiation – came in late 1829, when he was appointed to the chair of 'Estética y Literatura' (Aesthetics and Literature) in the Colegio de Humanidades of the neighbouring town of Cáceres in Extremadura. This position had been offered first to Quintana who, in turn, recommended the twenty-year old and initially reluctant Donoso for the post (Graham 1974: 28). The speech that inaugurated the activities of the Colegio was entrusted to Donoso who decided to address a monumental topic: the origins of modern European civilisation. He mainly focused upon the Middle Ages, in order to highlight the cohesive powers of Christianity, conceived of in terms of a moral revolution, one which had allowed Europe to overcome the chaos which came from the fall of the Roman Empire. Revealing his readings of Chateaubriand and Guizot, Donoso asserted the idea that Christianity had then been a crucial element in keeping Europe together, because 'their religion was one, one the head of the Church, one the interest of the religion and one the interest of Christians' (Donoso 1829b, OC I: 186, 194). As Graham insists, Donoso, guided by his readings of Madame de Stäel, Byron and Durán, made here a crucial distinction between Christian and pagan (or rationalistic) civilisations – one with long-lasting consequences in his oeuvre. This led Donoso to chastise eighteenth-century classicist literature, which he saw as an aesthetic and philosophical regression to pagan antiquity and praised instead the revival of older Christian traditions of Europe allegedly contained in contemporary Romantic literature (Graham 1974: 29–30).

Shortly afterwards, Donoso forsook poetry for politics. In the first half of 1832, he moved to Madrid. The political circumstances of Spain were about to change dramatically. Fernando VII had been confronted by the key issue of his own succession, as he had had two daughters in the course of his four marriages. He decreed a Pragmatic Sanction (1830) which, by allowing female succession to the throne, implicitly excluded his brother Don Carlos from power (Canal 2000: 52–3). Following the death of Fernando in 1833, the Bourbon family split into two contending branches, thus providing the basic lines in which political conflict would develop during the following decades. The king's widow, María Cristina, would act as queen regent until the majority of age of Isabel, who came to the throne in 1843. The king's brother, Don Carlos, would resort to violence in order to oppose Isabel's right to succession, as shown in the First Carlist War (1833–1840). Although she was far from being enthusiastic about liberalism, the threat represented by Carlism forced María Cristina to enter into an alliance of convenience with liberal political groups, from radicals to moderates. So, thanks to the divisions in right-wing politics, moderate liberal ideals were able to be asserted within the political scene (Burdiel 1998: 904).

In a context in which expressing one's political allegiance was crucial to social advancement, Donoso began his career with a statement, a *Memoria sobre la situación actual de la Monarquía [Statement on the Current Situation of the Monarchy]* addressed to the king (Donoso 1832, OC I: 213–23). Donoso depicted himself as a moderate and a supporter of Isabel's right to the throne, and skilfully argued that Spain was threatened less by the leftist and liberal-minded revolutionaries than by the rightist partisans of Don Carlos. He also emphasised that the bourgeoisie and the bureaucracy ought to be the pillars of the monarchy, and even suggested the convocation of Cortes (Graham 1974: 32–3). By February 1833, Donoso fully reaped the fruits of this intervention, as he entered the civil bureaucracy in the Ministry of Grace and Justice (Secretaría de Estado y del Despacho de Gracia y Justicia de Indias), where he passed from being fifth clerk to head of his section in just three years (Dardé 2015: 11–12; Graham 1974: 34). Every advance in Donoso's political career would have, from now onwards, a written counterpart: a rhetorical, literary statement of his political ideals.

II. Donoso: a politician with a European outlook

Finding a *juste milieu* between tradition and modern developments in political thought was a central question for contemporary Spanish writers. For those of a liberal orientation, the 1830s marked a key transition from a revolutionary to a post-revolutionary understanding of liberalism (Suárez Cortina 2006: 12). For the two main families of Spanish liberals, *progresistas* and *moderados*, it was fundamental to maintain a constitutional and representative government in Spain – their disagreements stemming mostly on how much weight to give to both the Church and the monarchy, and on how to reconcile central with local and regional politics. At the same time, both liberal families were convinced that such government was in urgent need of a more stable basis. The most vivid feature of this passage to a post-revolutionary liberalism was the gradual abandonment of the principle of popular sovereignty, once enshrined in the Constitution of 1812. In the 1830s, this principle came increasingly under suspicion. It was seen as leading to a potentially dangerous extension of political rights to broad segments of society: if taken to its very last (i.e. democratic) consequences, it would be translated into universal (i.e. male) suffrage and even to a republican form of government. Therefore, in the 1830s, the liberal revolution was the subject of a reinterpretation in what Fuentes labels a 'mesocratic key'. Hence, in the political writings of this period, the 'virtuous middle classes' would take a leading role as mythical protagonists of Spain's political life, thus displacing the 'heroic people' that had once led the independence struggles against the French from centre stage (Fuentes 2006: 298).

A good illustration of how Donoso was influenced by these developments is his first serious political writing, *Consideraciones sobre la diplomacia [Considerations on Diplomacy]* (1834), an essay that served the purpose of symbolically uniting the cause of Spain with that of the most forward-looking part of Europe. It was spurred on by the signing of the Quadruple Alliance in 1834 between Britain, France, Spain and Portugal. This pact aimed at defending the constitutional regimes of the Iberian Peninsula from disruptive legitimist and absolutist movements such as Spanish Carlism and Portuguese Miguelism (Jover Zamora 1991: 254). This allowed Donoso to insist that Spain was not the backward and absolutist country identified with Don Carlos and the Holly Alliance but a country which willingly supported a 'free and moderate government' (1834, *OC* I: 255). He further dwelt upon the exemplariness of Spain within the European context, describing Rafael de Riego's revolt in 1820 against Fernando VII and demanding the return of the 1812 Constitution, as having been a 'great example' of the modern battle against absolutism (1834, *OC* I: 255). Nonetheless, Donoso clearly distanced himself from Riego and from early Spanish liberalism. The democratic nature of the Constitution of 1812, he argued, was a reflection of the historical moment in which it had appeared, as the common fight against the French had blurred social differences (Donoso 1834, *OC* I: 246–50). When the power returned to the throne, as the argument went, neither king nor people had been able to reach a compromise. According to Donoso, neither the Constitution of Cádiz nor absolutism corresponded to the present needs of Spain. His middle-of-the road perspective was best expressed in his idea of sovereignty: it was not to be found in the general will or in the divine right of kings, but in the incarnation of intelligence and justice at a specific historical moment (Donoso 1834, *OC* I: 264–5). Defining sovereignty, or *who* was entitled to embody the spirit of the present age, became the crux of his early works.

The idea that, at moments of profound historical change, a specific social class ought to play the role of embodying and materializing a series of collective aims, was far from being exclusive to Donoso (Fuentes 2006: 295). In fact, these reflections around what was incipient theory of class struggle were a common feature of contemporary Spanish liberal thought. As mentioned before, this led to an increasingly positive depiction of the urban middle classes in speeches and press articles, thus mirroring the prevailing idea of progress, seen as an ever-ascending march to a future of wealth, prosperity and freedom (Fuentes 2006: 291). The association between 'middle classes' and 'progress', however typical of mid-nineteenth century political writings, should not be taken – from today's perspective – at face value. Recent historiography has departed from the idea that liberalism was the ideological counterpart of the rise of the middle classes into power – that is, after the concomitant demise of the feudal aristocracy. In nineteenth-century Spain, as the work of Cruz has demonstrated, there was a high degree of continuity in the social composition of politically and economically dominant groups. Despite the liberal legal framework that recognised the equality of citizens before the law, the road to power and wealth continued to be based 'on the privilege of belonging to a family or to a network of mutual solidarity' (Cruz 1996: 2006). At the same time, however, Cruz highlights this period's increased fluidity within the 'mechanisms of social promotion', as well as the intense 'rural-urban interaction' that took place, as locally dominant elites acted as a bridge with central power in Madrid (Cruz 1996: 194–5).

The path taken by Donoso mirrored these developments. His position as member of an affluent and influential family of Extremadura was strengthened by his marriage in 1830 to Teresa García Carrasco, a union in which 'profession and land joined to commerce and land' (Graham 1974: 30). Although full of tragedies, such as the death of a first child at two years of age and the death of Teresa herself in 1835, this marriage certainly facilitated the road that led Donoso to the epicentre of politics in Madrid. There, as it will be seen, Donoso developed an acute interest in shaping the very definition of who should be in – or, to be more precise, who could join – the ruling classes in liberal Spain. Like many of his contemporaries, he was driven by the conviction that 'the divorce between freedom and order has produced all the catastrophes in human societies' (1834, OC I: 280).

The way in which Donoso would frame this question (liberty & order) shows clearly the nature of his desire to think about Spain within a European context. Generally speaking, the influence of French and British authors upon Spain's political thinkers was facilitated by the liberals' experience of exile during the two reigns of Fernando VII: 1814–1820 and 1823–1833

(Fernández Sarasola 2005: 74). For moderate liberals, from Martínez de la Rosa to Alberto Lista, it was essential to reconcile both the monarchy and the representative system, mainly by addressing the imbalance which the 1812 Constitution had created between the executive and legislative powers, given that it favoured the Cortes at the expense of the king. The transition to a post-revolutionary liberalism can be vividly illustrated by the former *exaltado* (radical) liberal Martínez de la Rosa, who became the author of the *Estatuto Real* (Royal Statute) in 1834. Promulgated in the midst of a civil war, this semi-constitutional document was conceived of as a compromise between 'mild absolutism and the most moderate liberalism' (Burdiel 2010: 34), with the aim of securing liberal support for the fight against Carlism (Estrada 1998: 244). It granted the monarch a leading role in conducting the State's affairs and made suffrage heavily dependent upon property ownership, but ultimately stood for a defence of the parliamentary system (Mücke 2008: 426–427). Writing in 1835, Martínez de la Rosa referred to what he regarded as being mankind's key concern: 'what are the means of pairing order with freedom?' (1835: xiii). In his view, society could never reach an agreement on the grounds of political theories, nor did it make sense to argue on the basis of ancient privileges or primitive rights. The task ahead was mainly a practical one: to harmonise the interests prevailing in society.

A similar pursuit, the transformation of what had been revolutionary goals into peaceful and stable institutions, was shared by the so-called French *doctrinaires*, whose ideas exercised a strong influence in Spain. The *doctrinaires* had actively espoused the cause of constitutional monarchy since the Bourbon Restoration (1814–1830), presenting themselves as an alternative to the extremes represented by the ultra-royalists and the republicans (Fernández Sebastián 1997: 132; Gunn 2009: 399). This was a project which would roughly crystallise in the reign of the 'citizen king', Louis Philippe (1830–1848). The *doctrinaires* were not a political party as such, but an elite movement formed by 'intellectual politicians' who occupied important posts both in the government and the university (Díez del Corral 1956: 15). Due to its small size, the *doctrinaires* were once ironically described as *le parti sur le canapé* (Craiutu 2004: 40); however influential, it was composed of a few members: Pierre Royer-Collard, Prosper de Barante, Victor de Broglie, Victor Cousin, Camille Jordan, François Guizot and Charles de Rémusat. Theirs was a 'liberalism under siege', that is, compelled to find a middle ground between those who wanted to continue the Revolution and those who dreamt about a return to the Old Regime (Craitu 2003: 8–9).

Under the motto 'liberty without anarchism, order without despotism', the *doctrinaires* favoured a constitutional monarchy based on limited suffrage (Craiutu 2003:14, 280). Their political ideas were aimed at finding a *juste milieu* (i.e. being anti-revolutionary without being reactionary) and therefore shared a series of similarities with the Spanish moderate liberals, mainly: the desire to empower the upper middle classes, the emphasis upon Christianity and monarchy as being the pillars of the European civilisation, and the rejection of the 'extremes' represented by both despotism and democracy (Fernández Sebastián 1997: 134–5). Reception of the *doctrinaires*' ideas had already begun in Spain after the Liberal Triennium (1820–1823) especially within the intellectual circle of Alberto Lista; moreover, liberals such as the Count of Toreno and Martínez de la Rosa had actively sought Guizot's friendship (Fernández Sarasola 2005: 66, 73). But the influence of the doctrinaires only took shape from 1833 onwards, as the death of Fernando VII opened up once again the possibility of returning to a constitutional regime.

Perhaps the most characteristic feature of the *doctrinaires* was their theory of sovereignty, regarded not as a divine attribute or the result of a primeval social contract, but as the outcome of a long-standing historical process. In other words, through a series of delicate intellectual manoeuvres, the *doctrinaires* adhered to representative government insofar it was the legitimate consequence of a series of events (i.e. at some points in history, certain social classes were bound to be the historical incarnation of the 'sovereignty of reason'), and not because it stood for a timeless, abstract popular will. Their main preoccupation was, in a nutshell, to prevent arbitrary power exercised either by the monarch or in the name of the people. There is a degree of controversy among scholars as regards the influence exercised by doctrinaire theory on sovereignty upon Spanish thinkers (Díez del Corral 1956: 400, 440; Craitu 2003: 141–143; Fernández Sarasola 2005: 76). Nonetheless, the fact remains that *doctrinaire* ideas were in vogue in Spain during the 1830s, and their influence can be traced in the debates staged within a unique institution: the Ateneo of Madrid.

Founded in 1820 and reopened in 1835, the Ateneo was a meeting point for the Spanish intellectual elite: it hosted 'chairs' delivered by distinguished personalities and provided 'sections' for the study and debate of specific topics, mostly related to economic and political reform (Fox 1998: 28). The Ateneo eventually became the 'anteroom of Parliament' (Fernández Sebastián 1997: 32), especially for the supporters of liberal moderate ideas, whose views predominated in the Ateneo between 1835 and 1868. The Ateneo would play a similar role to the University of the Sorbonne which, due to the immense popularity of the lectures given by Cousin and Guizot, was crucial in the diffusion of the *doctrinaire* political ideas. In Madrid, the interplay between French and Spanish influences was especially reflected in a series of lectures delivered on what was a relatively new development within Spanish (legal) history: constitutional political law. In fact, the constitution of 1812 had made provisions for the education of Spanish people in constitutional matters (article 368), so that the constitution would be the matter of study in universities and literary establishments (Garrorena 1974: 21–22).

In the case of the Ateneo, the chair of constitutional law, the most prestigious of all, as well as symbol of the tensions between progressives and moderates, was occupied successively by Juan Donoso Cortés (1836–1837), Antonio Alcalá Galiano (1843) and Joaquín Francisco Pacheco (1844). In the case of Donoso, the spirit of his *Lecciones sobre derecho político constitucional [Lectures on Constitutional Political Law]* (1836–7) had already been heralded by a pamphlet: *La ley electoral considerada en su base y en su relación con el espíritu de nuestras instituciones [The electoral law from a legal standpoint and in relation to the spirit of our institutions]* (1835), written in response to the government's plan for electoral reform. In short, Donoso argued here that the right to vote should be given according to income. Whereas this only confirmed what was already a fact (only 0,1 % of the Spanish population could vote, a percentage that was raised only to 2.2 % in 1837), the true novelty was in *how* this was justified (Pro 2019: 540). As Donoso claimed, the educated and property-owning middle classes were the country's 'legitimate aristocracies' and, as such, the most capable of embodying the sovereignty of intelligence in the direction of the State. He regarded the deputies to the Cortes much less as representatives of the people than as the historical incarnation of intelligence (Donoso 1835, *OC* I: 309, 311).

The first of Donoso's *Lecciones* at the Ateneo began, with a passionate defence of representative government, seen as capable to 'respect human individuality without loosening the social bond and to preserve this bond without mutilating the individual' (Lección I: 22-XI-1836; *OC* I: 336). In the third lecture, using an eclectic approach, highly reminiscent of what Royer-Collard thought the role of modern philosophy was, Donoso was even more emphatic about the historical task which representative government ought to accomplish: 'it must bring together all the truths that exist in a state of dispersion, it must complete all the incomplete truths, it must draw limits to all the exaggerated truths' (Lección III: 6-XII-1836; *OC* I: 349).

By redefining the very essence of representative government, Donoso was expressing the desire of himself and other *moderados* to find an alternative to both reactionary Carlism and radical, revolutionary liberalism. In an implicit attempt to debunk the views of Don Carlos' followers, Donoso expressed his mistrust of the French traditionalist thinkers, namely De Maistre, Bonald, and Chateaubriand. Their school of thought upheld divine revelation and the authority of the Church at the cost of human reason (Lección IX: 14-II-1837; *OC* I: 421). In denying the perfectibility of men, Donoso argued, traditionalist thinkers denied the possibility of human progress and therefore condemned society to immobility:

...then doubt, that morass of the moral world, takes control of certain intelligences which, endowed with a weak faith in the perfectibility of man, do not believe in liberty, because they look at it in a moment of eclipse, and seeking a new faith and a new belief that might be more solid and firmer, they find them at the foot of altars and in the concept of divine right. This situation is horrible, gentlemen; this divorce between liberty and intelligence is a sacrilege (Lección III: 6-XII-1836; *OC* I: 358).

Above all, Donoso's attempt at tempering revolutionary liberalism was expressed in his own definition of sovereignty. This involved, in the first place, making a sophisticated intellectual manoeuvre. Hence Donoso described both popular sovereignty and the divine right of kings as being 'reactionary principles'. It must be taken into account that he had defined reactions (i.e. extremes in political thought) as being either 'an exaggerated truth or an incomplete truth' (Lección II, *OC* I: 349). Donoso skilfully argued that both despotism and democracy led to tyranny, being political systems which were supposedly based upon an identical claim: the right of the king and the people, respectively, to exercise an omnipotent power over society (Lección V: 3-I-1837; *OC* I: 375–6).

It was an uneasy equilibrium that Donoso was able to reach with his own concept of sovereignty, deeply anti-democratic and yet not aristocratic in the traditional sense. He stated that 'the most intelligence have a right to lead; the less intelligent have a duty to obey' (Lección VI: 10-I-1837; *OC* I: 389), later explaining how intelligence had been 'inoculated' into the middle classes from the eighteenth century onwards (Lección VIII: 31-I-1837; *OC* I: 416). Interestingly, according to what Garrorena states, a similar point would be made by the former *exaltado* liberal Alcalá Galiano, who in 1838 succeeded Donoso at the Ateneo's chair of constitutional law. Instead of resorting to Donoso's historicist and even theological arguments, Alcalá Galiano resorted to a sort of sociological realism to make the same point as his predecessor: that the government should be an expression of the predominant interests within society (Garrorena 1974: 160–161).

It might be tempting to conclude that Donoso was an unaccomplished historian, given that this lack of accuracy was a recurrent feature in his historical writings, 'which are only excuses to present theoretical points of view' (Díez del Corral 1956: 490). Or, more significantly, it is tempting to argue that Donoso *misinterpreted* liberalism. This is the view held by Díez Álvarez, who suggests that Donoso rejected the 'socialisation' of political power inseparable from liberalism, so that he might have merely used a liberal robe to cloak his own 'traditionalism', rooted in an alleged desire to reform absolutism in Spain (2003: 311–312). Yet it is important to highlight the position from which Donoso was speaking. His celebration of the role of the upper middle classes in Spain was indeed self-interested. But his role as a *moderado* did not lie in the past, but in the future. It would gain its full meaning in the decade to come, as the *moderados* rose to power and gave a decisive impulse to the construction of the liberal State in Spain. This State, as Pro convincingly demonstrates, was not a mere update of the eighteenth-century monarchy to changing circumstances, but a novel and revolutionary development set against a context of crisis and war (Pro 2019: 51–52, 83).

Donoso's profile fulfilled that of the archetypal *moderado*: a well-off law graduate with literary interests and anti-absolutist outlook who, after a stint in a law firm or a university, made his way into politics (Fox 1998: 29). As it had happened during Spain's 'first' liberalism, the political and administrative elite continued to be overwhelmingly composed by lawyers – who, in addition, were the main and often the only alternative to military men in high-profile posts (Pro 2019: 168–169). They shared a specific and elitist 'legal culture', that is, a cultural predisposition to think about politics in legal terms, as well as a rhetorical type of argumentation, one which invoked a vast catalogue of 'authorities' past and present in its support (Pro 2019: 179–182). This cultural milieu explains, to a certain degree, Donoso's tendency towards grandiloquence in both historical and philosophical matters – a trait that was often ridiculed by his contemporaries. For example, the poet and moderate liberal Ramón de Campoamor wrote a humorous portrait of the speeches given by Donoso in his role as a deputy to the Spanish Cortes (1845: 99):

In the field of history Mr. Donoso is as efficient as Napoleon, as devastating as Attila, and as invincible as both of them. He bridges historical abysses with philosophical-novelistic induction, bypassing the mountains that hinder him, hiding a thousand years between two commas, or eliminating a dynasty by means of a parenthesis.

The *Lecciones* left no doubt of Donoso's erudition in historical and philosophical matters while, at the same time, showing its author's pragmatism on occasions in which rhetoric prevailed over historical accuracy. But Donoso's erudite references to Greece, Rome and the Middle Ages also served a higher purpose: to constantly remind the reader (or listener, in this case) of his conviction that Spain shared a common European heritage. He thus expressed his awareness of the recent development of historical studies in Europe, mentioning the names of Niebuhr, Ferguson, Michelet, Gibbon and Montesquieu (Lección VIII: 31-I-1837; *OC* I: 405). Moreover, Donoso highlighted the intellectual exchange between European countries, implicitly revealing his own vision of Europe, as composed of France, Britain, Germany... and Spain. He mentioned several instances of fruitful intellectual exchange, such as the interest of Montesquieu in the workings of the British Constitution, the influence exercised by Locke upon Condillac and Rousseau, the fact that Royer-Collard had translated the works of Thomas Reid and thus introduced the Scottish School of common sense into France, and the influence which Immanuel Kant's idealism had exercised upon Benjamin Constant and Victor Cousin.

In addition, Donoso was aware of the most recent developments in radical political thought, such as the Utopian socialism of Saint-Simon which connected ideas of the liberation of the exploited classes with Christian views on brotherly love (Lección IX: 14-II-1837; *OC* I: 422–8). What Donoso's impressive display of erudition actually mirrored was a thriving network of cultural transfer between European countries, marked by a process of mediation, reception and especially translation: into different languages, as well as across a wide range of contexts. For example, Donoso is credited with having first introduced Giambattista Vico's philosophy of history in Spain, as well as with having been one of the first Spanish authors to engage with the ideas of Fichte, Schelling and Hegel. Yet it was thanks to French sources, namely the works of Victor Cousin, Jules Michelet and Madame de Staël, that Donoso became acquainted with these Italian and German authors (Garrorena 1974: 258–259, 266–267). Through indirect means, Donoso would owe to German idealism – and especially Hegel – the idea that reason is ultimately social and collective, and thus different to individual free will, as well as a belief in the possibility of discerning a series of laws ruling the course of history (Garrorena 1974: 282–283).

The last of the *Lecciones*, dwelling upon the importance of political reforms, proved to be momentous for a variety of reasons. According to Graham, the position taken by Donoso was controversial to a point that it prompted the cancellation of subsequent lectures (Graham 1974: 43). In this last lecture, Donoso asserted that if the cause of revolutionary turmoil was found in imperfect and faulty social habits, there could be only two remedies: the less stringent if gradual correctives afforded by legislation, and the expedient solution of a dictatorship. Apparently, Donoso abruptly switched to a theory of dictatorship as a way of proving his independence from *doctrinaire* ideas, as a reply to the harsh criticism of the radical liberal Gallardo who had nicknamed him as *Guizotín* (Graham 1974: 44–5). Yet, in previous lectures, Donoso had carefully stressed that 'social omnipotence', namely a dictatorship, was an emergency measure in moments in which society was threatened by a cataclysm. Hence a dictatorship exercised by a given people, man or king would be legitimate insofar it saved society from being wrecked. A dictator's legitimacy would be directly proportionate to its *expediency*: 'in such cases, victory alone confers the rights and makes power legitimate' (Lección VI: 10-I-1837; *OC* I: 391).

According to Garrorena, neither the Ateneo nor the government of José María Calatrava were to be blamed for the cancellation of Donoso's course of lectures. Apparently, he took the decision himself out of concerns for his personal safety. Sparked by his provocative critique of the *progresistas* during this last lecture, Donoso received a series of anonymous letters threatening his life (Garrorena 1974: 123–4). He had drawn a comparison between the 'bloody demagogues' of the French Revolution and the *progresistas*, whom he accused of engineering the so-called Mutiny of La Granja – a royal palace at the outskirts of the city of Segovia, north of Madrid. In August 1836, a group of sergeants declared themselves against the regency of María Cristina, forcing her to declare a return to the constitution of 1812, which ought to remain in vigour until a new constitution – as it happened in 1837 – was drafted and promulgated (Barrios 2016: 261–262). During the Reign of Terror in France (1793–1794), Donoso had claimed, implicitly inviting his listeners to draw a parallel with current circumstances, 'the people were given neither bread nor freedom, and instead they were deprived of their God' (Lección X: 21-II-1837; *OC* I, 444). Writing in 1837 for a *moderado* paper, *El Porvenir*, he also accused the progressive liberals of being 'atheist' due to their supposed failure to proclaim their Catholic faith publicly. Ultimately, what Donoso criticised was the *progresistas*' attacks on the material wealth of the Church, which he interpreted as being a denial of the strongly religious character of the Spanish people to whom 'worship, religion and its ministers are one and the same thing' (Donoso 1837a: 490).

The reality was more complex and went well beyond a supposed façade of anti-clericalism. On the one hand, it was true that the *progresistas* – in power since 1835 – would put an end to the structural foundation of the Old Regime in Spain (Burdiel 2008: 48–49). This meant, among other things, equality before the law and freedom of expression, but also the abolition of tithes and a massive disentailment (*desamortización*) and subsequent sale of Church properties. Up to a certain point, these measures were not new; they were part of the spirit of regalism which had been present in Spain since late eighteenth century – that is, liberal governments attempted at doing what monarchs had done before: moulding the Church according to their own interests. Yet the *progresistas* did much more than that: they consolidated Spain's constitutional regime and, in the process, set the foundations of the modern liberal State. With civil war raging throughout the country, these measures not only ameliorated the financial penury of the State but facilitated the creation of both a permanent army and an incipient civil administration (Pro 2019: 241–242). In the specific case of Donoso, his position vis-à-vis the *progresistas* was far less simple as his rhetoric suggests. In late 1835, he did not object to the sale of ecclesiastical properties undertaken by the government of Mendizábal and, as a proof of his disposition as 'loyal government employee', was even entrusted with the mission of ensuring loyalty towards the government in Extremadura (Graham 1974: 39; Dardé 2015: 12).

By the late 1830s, Donoso combined his role as a journalist and deputy to the Cortes. In his speeches and articles, he shared his thoughts on how to overcome revolution and achieve the regeneration of Spain. In 1838, his disenchantment with *doctrinaire* ideas became all too evident when, in a series of articles published in *El Correo Nacional*, he publicly severed his links with this school of thought. At first, Donoso had paid due credit to the doctrinaires for having raised a voice of peace and concord at a moment when France was being torn by antagonistic political groups, referring to them as 'representatives of common sense' (Donoso 1838a: *OC* I: 495). Yet Donoso thought that their ideas were ill-suited to the present times; in other words, he believed the *doctrinaires* could be labelled 'doctors of an impotent science' because they were not *dogmatic* enough. Royer-Collard and Guizot could not teach societies how to move forward because they lacked a dogma which, in Donoso's terms, accounted for a set of political beliefs which could solve 'the problem of human perfectibility' (Donoso 1838a: *OC* I: 497–9). Consequently, Donoso argued, their ideas were not a sure guide to follow in either everyday politics or exceptional circumstances. At any rate, he claimed, it was impossible for the *doctrinaires* to keep forever the balance between monarchic and democratic elements: 'occupied in putting the claims of the Throne and the claims of the people at bay [...] they are looked upon with disgust by the people, and are frowned upon by the king' (Donoso 1838a: *OC* I: 501).

Exploring Donoso's rejection of the *doctrinaires*, based mainly on their lack of dogmatism, leads to an important aspect of their thought which he left mostly untouched: Guizot's idea of European civilisation. It is important to mention that a book by Guizot, *The History of civilisation in Europe*, which captivated Spanish intellectuals during the mid-nineteenth century to the point that, in the ironic phrase of Menéndez y Pelayo, it became 'the Koran of our publicists and statesmen' (1958, VI: 29). This book was the published version of the lectures which Guizot delivered at the Sorbonne between 1828 and 1830. He had written them with the immediate aim of opposing the ultra-royalists' intentions of recreating an aristocratic society in France, proving that French institutions had been transformed long before 1789 (Siedentop 1997: xv-i). In just a ten-year period, several Spanish editions of Guizot's *History* appeared in Madrid (1839, 1840, 1846, and 1847), Barcelona (1839 and 1840) and Cádiz (1839); additionally, his ideas were spread in periodicals such as *Revista de Madrid [Journal of Madrid]*, *El Correo Nacional [The National Post]* of Madrid and *El Guardia Nacional [The National Guard]* of Barcelona (Flitter 2006: 40; Fernández Sebastián 1997: 33). Moreover, Guizot would be the inspiration behind the work of several Spanish historians who, in turn, helped to consolidate the idea of civilisation was an appropriate means of measuring a collective historical experience, while nevertheless tracing a strong link between 'civilisation' and their own Catholic values (Fernández Sebastián 2014: 208–210).

Making a crucial distinction between social structure and political order, Guizot sought to demonstrate that the Revolution had not been a complete break with the past, but an adjustment of the political institutions to the new social condition that had developed over time (Craiutu 2004: 43–5). Guizot made a comprehensive account of the history of individual countries of Europe (i.e. France, Britain, Germany, Spain and Italy) in order to prove that the rise of the third estate over the aristocracy and the clergy had been

SPAIN BELONGS TO EUROPE

an inevitable and legitimate phenomenon, representing a triumph over, privilege and absolutism. In sum, Guizot portrayed the history of Europe as the history of liberty. Yet he made clear that what distinguished Europe from other civilisations was its pluralism (Rosenberg 2020: 134). Based upon a never-ending struggle of its constitutive elements, freedom and diversity were guaranteed insofar as no value, class or institution won complete supremacy over the others:

Now nothing but the general freedom of all rights, all interests, and all opinions, the free manifestation and legal coexistence of all these forces, can ever restrain each force and each power within its legitimate limits, prevent it from encroaching on the rest, and, in a word, cause the real and generally profitable existence of free inquiry (Guizot 1828: 244).

Guizot's conception of European civilisation as an arena of free enquiry led not only to an idea of separation of powers, but also to a firm defence of religious toleration. In his view, one completely different to that of eighteenth-century Spanish reactionaries, the Reformation heralded the French Revolution insofar 'it was a great attempt at the enfranchisement of the human mind; [...] an insurrection of the human mind against absolute power in the spiritual order' (Guizot 1828: 203). The fact that Guizot himself was Protestant did have a significant impact in the reception of his ideas in Spain. For many Spanish liberals, who were overwhelmingly Catholic, Protestantism exercised nevertheless a particular fascination. For them, protestant spirituality appeared to have a higher degree of compatibility with liberal principles such as progress and the independence of individual consciousness (Fradera 2003: 283). Even Donoso would endorse then Guizot's approval of the Protestant Revolution by stating that Martin Luther 'concluded, indeed, the great work of secularizing human intelligence' (Lección II: 29-XI-1836; OC I: 341). In addition, echoes of Guizot would be felt in Donoso's depiction of the French Revolution as a 'humanitarian revolution' (Lección IV: 20-XII-1836; OC I: 367). In 1789, Donoso further claimed, the democratic spirit of Christianity had reached a peak by emancipating all classes in society, thus consummating 'the great drama beginning with the crucifixion of Jesus and concluding in the atonement of Louis' (1835: 307).

But whereas Guizot had emphasised that the representation of *all* interests and opinions was the essential characteristic of the European civilisation, Donoso tended to isolate the Christian factor from the rest of the equation which according to Guizot had brought about modern Europe. By the end of 1838, in a series of articles published in *El Correo Nacional*, a monarchic and constitutionalist paper, Donoso advanced the view that, after years of political unrest, European peoples had finally realised that only religious truth could serve as the indestructible foundation of society, that Christianity – understood of as Catholicism – in itself constituted a 'complete civilisation' (Donoso 1838b: 653). In doing so, it appears that Donoso ignored Guizot's comments on how the overwhelming presence of the Catholic Church in Spain had stifled the country's intellectual and scientific life. Yet Donoso cannot be blamed for failing to understand the benefits associated with the free discussion of ideas, as well as with freedom of worship. In the context of Hispanic political culture, '[religious] intolerance meant literally unity of the body politic; tolerance, on the other hand, meant disunion, illegitimacy, even civil war' (Fernández Sebastián 2008a: 21). Consequently, Donoso was eager to stress that political unity was attained when citizens shared not only a common legal framework but also the same religion. As will be explored in the next section, it would be Jaime Balmes who would epitomize the reaction against the influence exercised by Guizot upon Spanish intellectuals. And, in doing so, he would put forward what was then a novel intellectual construct: a distinctively Catholic idea of the Spanish nation.

III. Balmes & European civilisation

What Balmes found inaccurate and ultimately offensive in Guizot's *History of the civilisation in Europe* was his appraisal of the Catholic Church. Guizot did acknowledge the fact that this Church had been 'the bond, the medium, and the principle of civilisation between the Roman and barbarian worlds' (Guizot 1828: 39). Yet he stressed how the Catholic Church had eventually denied the right of individual reason by forcing belief and physically punishing heresy; moreover, he stressed how the Church had also attempted establishing its domination over the secular authorities (Guizot 1828: 92–7). Consequently the Reformation had restored the independence of both individual thought and the temporal power, while banishing religion from politics. Following the very same steps of late eighteenth-century French critics such as Masson de Morvilliers, Guizot referred to Spain as a country in which the human mind had not been 'enfranchised', something which accounted for its having fallen into 'effeminacy and indolence' for the last three centuries (Guizot 1828: 207).

Balmes' adverse reaction to Guizot can be regarded only partly as forming part of the long-standing genre of the *apología* (apology), as reflected in the works of Juan Francisco Masdeu (*Historia crítica de España y de la cultura española [Critical History of Spain and Spanish Culture]*, 1783–1805) and Juan Pablo Forner (*Oración apologética por la España y por su mérito literario [Apologetic Oration for Spain and Her Literary Merits]*, 1786). Balmes did more than simply vindicate Spain in the face of the criticism of yet another foreigner: he actually contested Guizot's usage of the term *civilisation*, and pronounced his own judgement on what should be regarded as belonging to the truly civilised European world. The fact that Balmes resorted to historical rather than to theological arguments, mirrors an overall European trend now that church history had started to replace theology as 'an authoritative medium for religious argument' (Bennett 2019: 16–18).

The concept of civilisation was linked to the debate that took place in Spain from the late eighteenth-century onwards on the 'benefits and drawbacks' of catching up with the rest of Europe (Fernández Sebastián 2008b: 85). It was defended by those who were in favour of the modernisation of Spain, insofar as it synthesised their aspirations toward reform; it was attacked by those who felt it posed a threat to authentic Hispanic values. In the 1830s, the debates on *civilisation* gained a new prominence, partly due to the influence of Guizot and partly due to the new Romantic sensibility. With the transition from the Enlightenment to Romanticism, the concept was pluralized and fragmented: moving away from the idea of progress and entering into the realm of identity, *civilización* became *civilizaciones* (Fernández Sebastián 2008b: 87, 102). On the one hand, by seeking to describe the peculiarities of a given people's historical development, the concept of civilisation acquired an 'ethnographic' and 'relativistic' connotation; on the other, its usage became more nuanced, insofar as 'material' civilisation (i.e. technical progress) was not always regarded as being identical to 'moral' civilisation (i.e. a higher degree of civility or morality). As Fernández Sebastián concludes, in mid-century Spain, a strong tendency to trace a link between civilisation and religious values prevailed (2014: 8–10).

The new Romantic emphasis upon the authentic and the peculiar can be illustrated with the creation of a chair of 'Historia de la civilización española (History of Spanish Civilisation)' in the Ateneo of Madrid, between 1839 and 1840. As shown in the lectures of its first holder, Fermín Gonzalo Morón, any assessment of what it meant to be Spanish was inseparable from an idea of Europe, one which could be either positive or negative. Interestingly, these lectures also illustrate that Morón and his contemporaries had a quite limited idea of Europe, geographically speaking, as being circumscribed to neighbouring France and Britain. Faithful to a providentialist view of Spanish history, Morón affirmed there had once been a true Spain uncontaminated by foreign influences, specifically in times of the Catholic Kings before the advent of the Habsburg and Bourbon dynasties. This stemmed from his conviction that peoples could not be civilized by decree (Fernández Sebastián 2014b: 208), so that neither despots nor revolutionary assemblies could ever alter the very essence of the Spanish nationality. More significantly, Morón suggested that a return to such a pristine state was possible:

But without disregarding the services rendered by France, it is my intimate conviction that Spain will not be what it should be, as long as our men heading our government and parties do not abandon the servile and ridiculous parody they make of French ideas and laws, that is, as long as they do not study our history and civilisation in depth; as long as, to say it once and for all, Spain is not exclusively Spain (Gonzalo Morón 1841: 228–9).

What is remarkable about Balmes is not only that he shared in the new Romantic sensibility, but that he used it to argue that Spain should set itself free from French influence. Literature, he argued, should not consist of imitation but rather be an expression of originality, of a national spirit (Batllori 1943: 7). Balmes lamented the *afrancesamiento* (Frenchification) of Spanish literature as, in his view, the strict rules of neoclassicism had prompted Spanish writers to appropriate – albeit uncritically – French models. But Balmes did not remain in the sphere of literary criticism. His point was that 'when there is imitation at the level of language, it is because there is imitation in the realm of thought' (Balmes 1842a, *OC* VIII: 236). This could bring along, he warned, a dangerous divorce between Spanish literature (and thought) and the 'social needs' of Spain. Balmes heralded the Romantic school insofar as it was a vehicle towards the creation of an authentic social literature, therefore bringing about 'a reciprocal exchange in which society influences literature and literature influences society' (Balmes 1842a, *OC* VIII: 241). He consequently planned a series of novels with the aim of demonstrating to the broadest possible audience, through fictional characters, the benefits of religion. Only a few sketches remain of this project (OC VIII: 436–5), but it is highly reminiscent of a previous work, *El Evangelio en triunfo. Historia de un filósofo desengañado [The Gospel in Triumph. History of a Disillusioned Philosopher]* (1798) by the repentant *ilustrado* Pablo de Olavide. The fact remains that this didactic aim, along with an emphasis upon the need to adapt culture and politics to the *true* needs of the Spanish nation, became the trademark of Balmes' writings.

It was an article published in *La Paz* [*The Peace*] (Barcelona, April 1838), written in praise of Guizot's *History of civilisation*, that prompted Balmes to publicly engage with current affairs and emerge from the relative obscurity in which he had spent his first youth. The anonymous author of this article, an admirer of Guizot, described the Reformation and the French Revolution as great historical achievements, while attributing Spain's backwardness to the Inquisition and to political despotism. In a letter addressed to the editors of *La Paz*, Balmes complained of their having implicitly endorsed an article which had outraged Catholicism and destroyed historical truth (Casanovas 1948: 324–5). This was the beginning of a series of works in which Balmes vindicated Catholicism as a vehicle for civilisation. What distinguishes him most from Guizot is the belief that Christian values, thought of as the basis of social order and common good, could only be put into practice through *organised* religion. After all, Guizot had not called into question the values of Christianity, thought of as the foundation of modern liberties, but rather the institutional Church. Guizot became aware that, in modern Europe, values which once belonged to an originally corporate society were now a matter of individual choice and could only depend upon individual freedoms for its sustenance (Siedentop 1997: xxxvii). In contrast, Balmes was convinced that only Catholicism was the accurate expression of divine truth and therefore could not allow such freedom to decide. Nonetheless, his own views on the role of the Church did not exclude a discussion of issues related to political freedom, intellectual enquiry and even modern developments in science. Balmes was a priest and, as it will be demonstrated with reference to his biography and his intellectual formation that, being mostly the result of personal effort, was certainly exceptional for his time.

In February 1835, Balmes received the degree of Doctor of Divinity from the University of Cervera. On receiving his degree, Balmes was expected to give a speech praising the ruling monarch, something which was normally used to pass a judgement on the current political circumstances. Strife waged between *cristinos* and *carlistas* had been particularly acute in Catalonia, but Balmes decided to remain neutral and spoke instead about the need for educational reform in Spain (Casanovas 1948: 89–91). Between 1835 and 1838, roughly until the end of the First Carlist War (1833–1840), Balmes kept mostly away from public life and remained in his native Vic (Balmes 1846c: 518). Despite suffering from several tuberculosis crises, Balmes engaged in a wide range of activities throughout this period: reading indefatigably in the episcopal library, writing poetry, giving private lessons, and helping out with his family tannery business (Casanovas 1948: 127–8, 146). In the speech that inaugurated his acceptance of a chair of mathematics in Vic in 1837, Balmes argued that ignorance was to be blamed for both the economic problems and the religious shortcomings of Spain. Consequently, Balmes plainly stated that it was absurd to believe that scientific knowledge necessarily led to scepticism and immorality. Striking an autobiographical note, he declared that in discovering the regularities and patterns behind nature the learned man could not but acknowledge the authorship of God (Balmes 1837, OC VIII: 570–1). Only through education, Balmes promised to his listeners, would Spain be able to overcome its scientific and material backwardness. In turn, this would allow Spain to recover an independence stance within the international arena:

Let us erase that stain with which foreign pride and slander has sought to cover us, that we Spaniards belong to Africa, that we are incapable of matching them in their advances. Do not listen to those Spaniards who speak to you with contempt of our national genius and who look with a derisive smile at any establishment that is not located in France or England (Balmes 1837, OC VIII: 575).

Balmes' insistence upon the positive relationship which needed to exist between a Catholic order and intellectual advancement also informed his views on how to address the shortcomings of the Spanish Church. According to Balmes, only an enlightened and well-prepared clergy would allow Spain to put into practice the values of Catholicism. He put forward an ideal of priesthood which implicitly contested the views of both eighteenth-century *ilustrados* and nineteenth-century *liberales* who had consistently charged the Catholic clergy with two main flaws: idleness and ignorance. He thus claimed in a speech delivered in Vic between 1838 and 1841 and titled 'Discurso sobre los males causados por la ociosidad' [Speech on the evils produced by idleness]:

What would become of religion if you, the chosen portion of the priesthood of Jesus Christ, should now give yourselves up to idleness? It would not be enough, no, to fulfil your high ministry or, prostrated between the vestibule and the altar, that you should weep for the sins of the people; it is necessary that you attract the respect of the people, by combining the censer waving in our hands with the prestige of wisdom; [...] so that you may be able to shine rays of truth and eloquence to pulverise the sophistry of impiety and ignorance (Balmes 1838 ca., OC VIII: 581).

These were times in which the role of the Church within Spain came increasingly into question. Balmes was aware that the clergy could only maintain its claim to the moral leadership of the country if this was justified by an adequate education. The problem was that after a massive loss of both personnel and wealth, now that the male regular orders had been suppressed and a massive sale of ecclesiastical properties had taken place, the position of the Church had been significantly downgraded. Between the 1800s and 1830s, anti-clericalism had been a significant component of liberal ideology, as the Church was seen as a roadblock in the way of modernization (Smith 2017: 48–49). Its secular power, as well as its intervention in civil affairs, were significantly curtailed by contemporary liberal legislation. Seen retrospectively, what the Spanish revolution actually pursued was the creation of a national Church, one compatible with – and financially maintained by – the liberal State (Pro 2019: 349–350). Balmes rejected the concomitant view of the clergy as civil employees and – to use Callahan's expression (1984: 162) – fought consequently against such 'domestication of the Church' by the State. In fact, the book that marked the entrance of Balmes into the scene of national politics, *Observaciones sociales, políticas y económicas sobre los bienes del clero [Social, Political, and Economic Observations on Clerical Property]* (1840), was a discussion of the situation of the Spanish Church. The success of this book was partly due to the clever strategy concerning its dissemination: two thousand numbers of the *Observaciones* were printed in Vic and distributed in the whole of Catalonia, plus Valencia and Madrid, reaching a second edition by the end of 1840 (Casanovas 1948: 330–2).

Yet its success was mostly due to the originality of Balmes' approach to the controversial question of ecclesiastical property. Instead of resorting to lengthy quotations from the Bible or from treatises on canonical law, the arguments of the *Observaciones* were grounded upon facts and pragmatic reasons. Balmes objected to the sale of ecclesiastical properties which had taken place in the mid-1830s not only because it had impoverished the Church, but because it had made it increasingly dependent upon the State. In his view, the Church could only become an 'organising and civilising association' insofar as it had a material foundation (i.e. properties) which provided it with both stability and the means for an independent course of action (Balmes 1840a, *OC* V: 687–90). With characteristic pragmatism, Balmes believed that the ability to turn this ideal into reality depended upon the union between moral and material means. In sum, according to Balmes, the Church would be an agent of civilisation only if it had an independent standing as an institution.

The concept of civilisation, in the works of Balmes, was inseparable from a religious content; in other words, the overview of historical facts was necessarily accompanied by a series of moral imperatives. This was shown in the case of *La Civilización [The Civilisation]*, the first periodical publication that Balmes edited and coordinated. It appeared fortnightly in Barcelona, between 1841 and 1843 (Casanovas 1948: 345–6). In a series of four articles, written in 1841, Balmes returned to Guizot and his idea of civilisation. He started from the assumption that all the meanings given to the word civilisation, according to a variety of philosophical schools, had nevertheless 'a central idea: the perfecting of society' (Balmes 1841, *OC* V: 457). Then he focused upon the answer given by Guizot to this question in *The History of civilisation in Europe*, where civilisation had been defined as consisting of 'two principal facts: the development of human society, and that of man himself; on the one hand, political and social development; on the other, internal and moral development' (Guizot 1828: 245). What made Guizot's definition a problematic one, Balmes argued, was the (lack of) meaning of the word 'development'. It precluded judgements about the value of such development, as it was unable to answer the following questions: 'are there different kinds?, are all of its variants equally good?, what is good and what is bad? and what is best and what is worst?' (Balmes 1841, *OC* V: 458).

According to Balmes, who portrayed himself as someone appreciative of his age and who entertained no pessimism regarding the future, Europe nevertheless appeared as being in bad need of 'regularising principles of movement' (Balmes 1841, *OC* V: 462). This statement, as it focused upon the normative and the prescriptive, was reminiscent of Donoso's critique of the *doctrinaires'* lack of 'dogma'. Not surprisingly, the principles which Balmes had in mind were linked to religion, starting from the assumption that it was unwise to found societies upon 'the unsteady foundation of human reason' (1841, *OC* V: 463). Notwithstanding this, Balmes put forward an eminently practical (rather than a religious or moralistic) definition of civilisation, one which contained its own standards and measures of success and used a utilitarian approach:

There will be the maximum of civilisation when the greatest degree of intelligence is found in as many people as possible, the greatest degree of morality in as many people as possible, the greatest degree of well-being in as many people as possible, and the greatest degree of civilisation in as many people as possible (Balmes 1841, *OC* V: 463–4).

Balmes also believed that Guizot's idea of development, here taken as 'the development of intelligence', was elitist and narrow. Intelligence as furthered by a few 'elevated intellects' was not necessarily identical to that of the majority of the population; in other words, it referred to the few and did not necessarily translate into the well-being of the many. Therefore high culture could be misleading; it could hide deeper social problems by acting as 'a magnificent curtain concealing the bed of a dying person' (Balmes 1841, *OC* V: 469). Balmes characterised eighteenth-century France as a perfect illustration of such a situation; despite the brilliance of the *philosophes'* culture, the divorce between intelligence and morality had led to the Revolution, that is, to the end of the monarchy, to war at home and abroad and eventually to Jacobinism and Terror (Balmes 1841, *OC* V: 472). Moreover, in contrast to Donoso (and the *doctrinaires*) who had linked the concept of intelligence with that of social predominance, Balmes conceived of intelligence as inseparable,not from a social class, but from those ideas and institutions that could exercise a great influence upon the vast majority – that is, the Church and its idea of morality (Balmes 1841, *OC* V: 469–70, 474). Lastly, Balmes strongly criticised moderate and progressive liberals for their misleading definition of the 'middle classes' as being the embodiment of progress. Such definition catered to city dwellers, ranging from urban professionals to those who made a living out of commerce and industry, but left the rural middle classes outside the picture. This was seen by Balmes as a token of radical liberals' individualism and tendency to blur social hierarchies, one that carried a significant risk: that of turning 'progress' into a mere euphemism for 'revolution' (Fuentes 2006: 301).

The originality of Balmes' approach in his articles in *La Civilización*, despite his traditional defence of the authority of the Church, lies in his insistence upon addressing the topic of modern civilisation from an economic point of view. The fact that Balmes wrote from Catalonia, a Spanish province with a unique combination of rural discontent and urban conflict, ought to be highlighted. Throughout the mid- and late-nineteenth century, only the region around Barcelona mirrored the industrialisation processes characteristic of north and central Europe (Fradera 2012: 139). For Balmes, who was a first-hand witness of the social tensions which had arisen in the region as a consequence of early industrialization, it was evident that this went hand-in-hand with an astonishing increase of the 'proletarian classes' (Balmes 1841, *OC* V: 488). Later, during a trip to London, Balmes was strengthened in his conviction that modern societies should urgently address the spread of abject poverty – claiming, for example, that the growth of pauperism in Britain was on the brink of making this country's civilisation a 'solemn imposture' (Balmes 1841, *OC* V: 488–9). From this we can see how Balmes, when discussing the role of the middle classes in modern Europe, privileged issues of responsibility and even of distributive justice over the mere right to rule, as Donoso had done in his *Lecciones sobre derecho político constitucional [Lectures on Constitutional Political Law]*. The duty of the middle classes was, according to Balmes, *to civilize*: 'the duty to be civilising; that is, to procure instruction, morality and welfare to the greatest number of people' (Balmes 1841, *OC* V: 489). Yet he cautiously stated that it was pointless to promote the message of Christian fraternity outside the framework of the Church, as some modern reformers were trying to do, emphasising that Catholicism preached against the use of violence by both the rich and the poor when addressing social conflict. Balmes concluded that:

...many of the questions that today are called high politics could be simply resolved by tackling material needs, and most of the major political upheavals would have been easily remedied by some increase in the means of subsistence (Balmes 1841, *OC* V: 485).

IV. Balmes: Spain as a Catholic nation

Balmes in his historical magnum opus: *El protestantismo comparado con el catolicismo en sus relaciones con la civilización europea [Protestantism compared to Catholicism in its Relation to European Civilisation]* (1842–1844) reasserted the link that ought to exist between civilisation, understood as the most important ideal for a society to strive towards, and Christianity. This work dealt in detail with Guizot's negative views on the Catholic Church; in particular, Balmes challenged Guizot's interpretation of the Reformation as having been *the* major turning point in European history. Balmes did not regard his work's conclusions as restricted only to Spain; in fact, he intended to reach a European audience with what was conceived of as 'a work of universal apologetics' (Casanovas 1948: 360–2). Once the first volume of *El protestantismo* appeared in Barcelona, Balmes headed to Paris to prepare its French edition. The translator was Albéric de Blanche-Raffin who, along with Louis Veuillot, became one of the long-time editors of the ultramontane periodical *L'Univers* between 1843 and 1883 (Dupont 2011: 85). During his stay in Paris, he made contact with key Catholic personalities such as the preacher and theologian

Henri Lacordaire, the scholar Frédéric Ozanam, the future bishop Félix Dupanloup, the Jesuit preacher Gustave Delacroix de Ravignan, the writer and politician François-René de Chateaubriand and the Benedictine monk Dom Guéranger (Casanovas 1948: 369–70). But Balmes avoided the acquaintance of Guizot – then Minister of Foreign Affairs – for fear of risking his reputation by finding himself associated with a political party. He invoked the same reasons for not meeting Donoso, part of the *moderado* émigré circle in Paris. As many other *moderados*, he had gone into exile after a revolution in late 1840 forced Queen María Cristina to renounce to the regency, replacing her in that role with the *progresista* general Baldomero Espartero until 1843 (Burdiel 2008: 74). In mid-1842, Balmes went to London. He had been furnished by Martínez de la Rosa with a recommendation letter, addressed to the cultural entrepreneur and man of letters José Joaquín Mora, asking for his help in promoting Balmes' work in England (Casanovas 1948: 362–5). During his stay in London, Balmes noted the rising fortunes of the Anglican scholar John Henry Newman and followed carefully the development of the Oxford movement (1833–1845), a religious movement within the Church of England that called for a revival of its Catholic heritage (see Nockles 1994).

When writing his magnum opus, *Protestantism compared to Catholicism*, Balmes had less a historical than a polemical work in mind. As shown above, Balmes did not write from a position of obscurity; he was aware of developments already taking place in Europe and hoped to make his own contribution to the Catholic cause. As a result, the strength of his arguments in *El protestantismo* derives less from their historical accuracy than from their being all-encompassing generalizations, useful when deployed in a controversy. It can be said that, by positioning himself within a longstanding historical process, Balmes created an 'ad hoc past, tailored to suit his vision of future' – to use an expression that Fernández Sebastián uses in reference to the first Spanish *liberales* (Fernández Sebastián 2014: 41). The overarching objective of his book was thus to establish a causal link between Protestantism and what Balmes identified as modern evils: the proliferation of sects, laxity of conduct and revolutionary upheavals (1844i: 587). Balmes disregarded any distinction between the different branches of Protestantism; in his eyes, their separation from Catholicism already made them incapable of producing any valid religious judgement. He even stated that the first reformers' intention had never been to correct abuses within Catholicism but simply to break away from the Church's discipline and then introduce disorder and licentiousness (Balmes 1844i: 37).

In stark contradiction with Guizot's interpretation of the Reformation as an emancipation of the human spirit, Balmes believed that it had been nothing but 'the mere outcome of human passions' (1844i: 98). Even if he resorted to an argument that far from being a novelty among Catholic apologists, keen to discredit real and imagined adversaries, Balmes did engage profoundly with Guizot's ideas. Interestingly, he ended up borrowing a great deal of his ideological rival's characteristic patterning, 'apparently without irony or reserve' (Flitter 2006: 57–58). However, despite his many debts to Guizot, Balmes nevertheless arrived at the opposite conclusion, namely that Protestantism had been a deviation from true civilisation. His idea of Europe was consequently narrowed in order to fit his ideal vision of a (supposedly) harmonic, pre-Reformation order. The downside of such an argument was that it made it practically impossible to account for the positive developments which had taken place in Europe between the sixteenth- and nineteenth-centuries.

In short, Balmes blamed on Protestantism the demise of representative forms of government in Europe. To summarize, he described a sequence of events: Protestantism's hatred of authority produces anarchy; the confusion in religious and moral ideas soon leads to chaos in the political realm; public order can only be restored by a despotic government; finally, absolute rule ends up prevailing over previous representative forms of government. This sequence confirmed, according to Balmes, that Protestantism should not be regarded as the forerunner of the modern political liberty. Yet Balmes claims about the 'immutability of Catholicism', as Lawless notes, were not accepted without qualifications by his international audience. Spurred on by a translation into English of *El protestantismo*, a British commentator wrote in 1855 that 'as M. Balmes delights to throw around Catholicism the garb of antiquity in order to render it respectable, so he likes to keep Protestantism in the cradle, that he may taunt it with the faults of its infancy' (cit. by Lawless 2018: 65).

Following in the steps of previous reactionary thinkers, Balmes believed that the Protestants' rebellion against the 'legitimate authority' of the Catholic Church as the only valid interpreter of religious truth, along with their emphasis upon the free examination of the Scriptures, had introduced a degree of relativism and uncertainty in every sphere of human thought. Balmes believed that a free-thinking attitude, as it implied the rejection of any fixed ideas (i.e. on good and evil), would necessarily lead towards to moral depravity. The natural and direct consequence of the Reformation, according to this reasoning, had been the impious ideas of the Enlightenment. Hardly original, Balmes used the term 'false philosophy' to discredit the thinking of either sixteenth-century Protestants or eighteenth-century *philosophes*, and chose Voltaire as his *bête noire*; also, like Forner and Vélez had done before him, Balmes used the word 'preservative' in order to describe the protective qualities associated with religion (1844i: 86, 98). Yet, unlike the *reaccionarios*, Balmes did not label his ideological adversaries as being 'pure evil' and, as such, deserving only the treatment of 'enemies' at war (Mücke 2008: 78–79). Similarly, he did not indulge in conspiracy theory, and thus refrained from raising alarm about the covert action of whatever Protestants, freemasons or liberals who might engage in to encourage the unsuspecting Spanish people to rebel against their lawful rulers (López Alós 2011: 182). Nonetheless, a key aspect of this narrative – the many at the mercy of the few – continued to be present in Balmes, as well as in other authors close to conservative and right-wing positions (Kolar & Mücke 2019: 27). As will be explored in the next chapter, such portrayals of an innocent people prone to manipulation often meant denying historical agency to this very people.

Arguing that Catholicism was the single unifying element in the development of European civilisation became, in the case of *El protestantismo*, a way of justifying Spain's staunch adherence to Catholic unity. Here Balmes made a very practical point: unity in religious matters led to stability in political affairs. He was convinced that 'it is the unity of religious thought what turns a whole people into a single being' (1844i: 109). However, there was a condition to fulfil: the maintenance of religious intolerance. Interestingly, Balmes invoked political rather than religious reasons to defend Catholicism's intolerant reactions against heresies. Referring to the Albigensian heresy which tore France apart between the 11th and 13th centuries, Balmes stressed that 'it was not a dispute over this or that point of dogma, but the entire existing social order was in danger' (1844i: 322). He used a similar reasoning to justify the creation of the Spanish Inquisition in 1478. It had been established by the Spanish monarchy in order to consolidate its power, as it feared a potential union between Jews and Moors which could threaten its existence (Balmes 1844i: 323–8).

In contrast to those who blamed the country's evils on religious intolerance, therefore attributing its scientific backwardness to the censorship exercised by the Inquisition, Balmes believed this unity of belief to be Spain's greatest political asset. In his view, religious intolerance turned Spain into an exceptional country within Europe: in times of revolution and distress, the purity of its faith gave an unusual strength to its social fabric, making it more resistant against social upheavals (1844i: 106–7). Faithfulness to the Catholic religion brought Spain close to both liberty and civilisation because, throughout the course of European history, 'it [the Catholic religion] has civilised the nations that have professed it; and civilisation is the true liberty' (Balmes 1844i: 116). By establishing a close link between Catholicism and civilisation, Balmes implicitly freed Spain from the need to accomplish tasks which others considered urgent or necessary, such as sanctioning freedom of religion or, more importantly, "catching up" with Europe. Instead, Balmes focused upon the idea that solutions to country's problems could be found within Spain. The counterpart to his discourse of Spanish *exceptionalism* (Spain as a self-sufficient culture) was a heroic reading of the country's history, one in which Catholicism appeared as the exclusive inspiration behind the nation's greatest deeds, both ancient and modern:

.... that religious unity, which is closely identified with our habits, our usages, our customs, our laws, which guards the cradle of our monarchy in the cave of Covadonga, which is the ensign of our banner in a struggle of eight centuries with the formidable power of the Crescent Moon, which is the bright unfolding of our civilisation in the midst of so laborious a time, which accompanies our terrible *tercios* [military units] when they imposed silence on Europe, which leads our sailors to the discovery of new worlds, which leads them to first circumnavigate the round of the globe, which encourages our warriors in carrying out heroic conquests, and which in more recent times seals the accumulation of so many great deeds by overthrowing Napoleon (Balmes 1844i: 112).

Balmes thus set the foundation stone of the 'historiographical myth of the link between Spanish nation and Catholicism' (Álvarez Junco 2007: 417), deriving from the conviction that the Catholic religion had created the Spanish *nation*. This myth would eventually culminate in the oft-quoted words of Menéndez y Pelayo: 'Spain, evangeliser of half the world; Spain, hammer of heretics, light of Trent, sword of Rome, cradle of St. Ignatius' (1958, VI: 506–9). Yet, in the times of Balmes, this was an unusual development. Previous reactionary and conservative writers had enthusiastically embraced the closeness between Catholicism and Spanish *identity*. Yet they had been staunch opponents of the (liberal) idea of a nation which derived political power from a secular source: a political community whose existence did not depend upon any religious validation (Álvarez Junco 2007: 305–6; Villalonga 2014: 325). In the eyes of earlier conservative thinkers, the legitimacy of the liberal state had appeared as being something independent from religion because it was founded upon popular sovereignty rather than upon a divinely appointed authority.

Balmes became 'the first and most important Catholic thinker to build a consistent Catholic nationalistic theory' (Villalonga 2014: 311). In his view, a nation was not a mere aggregate of autonomous individuals, but rather the result of a collective experience. It was a historical entity characterised by its religious, cultural and political unity, attributed to the combined action of the monarchy and the Church (Pro 2006: 281–282). Despite his insistence upon the immutable values of Catholicism, Balmes steered away from an essentialist perspective, asserting instead that nations were 'always in the process of being made' (Villalonga 2012: 60). Within Europe, Balmes inspired contemporaries such as Félix Dupanloup and Cesare Cantù, whose works would further elaborate on the compatibility between Catholicism and modern nationhood. It can thus be argued that Balmes anticipated the turn given by the Papacy under Leo XIII (1878–1903) who, unlike his predecessors, finally envisioned a peaceful coexistence between Catholicism, on the one hand, and liberal regimes and nation-state projects, on the other (Villalonga 2014: 330).

Within Spain, Balmes is often regarded a having been a forerunner of *nacionalcatolicismo* (National Catholicism). This would be a political-religious ideology as well as a model of nation-building, first essayed during the dictatorship of Primo de Rivera and taken to its zenith by Francisco Franco. It was cemented by a close link between the Church, seen as the moral leader of the (necessarily and providentially) Catholic nation, and the State, whose corporative structure revealed an organic view of society, one in which the heterodox views of the so-called "anti-Spain" had no place (Romeo 2021: 78–81; Botti 2008: 51, 70). Whereas the role played by Balmes – albeit posthumously – in these developments is outside the scope of this book, it is worth analysing further how Balmes positioned himself within contemporary political debates, at moments in which Church-State relationships were undergoing a profound transformation.

In order to arrive at the idea of Spain as a Catholic nation, Balmes had to deal with what was one of the fundamental issues of his day: sovereignty – or the origins of political power. The answer given by Balmes to the key question of sovereignty in *El protestantismo* is a clear example of how his thought, despite what his pro-clerical orientation might suggest, was nonetheless deeply embedded within the 'political languages' of contemporary Hispanic liberalism, to use Palti's expression (2006: 73). In the context of the unprecedented crisis of the Spanish monarchy, the first *liberales* had staged a comeback of the sixteenth-century 'pactist tradition' represented by neo-scholastic thinkers such as the Dominican Francisco de Vitoria (1480?-1546) and the Jesuit Francisco Suárez (1548–1617). According to Palti, the legacy of these thinkers was less a fixed theory than a characteristic way of thinking about the origins of political power. Such power was seen as embodied in the monarch, whose authority stemmed from God and yet had been confirmed by a 'primeval pact' with his people (Palti 2006: 106–7). In the nineteenth century, this argument was revived to justify the sovereignty of a third entity, that of the nation, half-way between the people and the monarch. Interestingly, Balmes went back to the works of two sixteenth-century Jesuits, Francisco Suárez and Roberto Bellarmino (1542–1621), in order to prove that it was possible (and essential) for a regime simultaneously to protect the people and the Church. Just as his predecessors had before, Balmes looked back on the teachings of Thomas Aquinas, including the idea that any government should reflect the rational nature of man, and that there was a natural law with a 'directive power toward the common good' in society (Wilson 2004: 37, 46).

In positing a Catholic nation as *the* alternative to a liberal one, Balmes was keen to prove wrong those 'modern demagogues' who believed that a defence of popular sovereignty, as embodied in the nation, necessarily involved reducing the Church's sphere of influence. He therefore emphasised how Suárez and Bellarmino had declared that, in contrast to the authority of secular rulers, the Church's authority had an unquestionably divine foundation (Balmes 1844i: 493–5). This supernatural quality was supposed to safeguard the Church from any encroachments on its privileges by the civil authorities. After all, he claimed, Suárez and Bellarmino had envisaged a particularly dangerous situation, one in which 'by arrogating to itself unlimited supremacy even in ecclesiastical affairs, a monarchy would degenerate into oriental despotism, where one man is everything while all things and all peoples are nothing' (Balmes 1844i: 495). Balmes desired to prove that secular rulers had a double task: to protect their people's rights and to maintain the independence of the Church.

This complex argument paved the way for Balmes' plea for the 'public ministry' of the Catholic Church in Spain's political and social life (1844i: 131). Moreover, anticipating the language of reformers in late nineteenth-century Spain, Balmes spoke of 'matrix ideas' which served as a moral foundation to the social edifice and, in the case of Spain, referred to Catholicism as the 'only national and regenerative idea' which had survived decades of civil strife and political instability (1844i: 92, 108). According to him, the influence of the Church in Spain would ensure that a 'Christian' interpretation would be given to the word 'democracy': ruling out the arbitrariness of power, while guaranteeing the prevalence of the common good and the rule of law (Balmes 1844i: 580–2). Interestingly, regardless of his acknowledgement of the community as the source of political power, Balmes refused to admit that the liberal Cortes of 1812 and 1820 had been the rightful heirs to the medieval Cortes of Spain – as the *doceañistas* and *exaltado* liberals once claimed (Pro 2019: 118). He believed their projects to have been nothing but a bad imitation of foreign ideas, as they went against the religion professed by the 'true Spaniard' while threatening the nation's stability (Balmes 1844i: 578). At this point, Balmes made a sweeping judgement: if the current government exercised little influence upon the people of Spain, it was because it had neglected its true interests and Catholic beliefs (1844i: 111).

During the following years, Balmes' own political project would essentially consist of the attempt to bridge the gap between the 'political sphere' composed by the representatives of the people, and the 'social sphere' that was formed by the actual people. Such an attempt rested upon an idealised vision of the Spanish people as naturally religious and politically conservative. Keen on engineering what he regarded was a much-needed adjustment between political institutions and social structures, Balmes sought to exercise a direct influence on Spanish public life. This pitted him not only against the progressive liberals but against the *moderados* too, including Donoso, who then gained the upper hand in Spanish politics. Ultimately, what the interventions of both Balmes and Donoso into the world of statesmanship reveals is the extent to which their political projects – a conservative vision of Catholic Spain – could still be compatible with what possibly was the most significant legacy of the country's liberal revolution: constitutional and representative government.

Chapter 2: Varieties of Spanish Liberalism

In this chapter, I will explore the contrasts and similarities between Balmes and Donoso, in terms of their respective political projects, during the *moderado* decade of power (1843–1854). This had come in after a successful *pronunciamiento* put an end to the progressive liberals' government under General Baldomero Espartero (1840–1843), and the *moderados* came to power. An analysis of the differences between the two main liberal families in Spain, *moderados* and *progresistas*, raises doubts about the plausibility of reading this period's history in terms of only *two Spains*, one liberal and one conservative, fighting against each other. The reality was much more complex, as the tensions present within contemporary Spanish liberalism show: on the one hand, moderate liberals who aimed at strengthening the role of the monarchy and sought a *modus vivendi* with the Church, all while building a powerful State controlled by a minority; on the other hand, progressive liberals who, although no fully-fledged democrats, were willing to reach out to broader sectors of society, and defended local political autonomy vis-à-vis an increasingly centralized and militarized State.

Running along these two main liberal families, there were smaller political groupings that incarnated a more radical version of their respective ideals. Within the *moderados*, for example, there were political factions whose conservative outlook often acquired authoritarian and even pro-absolutist undertones. Among the *progresistas*, there were also radical liberals who aimed for a more democratic political system, while pursuing an openly anticlerical and secularizing agenda. Here I will concentrate on how Balmes and Donoso positioned themselves within contemporary Spanish politics. It might be stressed that one of the most striking facts in the lives of Jaime Balmes and Juan Donoso Cortés, always presented as brothers-in-arms in general histories of nineteenth-century Spain, was that they never sought the acquaintance of one another (Núñez Florencio 2018: 232, Graham 1974: 236–7).[1] How can we account for the admiring if cautious distance that Balmes and Donoso kept between them? As I shall seek to demonstrate, Balmes and Donoso came to be set against each other, because their respective ideal of Church-State relations diverged significantly. In turn, looking at this phenomenon will raise a fundamental question: how much monarchical and clerical influence could the the Spanish regime bear without losing its liberal, parliamentary and constitutional character?

Betweeen 1843 and 1854, the *moderados* continued to support 'a liberal parliamentary regime, [albeit] politically restrictive and socially oligarchic' (Burdiel 1998: 892). As Pro has cogently argued, the *moderados* excelled at State-building, guided by the idea that the best antidote against revolution was an enhanced public administration (Pro 2016: 27). Revolution was understood by the *moderados* as being a threat to the institutional order and as a challenge to the throne of Isabel II – that, as it will be explained, was symbolically and practically appropriated by the *moderados*. Donoso played a key role in these developments, becoming one of the most influential figures of the *moderado* party during the mid-1840s. Speaking from the sidelines of power, Balmes became an outspoken critic of the exclusionary character of *moderado* politics, and thus tried to broaden the scope of Spanish politics, giving a voice to those whom he believed were neglected or underestimated by the current government. In order to appreciate the relevance of their ideas fully, it is essential to set both thinkers against the context of Spanish political life during the 1840s.

I. The ambiguities of the *moderados*

The fundamental question faced by nineteenth-century Spanish liberalism, and expressed in 1835 in the words of the politician Francisco Martínez de la Rosa, had been: 'what are the means of reconciling order with freedom?' (1835: xiii). The 1840s saw an increasing emphasis upon *order*, almost to the detriment of *freedom* (Comellas 1970: 6). This implied the acknowledgement that the instability and turmoil of the past decades, supposedly resulting

---

1 This is perfectly illustrated by the double portrait of Balmes and Donoso that Luis Brochetón y Muguruza (1826–1863) painted in 1848 for the Real Academia de la Historia in Madrid, and which adorns – not without irony – the cover of this book.

VARIETIES OF SPANISH LIBERALISM   75

from a quest for political freedom, had brought few material benefits to the majority of the population. The political writings of this period thus show a tendency to view *freedom* as being a broken promise, something which had brought only superficial changes. This feeling of disappointment was sharply expressed by Balmes:

> What are the benefits that freedom has brought us so far? If I pay as before, if I work as before, if I find less protection for my interests, given all the upheavals that have been taken place in the name of freedom, what have I gained from it? Why do I have to make costly sacrifices to attain it, when I see that, instead of true freedom, I have been given only a name? (Balmes 1840b, OC VI: 76).

The 1840s were a period of settling down. After decades of instability, and as the aftermath of the First Carlist War (1833–1840), peace became not just a goal but an imperative. This move towards the consolidation of the liberal State was especially reflected in the composition of the *moderado* party. Rather than being a new generation of politicians, the *moderados* were mostly former revolutionaries who had abandoned their radical views on becoming rich, powerful or respectable. Or, as Sierra put it, the moderate party also catered to a considerable number of 'recycled Carlists and absolutists' as well as to ageing survivors of the Cortes of Cádiz and authentic liberals (2018: 33). It might be noted that, in contemporary Spain, political parties were relatively loosely formed organisations, best described as an aggregate of personal networks. They did share a political outlook but, instead of a fixed ideological line, what often prevailed was allegiance to a certain parliamentary leader at a given time, prompted by patronage, family links and economic interests (Marcuello 2005: 14; Pan-Montojo 2006: 187).

The ideological flexibility of the *moderados* can be illustrated precisely by the fact that their movement also attracted men who had never been close to liberal ideas (Comellas 1970: 143; Marcuello 2013: 157–158). Such was the case of the so-called 'monarchical faction' that constituted the right wing of the *moderado* party. This was composed by the so-called 'Fernandine absolutists' who had always defended the throne of Isabel II, but did so less because they desired a modern constitutional monarchy than because they were faithful to the will of Fernando VII. They were aristocrats and landowners who, coming from a traditional mindset, nevertheless had points of coincidence with moderate liberals. These points of coincidence included, with varying degrees of emphasis, an alleged need to strengthen the Crown vis-à-vis the Cortes and a desire to restore the influence of the Catholic Church in Spain.

As I will show later, this monarchical faction, whose members became known as *vilumistas* thanks to the leading role played by Manuel de la Pezuela, Marquis of Viluma, would act as a platform for the dissemination of Balmes' ideas.

It is something of a paradox that it was thanks to Carlism, one of the most reactionary movements of nineteenth-century Europe, that a moderate form of liberalism was able to prevail in Spain. During the first Carlist war (1833–1840), Carlist intransigence had forced the regime of the Queen Regent María Cristina to seek the support of liberal groups in order to prevail over followers of Don Carlos. Only a few concessions were made which were limited by being centred upon the 'integration of the less radical and wealthier members of the middle classes into the new regime, while maintaining aristocratic hegemony' (Burdiel 1998: 904). The *década moderada* saw the consolidation of a new liberal establishment of the landed upper and upper middle classes which merged with the aristocracy, financially and politically (Payne 1984: 87). As Romeo concludes, the *moderados*' political project had an essentially oligarchic and anti-democratic character, and ultimately aimed at an 'apotheosis of authority', seen as incarnated in the monarch and executed by the State (1998: 46–47).

The throne of Isabel II was employed as a symbol of national identity by the *moderados* to neutralise the two extremes of the political spectrum: absolutist Carlism and revolutionary liberalism (Burdiel 2010: 23–4). Their formula of monarchy plus religion within a liberal State equals Spanish identity, was directly contested by Carlism, which had put forward the time-honoured union between Throne and Altar. The *moderados* put the legitimate monarchy, as embodied in Isabel II and the royal family, at the service of their own political project. Ultimately, the 'kidnapping' of the Queen by the *moderados* would prove to be a disservice to the monarchy itself, which then lost its ability to act as an arbiter above political parties (Burdiel 2010: 247; Sierra 2018: 34). In the short run, however, the *moderados* profited strongly from maintaining the monarchy's character as a rallying point, while undertaking the modernisation of the political system along moderate liberal lines. In practice, this approach was reflected in a cautious attitude when it came to extending political privileges from the top down. This was best illustrated by the type of State-building pursued by the *moderados*, that is, one in which administrative centralization was often achieved at the expense of local political autonomy.

Within Europe, a crucial way of bridging the gap between the old regime and modern political developments was to present the monarchy as an element of transition, namely from absolutism to constitutional government. The emphasis upon continuity and gradual change, a key feature of the writings of both French doctrinaires and Spanish *moderados*, ultimately led to a restrictive approach to political freedom. Yet in Spain, as in the rest of Europe, the aim of nineteenth-century liberals was not a transition from absolutism to democracy; in fact, 'the main political problem of liberalism had always been to control the revolutionary energy generated by the struggle against the old regime' (Burdiel 1998: 909). However, as their ascent to power was partly facilitated by their alliance with progressive liberalism, the *moderados* would perform the difficult task of emptying words such as 'democratic' or 'popular' of revolutionary content. During their decade in power (1843–1854), the monarch was still able to appoint and dismiss governments, and the *moderados* often used their privileged relationship with the Crown to sideline progressive liberals. In practical terms, this led to a 'vicious circle of exclusivity and political violence' (Pro 2019: 268–269). If progressive and radical liberals wanted to force their policies on the Crown and the moderates, they were often compelled to resort to insurrection and popular mobilization, through urban assemblies or *juntas*, or through military coups known as *pronunciamientos* (Barrios 2018: 261–262). However, it must be noted that there was no militarism in nineteenth-century Spain. Rather there was small group of officers who entered politics and who used the army's power and prestige in order to break the political stalemate (Tuñón de Lara 1973: 60).

Symbolic sanction for the *moderados*' political programme derived from Isabel II. After the exile of María Cristina who lived in Paris during the regency of the *progresista* General Baldomero Espartero (1840–1843), the question of who would exercise the tutelage of the young Isabel, who had remained in Spain, became a crucial issue. In the scramble to regain the control over Isabel, Donoso, who joined María Cristina's *moderado* entourage, played a key role. In Paris, Donoso developed a close friendship with Agustín Muñoz, María Cristina's second husband since 1833 – in fact, theirs was a morganatic marriage that only received the Pope's blessing in 1844, once Muñoz had been appropriately turned into Duke of Riánsares. As Pro argues, it was actually thanks to the efforts of the royal family, but especially of Muñoz, that the *moderados* emerged out of exile as a cohesive political force (Pro 2007: 32). The genius of Muñoz, for whom politics were inseparable from doing business, was to instil a sense of unity among moderate ranks by merging political interests with economic ones, thus creating a tightly-knit network of mutually beneficial relationships. According to Pro, Muñoz used financial incentives and rewards in order to strengthen the party's core. This allowed him to recruit key personalities within the army, as in the case of General Ramón María Narváez, as well as among the intelligentsia, as in the case of Donoso Cortés, who thus became the royal family's 'all-purpose scribbler' (Pro 2007: 33).

Donoso became 'the most faithful friend and correspondent' of Muñoz, having won his trust by showing him a loyalty without boundaries (Burdiel 2010: 84). By mid-1841, acting for the Queen Mother, Donoso tried, albeit unsuccessfully, to prevent progressive liberals from controlling the tutorship of the young Isabel (Burdiel 2010: 89–90). The subsequent loss of control over Isabel precipitated a failed uprising in October that same year. It was funded by María Cristina and staged by *moderados* in Paris, the Basque country and Madrid, with a significant participation of former Carlists and those who would later be known as *vilumistas*. The aim was to restore María Cristina as regent, under the assumption that only a strong monarch could act as a bulwark of the Church's privileges, while putting an end to conflicts between warring political factions. After the uprising failed spectacularly, so that many of its leaders were either shot or sent into exile, Donoso nevertheless managed to ensure that María Cristina would still, at least unofficially, be able to be in touch with her daughter. He did so by employing the services of Amparo Sorrondegui, a chambermaid who worked in the Royal Palace of Madrid and who served as a spy and a messenger (Burdiel 2010: 103–104).

Ultimately, the end of Espartero's regency was prompted by his growing unpopularity due, among other things, to his heavy-handed repression of an uprising in Barcelona towards the end of 1842, including the city's bombardment, an event witnessed by Balmes. More significantly, the *progresistas* became riddled with internal strife, a situation that enabled the *moderados* to forge an alliance with them against Espartero – a diplomatic enterprise in which Donoso, in the name of Muñoz, acted as a mediator (Burdiel 2010: 121). This involved trying to persuade *progresista* generals Serrano and Salamanca to renounce to their political ambitions in exchange of financial rewards (Pro 2007: 38–39; Borrego 1855: 83). Finally, in May 1843, an series of uprisings – started by the *progresista* generals Prim and Milans del Bosch, and joined in June by the *moderado* generals Nárvaez, Concha and Pezuela – led to the end of Espartero's regency.

In the actual story of how the moderates managed to displace the progressive liberals from the scene, so that they could keep the newly-won power for themselves, Donoso played a key role. During the uprisings in the summer of 1843, he had represented the interests of the royal family – who, it might be added, contributed with substantial sums to fuel the insurrection. Donoso was well aware that the coalition with the *progresistas* aimed, above all, at overthrowing Espartero, but not necessarily at enabling María Cristina's return to Spain, and even less at restoring her as regent. In fact, Isabel would have become officially queen in 1848. None of the political factions were willing, however, to wait for five more years, and even less to agree on a new regent (Comellas 1970: 26–7). The Cortes decided therefore, in November 1843, to declare the majority of age of Isabel II, then a thirteen-year old girl. Speaking before the Cortes, Donoso pronounced himself in favour of declaring Isabel's majority. Nakedly pragmatic, Donoso clothed his immediate political goal with the sanctity of tradition:

I do not believe in the divine right of kings, but I believe that in supreme majesty, considered in the abstract, there is something divine, and I believe that the person who exercises it, whether king, president, emperor or consul, is sacred. [...] What, then, gentlemen, is there in Doña Isabel II de Borbón anything to be considered but a thirteen-year-old girl? No, gentlemen; she is a thirteen-year-old girl, yes; but she is also something else: she is an institution that is fourteen-centuries old (Donoso 1843; *OC* II: 10).

As he wrote in his private correspondence, Donoso viewed Isabel II as a 'prey' to be won – or more precisely, to be snatched from the hands of the *progresistas* (Burdiel 2010: 131–132). Since the summer of 1843, as Narváez marched into Madrid, Donoso had used the services of the chambermaid Sorrondegui to inform Isabel that her mother supported the uprisings against Espartero – and, more importantly, he sought to mould her will, behaviour and political opinions in the *right* direction. Expecting to be named private secretary of the young queen, Donoso was very disappointed when the provisional government of the *progresista* Joaquín María López named a fellow *progresista*, Salustiano Olózaga, as tutor of the young Isabel instead. In November 1843, Olózaga also became president of the government. Despite an initial willingness to enable María Cristina's return, Olózaga nevertheless imposed his will and formed a *progresista* cabinet through and through. Hoping to obtain a parliamentary majority in the next elections, he obtained a decree from Isabel II that dissolved the Cortes.

This led to a major political scandal orchestrated by Olózaga's political enemies, beginning with Donoso, who accused him of having forced the queen to comply with his requests – an accusation not deprived of malicious sexual innuendo (Burdiel 2010: 143–145). The scandal became an international one, so that even Guizot, then France's president and close to the *moderados*, publicly expressed his concern through the French ambassador in Spain (Burdiel 2010: 147). Judging Donoso's actions on this occasion, Burdiel concludes that whereas Olózaga's behaviour towards the queen was that of a 'liberal gentleman', that of Donoso corresponded to a 'reactionary pimp' (Burdiel 2010: 136). Both Olózaga and Donoso were ambitious and cultured politicians who, coming from the educated upper middle-classes, despised the old aristocracy and felt entitled to become the country's new aristocracy. But whereas Donoso believed the monarchy ought to reign supreme, Olózaga defended a truly constitutional monarchy, one in which the Crown would remain accountable to its ministers and they, in turn, would be accountable to parliamentary constituencies. All in all, the smear campaign against Olózaga at the end of 1843, which included a backstage effort at inducing Isabel to lie convincingly, was 'the dirtiest manoeuvre in Donoso's political career' (Garrido Muro 2015: 48)

By 1844, the *moderados*, who now controlled both queen and government, implemented a series of measures aimed at the post-revolutionary stabilization of the country (Burdiel 2010: 153). Radical and progressive liberals were harshly repressed, while the freedom of the press was substantially reduced. A sense of constant threat moulded the regime's political programme and gave an excuse to support authoritarian measures if particular circumstances justified them. Between 1843 and 1844, 200 people were executed on conspiracy charges (Romeo 1998: 45); moreover, during the first five years of the *década moderada*, there was an attempt every seventeen days at overthrowing the regime (Comellas 1970: 140). The Guardia Civil, a federal police force, was created as an alternative to the Milicia Nacional of the *progresistas*, that was an aggregate of local volunteer corps (*milicias populares*). Yet the *moderados* succeeded at consolidating themselves in power. In March María Cristina returned to Spain; in April, Donoso was appointed private secretary to Isabel II and, later that year, even made a marriage proposal (albeit unsuccessfully) to Alejandra, sister of Muñoz (Burdiel 2010: 152, 220). More significantly, as architect of the Constitution of 1845, Donoso would be responsible for stamping the political ideals of the *moderados* into the fundamental law of the country: a temperate liberalism, a reinforced monarchy, minimal political representation and a centralized State.

By the mid-1840s, most *moderados* agreed that the reconstruction of Spain was to be achieved using the symbolic force of the monarchy, at the same time as restoring the relationship with the Church. Yet their party – in the sense described above, as a loose aggregate of personal networks – was nevertheless ridden by internal divisions. Among the divisive issues, besides the different degrees of importance assigned to the monarchy or the Church, was the question of just *who* was entitled to participate in the new political order. This was the main reason behind the divisiveness within the *partido moderado*, although its original name was actually *monárquico-constitucional*; in fact, its various factions can be seen as posing a different answer to this all-important question of political participation. There were three main groups within the moderate party: the main nucleus composed by the *narvaístas* (also known as *centristas* or *doctrinarios*), accompanied by smaller factions at the party's left and right, the *puritanos* and the so-called *fracción Viluma* (also known as monarchical faction).

The *narvaístas* were the strongest and most numerous faction, and it was one which included the most famous *moderados*: Alejandro Mon, Pedro José Pidal, Luis José Sartorius, Luis González Bravo and the general Ramón María Narváez. Characterised by their pursuit of expediency, they rejected coming to terms with those who were out of power – mainly Carlists and progressive liberals. According to Castro, the *moderados* continued to draw inspiration from the *doctrinaires* believing that, as in France during the Restoration, the time had come in Spain to 'make the throne national and the nation royal' (2011: 52–53). They established a mutually beneficial relationship with the monarchy: while the Crown was given an enhanced role in Spain's liberal political order, the *moderados* used the symbolic authority of the monarch to present their own project as a solid bulwark against revolution (Burdiel 2010: 186). The underlying assumption was that the *moderados* would be able to exercise an effective control upon the monarchy – or, to be more precise, upon the person of Isabel II (Marcuello 2013: 175).

Nonetheless, Pro holds that the moderate party was directed from within the court and by the royal family, with Muñoz acting as an executive leader of sorts (Pro 2019: 242, 266). Significantly, as he affirms, what really kept the moderates united as a party were the profitable businesses that served to create a community of both political and economic interests among politicians, army officers and journalists – with María Cristina and Muñoz at the head, acting as 'patrons' (2019: 266). Corruption ran rampant in areas such as public works, the stock market and rail-road construction. This corruption was socially accepted and kept out of view by restrictive printing laws, while scandals were occasionally 'denounced' in order to taint a political rival (Pro 2007: 40–1). It might be mentioned that, thanks to the famous speeches that he delivered at the Cortes towards the end of the decade, Donoso would gain a reputation as the scourge of corruption in Spain. Yet it is worth insisting that his reputation as scourge has less to do with the idea of 'fallen' human nature stemming from his renewed Christian faith, than to his firsthand knowledge of how the royal family and the *moderados* conducted their political and economic affairs.

What the other two *moderado* factions posited as the solution to political conflict was conciliation rather than expediency. Interestingly, both the extremes at the right and the left of the party shared an aspiration towards creating an overarching national party. On the one hand, the *puritanos* favoured dialogue between all the victorious parties of the civil war, that is, liberal groups of all shades. Figures like Joaquín Francisco Pacheco, Antonio Ríos Rosas, Andrés Borrego and Nicomedes Pastor Díaz believed that it was essential to bridge the gap between *moderados* and *progresistas* in order to establish a true liberal regime in Spain. Guided by the motto 'legality against arbitrariness', the *puritanos* often criticized the participation of the army in Spanish politics, believing that politics ought to remain in civilian hands (Burdiel 2010: 199). Nevertheless, the *puritanos* were against cooperating with Carlists, on the assumption that the latter's anachronistic ideas might act as a 'Trojan horse' within Spain's liberal regime (Castro 2011: 60–61). Convinced that the Constitution of 1837 ought to be maintained, the *puritanos* only became a separate group during the debates which led to the creation of a new constitution in 1845; in fact, their dissidence would then crystallise into a short-lived project, the creation of a new party under the name of the *Unión Liberal* (Koch 1993: 110).

The *vilumistas* – or the monarchic faction – were the least liberal-minded among the *moderados*. This group was led by Manuel de la Pezuela, Marquis of Viluma, together with a group of figures also referred to as 'Isabeline traditionalists', in attention to both their outlook and faithfulness to Isabel II (Urbina 1939: 120). Their number included the most ancient aristocracy (for example, the Dukes of Alba, Osuna and Medinaceli), as well as generals such as Serafín María de Sotto, Count of Cleonard, and Viluma's brother, Juan de la Pezuela, Count of Cheste (Castro 2011: 45–46). Viluma, according to Comellas, 'was liberal but with least possible amount of liberalism'; nonetheless, he did not envisage a return to the Old Regime but rather the strengthening of the aristocratic and monarchic elements within the new constitutional order (Comellas 1970: 180–1). In particular, the *vilumistas* sought to solve what continued to be an acute problem: to win the support of Carlism for Isabel's monarchy – not only of its leaders but especially in its broad social base. In particular, what separated Viluma most from the mainstream *moderado* programme was his marked deference towards the Church. He had strongly disapproved of the expropriation of Church properties which took place between 1835 and 1837, leading to a rupture with the Pope. Viluma believed that a reconciliation with the Church would provide in turn a firm basis for reconciliation among all Spaniards (Comellas 1970: 178–9). As it will be seen, it was among the *vilumistas* that Balmes found fertile soil for the dissemination of his ideas, to the point that he became this faction's 'brain', namely its leading intellectual figure (Marcuello 2013: 154–155).

Such was the complex background against which Balmes and Donoso charted their own political projects. The dreams of union among all Spaniards entertained by Balmes found a sympathetic echo among the followers of Viluma. Interestingly, the *vilumistas* served as a vehicle for Balmes' most ambitious political venture: the proposed marriage between Isabel II and the Count of Montemolín, son of Don Carlos. It was conceived of as a symbolic reconciliation not only between the two rival branches of the dynastic family, but also between the warring factions within Spanish society. In the case of Donoso, who found himself at the epicentre of the political game, the situation was more complex. The personal nature of his power gave him room for manoeuvre, making it easier for him to move easily among the groups of the *moderado* party. Donoso represented both the institutional and the unofficial aspects of the regime: on the one hand, he was a congressman and a journalist who tried to shape public opinion through reason and argument; on the other, he was a key member of the living centre of power, who obtained personal benefits from it and was prepared to set aside his political principles when expediency made it necessary.

II. A marriage of convenience

Balmes and Donoso constructed their political ideals upon the twin pillars of the monarchy and the Church. What is striking is that, while they basically made use of the same themes, their ideas led to divergent outcomes. The first and most obvious explanation of this divergence between Balmes and Donoso would focus upon the method employed in the pursuit of their political goals: the pragmatic Donoso working from within the political system while the idealist Balmes sought to influence policy-making mostly through journalism. I will illustrate this contrast with a crucial episode in nineteenth-century Spanish politics: the marriage of Isabel II. This was regarded as a golden opportunity by all political parties. The choice of the *right* husband for Isabel became a way of guaranteeing the continuation and importance of certain ideas and interests. Balmes and Donoso were among the many who, being aware of the potential of this marriage, moved accordingly.

The story, seen from the perspective of Balmes, centred upon his ambitious periodical publication: *El Pensamiento de la Nación [The Thought of the Nation]* (1844–1846). This put forward a devastating criticism of political parties – from the *progresistas* to the *moderados* – whose pursuit of partisan interests, according to Balmes, had blocked the emergence of a truly national government. Instead of establishing conciliation amidst the diverging elements of society, so the argument went, these parties simply acted for the sake of short-term goals, thus engaging into 'shameful transactions in which what was yesterday labelled wrong is now called right' (Balmes 1844a: I). As a remedy, Balmes invoked a return to those elements which he believed had a true standing in Spanish history and place in people's loyalties: the monarchy and Catholic religion. An important corollary of this argument was that both the Crown and the elements of the Church, but neither the constitution nor the current political factions, were the historical foundations of law and order in Spain. This stance was shared, to a certain extent, by the supporters of Don Carlos, yet with a substantial difference: Balmes was more interested in defending the monarchical institution as such than in expressing his allegiance to this or that branch of the royal family (Fradera 1996: 231). Ultimately, Balmes' position was not wholly dissimilar to that of the *moderados*. For them, it was crucial to counteract the idea, prevalent in progressive and democratic circles, that Isabel II owed her throne to the people who supported her cause during the first Carlist war. The *moderados* would argue instead that the monarchy existed in its own right, as well as being the true source of the people's liberties, because these had been generously granted from above (Burdiel 2010: 185). In a nutshell, what these arguments had in common was an explicit desire to severe the link – both in theory and practice – between the monarchy and the liberal revolution.

In January 1844, Balmes moved to Madrid and undertook the direction of *El Pensamiento de la Nación* as part of his strategic collaboration with the *vilumistas*. In Madrid, a city widely regarded as the country's cultural mecca, Balmes hoped – like many other aspiring writers and politicians from the provinces – to set the foundation for his career on the national stage (Smith

2014: 42). The political aim of his new newspaper was ambitious from its inception; as Balmes explained to his editor, Antonio Brusi, the ultimate goal was that *El Pensamiento* 'would lead the government' (Casanovas 1948: 421–422). In addition, Balmes ensured that his ideas would have an international reach; hence, the first number of *El Pensamiento de la Nación* offered subscriptions in Montevideo, New York, Rome, Paris and London. That Balmes felt confident enough to lead this project matches what, seen in retrospective, was a meteoric trajectory. In 1840, Balmes had sealed his national reputation with the publication of two works that minutely analysed two of the most contentious issues of the day: the *Observaciones sociales, políticas y económicas sobre los bienes del clero [Social, Political, and Economic Observations on Clerical Property]* considered, on the one hand, the precarious situation of the Spanish Catholic Church in the context of liberal land reform; on the other, he looked at the meaning of the liberal revolution in Spain in the *Consideraciones políticas sobre la situación de España [Political Considerations on the Spanish Situation]*. Moreover, Balmes had won a solid reputation in the burgeoning field of Catholic journalism. Together with representatives of the so-called Catalan school of apologetics such as Josep Ferrer i Subirana and Joaquim Roca i Cornet, Balmes had shone as co-editor of *La Civilización [The Civilisation]* (1841–1843).

What made Balmes absolutely unique in the whole of Spain, as Fradera claims, was that his defence of Christianity went well beyond doctrinal aspects and became thus inseparable from a broader debate about ongoing social and economic changes (Fradera 1996: 47). Nevertheless, Balmes' desire to depart from simple Catholic apologetics and enter the realm of politics instead, coupled with what was a characteristic stubbornness, created a certain discomfort among his friends and collaborators in Barcelona (Fradera 1996: 54–57). This was especially so in the case of Ferrer i Subirana, who felt betrayed by Balmes' decision to undertake alone publication of the journal *La Sociedad [The Society]* (1843–1844). Despite these problems, once the regency of Espartero came to an end and the *moderados* rose to power, Balmes believed the time was ripe to put his ideas into practice, and took the major step of leaving Catalonia to try his luck in Madrid.

Balmes' political project coincided ideologically with the group associated with the Marquis of Viluma, the extreme right of the *moderados*, keen on strengthening the monarchical and ecclesiastical elements of the regime. He had already established a contact with the *vilumistas* in late 1842, on his return from Paris and London. Interestingly, this acquaintance gave rise to a series of rumours that Balmes was now part of this political grouping and wanted to unite the rival branches of the Spanish dynastic family (Casanovas 1948: 377–9). Balmes' contacts with the *vilumistas* were resumed once the *moderados* regained full control of the political game. In May 1844, the Marquis of Viluma was offered the Ministry of State and used this position to spread his views on the topic that occupied centre stage: constitutional reform. According to Viluma, it was the monarch – rather than the Cortes – who should endow Spain with a new constitution. In his view, the Crown ought to reign supreme: it would keep for itself the faculty to create and modify laws and would exercise a strict control upon a bi-cameral parliament, that is, a high chamber composed by the old aristocracy and Church prelates, together with an elected low chamber consisting of major property holders (Marcuello 2013: 157; Urbina 1939: 123).

If this project had come to fruition, the liberal understanding of the Spanish regime as a constitutional monarchy that went hand-in-hand with representative government, would have been reduced to an absolute minimum. In July, Viluma quit his post as Minister of State, apparently due to the fact that the rest of the cabinet disagreed with his project of constitutional reform (Graham 1974: 57–58). Nonetheless, what really prevented the *vilumistas* from gaining the upper hand in the *moderado* regime were their views on the Catholic Church, as these stood at odds with those upheld by mainstream party leaders. Even if the government suspended the sale of the property of secular clergy in the summer of 1844, influential *moderados* such as Pidal and Mon were against calling into question the legality of previous sales, as this would affect a complex network of entrenched interests (Castro 2011: 46). In contrast, the *vilumistas* demanded compensations for the sales and made the case for a strong Church – that is, one that would be financially autonomous and independent from the State. In doing so, the *vilumistas* hoped to expand the social base of the regime, namely by incorporating former Carlists, on the assumption that they could in the last instance realise that Isabel II was preferable to the "revolution".

Writing from the pages of *El Pensamiento de la Nación*, Balmes enthusiastically embraced these views – and took them to new heights. As discussed in the previous chapter, Balmes projected a distinctive view of the Spanish nation, seen as a historical entity, born out of the interplay between monarchy and Church (Pro 2006: 281–282). He sincerely believed the *vilumistas* to be the vehicle for the creation of a truly national government, able to transcend partisan struggles. Interestingly, when the elections for the new Cortes were summoned in July 1844, Balmes promoted in Catalonia those candidates put forward by Viluma's faction, who bore the name 'monarchical' as distinct from the label 'monarchical-constitutional' preferred by most *moderados* (Casanovas 1948: 443–6). In December, as the crucial issue of the Church-State relationship was discussed in the newly-assembled Cortes, the *vilumistas* were unable to impose their views on the majority. Apparently it was Balmes who recommended them to leave the Cortes in protest (Fradera 1996: 256). Seen in retrospect, it was not a wise political decision: those who upheld the dream of uniting all parties in a single project were now just the 'Viluma faction', isolated from the rest. At this point, however, Viluma and his followers started their own movement, called Unión Nacional (National Unity). In a manifesto published in January 1845, they called for a reinvigorated Church as well as for the subordination of the Cortes to the monarch's authority (Castro 2011: 47). Significantly, they proposed the marriage of Isabel II with the son of Don Carlos as the best possible way to achieve the unification of all Spaniards.

The marriage of Isabel II had come to the fore immediately after her coming of age in 1844; it soon then became a double affair, as the marriage of her sister Luisa Fernanda came into consideration too. Having to orchestrate two marriages instead of one gave the *moderado* government some leverage in the face of heavy diplomatic pressure from Britain and France. This contributes to the idea that Isabel was not regarded as an autonomous entity; her marriage and future husband were by extension seen primarily as pawns in the political game. There were several candidates, including the Count of Trápani, brother of the Queen Mother, who was originally the first option of the *moderados*, and the two sons of Francisco de Paula, brother of Fernando VII: Francisco de Asís and Enrique whose liberal ideas made him the favourite candidate of both Britain and of Spanish *progresistas*. The overall impression of endogamy here can be explained partly as a result of the pressure exercised by France and Britain. In September 1845 and without taking Spain into account, these countries agreed on putting aside those candidates who were the closest to their own interests, as a sign of their willingness to prevent war, namely Antoine D'Orléans, Duke of Montpensier, the youngest son of King Louis Philippe of France and Leopold of Saxe-Coburg, first cousin of Queen Victoria. France and Britain also decided that, for the sake of peace in Europe, Isabel II should marry a Bourbon of the Spanish or Neapolitan branches (Comellas 1970: 329; Burdiel 2010: 165–166).

But there were those who believed that the royal weddings should be exactly that: a family matter, not an international affair. This was one of the reasons behind the presence of Count of Montemolín, son of the troublesome Don Carlos, in the list of potential husbands for Isabel. The campaign in favour of Montemolín became the principal aim of Balmes in *El Pensamiento de la Nación*. Bringing together Isabel and Montemolín was not a new idea; it had already appeared as a possibility when, during the first Carlist war, the followers of María Cristina were at their weakest. At this point, however, Balmes emphasised new aspects in a marriage he thought to be very advantageous. It offered the possibility of escaping from the diplomatic pressure of both Britain and France, thus achieving an independent international standing. More importantly, such marriage would become a powerful symbol of the reconciliation among Spaniards at its most profound level, that of ideology, thus enabling the establishment of a truly national government.

The commitment of Balmes to the cause of Montemolín was both deep and practical. Eager to disseminate his ideas, Balmes coordinated in March 1845 the setting up of a second newspaper: *El Conciliador [The Conciliator]*, directed by his friend José María Quadrado. This was directly aimed at winning the aristocratic elements of the *partido moderado* over to Balmes' cause; however, this project lasted only for a few months, as the middle-of-the-ground character of the publication was unable to satisfy either party: the *moderados* thought it absolutist, whereas those with Carlist and monarchic views believed it to be too liberal (Casanovas 1948: 467–70). More importantly, Balmes realised the need to act in accordance with Don Carlos' family, then exiled in Bourges, France. In April 1845, Balmes set off for Bourges; a month later, Don Carlos abdicated in favour of his son Carlos Luis, Count of Montemolín (Casanovas 1948: 458–61; Fradera 1996: 270–271). Balmes' influence was crucial on this occasion, to the extent that he actually wrote the manifesto which Montemolín addressed to all Spaniards on the 23rd of May (Balmes 1845 f, *OC* VII: 252):

I believe that the best way of preventing revolutions from happening again and again, involves neither destroying all what they have achieved, nor reconstructing all what they have destroyed. Justice without violence, reparation without reaction, prudent and equitable compromise between all interests, taking advantage of the much good that our elders bequeathed us without counteracting what is salutary in our age's spirit. This is my policy.

This manifesto condensed what Balmes had been constantly stressing in the pages of *El Pensamiento de la Nación*: the need to abandon all-or-nothing positions, in the crucial task of harmonising the old spirit, as embodied in traditional loyalty to both monarchy and Church, with the new spirit, characterised by modern political developments and novel ideas. But the practical means of attaining this noble goal, what Balmes called a marriage of conciliation, proved to be highly controversial. The *moderado* government, then headed by Narváez, reacted adversely to the publication in June 1845 of the 'Documentos de Bourges', a series of commentaries on the actions and manifestos of Count Montemolín, published by Balmes in *El Pensamiento de la Nación*. Balmes' paper was made subject to the action of the censor, and suspended for a short period of time, an action justified on the grounds that it had espoused a project which contravened the law which forbade Isabel to marry a person excluded from the line of succession, including members of the family of Don Carlos (Casanovas 1948: 475–7). Moreover, Don Carlos himself put an obstacle to the realisation of Balmes' project by demanding that his son, if he were to marry Isabel should be sovereign and not merely consort (Schramm 1936: 148–52). To further complicate things, the character of Balmes as 'priest-politician' was viewed with certain uneasiness (Graham 1974: 60). In fact, one of the harshest epithets ever applied to Balmes, seen as combining both religious and political pursuits, was that of being the 'Spanish Lamennais', a reference to Félicité de Lamennais (1782–1854) who had championed religious freedom in France and eventually separated from the Catholic Church. In a lengthy and passionate 'Vindicación personal [Personal vindication]', written in August 1846, Balmes clarified that he had no intentions of following a heterodox course in either politics or religion (Balmes 1846a, *EP*: 523).

On 10 October 1846, on her sixteenth birthday, Isabel was married to her cousin Francisco de Asís, Duke of Cádiz. Deprived of its reason to exist, *El Pensamiento de la Nación* soon came to an end. On 31 December, Balmes closed the publication with a farewell article which bore a rather pessimistic title: '¿Por dónde se sale? [What is the way out?]'. Balmes referred to his project as having been an attempt to stabilise the monarchy, implying that the *moderados* had not been wise in choosing their political allies. Balmes believed that instead of joining forces with the monarchist and traditional forces, so often dismissed due to real or imaginary links with Carlism, the *moderados* had opted for an alliance with the progressive liberals, whose revolutionary and democratic tendencies stood at odds with the idea of a monarchy. This is how Balmes described his failed plan:

It was deeply impressed on our minds that the throne of Isabel II had to be be freed from its association with revolutionary elements, as ever since she came to power, this has created discomfort among those who support her, and that it was necessary to bring the new Spain together with the old Spain; hence the need to provide the monarchy with the broad and solid foundation of national ideas and feelings, of Spanish traditions, believing that this was the only way to elevate the life-giving sap that circulates in the depths of society up into the regions of power (Balmes 1846d, EP: 784).

The story of the royal weddings, if we look at it from the perspective of Donoso, is significantly different. Soon after the wedding of Isabel II, as a reward for his involvement in the royal weddings, Donoso was raised to the nobility with the title of Marquis of Valdegamas (Schramm 1936: 148–52). Yet the contrast between Donoso's brilliant triumph and Balmes' utter failure can be explained by reasons other than their respective methods. It is true that the pragmatism of Donoso, who went gliding smoothly through intrigues and negotiations, was better suited to the occasion than Balmes' idealistic attempt at reconciling groups whose differences had led (and would lead again) to civil war. But the picture is not complete without taking into account the context and, more importantly, the balance of power between the different political groups.

By the mid-1840s, the *moderados* could afford to dispense with the Carlists, whose support was no longer necessary to consolidate the regime. This explains why, when it came to the royal marriages, the *moderado* government did not seek for the support of what Balmes called the 'the monarchical, absolutist, carlist, reactionary party – or call it what you will' (Balmes 1846d, *EP*: 784). Regardless of Balmes' conviction that such a party was the most accurate representation of the majority of Spaniards; the union between Isabel and Montemolín was championed only by a minority within the *moderados*, the Viluma fraction. Their efforts were consistently opposed by leading figures such as Pidal and Narváez, and even by inflexible and recalcitrant Carlists who protested against Don Carlos' abdication (Comellas 1970: 233). An alliance between *moderados* and Carlists had been tried once, as in the failed attempt to oust Espartero from power in October 1841, described above (Burdiel 2010: 98–100). However, as Balmes suggested when referring to the 'revolutionary support' which underpinned Isabel's throne, it was true that progressive liberals had been the main support of the *moderados* in their rise to power in 1843 (Romeo 2006: 92). This meant, in practical terms, a significant loss of political weight of those who, like Viluma and other traditionalists, were keen on reaching out to Carlism.

VARIETIES OF SPANISH LIBERALISM 91

The diplomatic pressure exercised by Britain and France exacerbated the struggles within domestic politics. The relationship of these countries with Spain derived from their place in the framework of the Quadruple Alliance (1834) which had assisted Spain in combating Don Carlos and Portugal in expelling Don Miguel, thus ensuring the prevalence of constitutional regimes. However, when dissension broke out among the adherents of María Cristina in Spain, Great Britain took the side of the *progresistas* and France that of the *moderados* (Jones Parry 1936: 2–3). The defeat of their common enemy, Carlism, did not put an end to their differences, differences which were exploited by France and Britain to serve their own interests. These constraints explain why Donoso initially supported the Count of Trápani, the younger brother of Queen María Cristina, as a suitor, as he would then be able to exercise a tighter control over Isabel and the nucleus of the royal family (Burdiel 2010: 166–167). Some circumstances made Trápani an attractive choice; for example, the Constitution of 1837 was modified in order to enable Spanish monarchs to marry without previous discussion in the Cortes. By early 1846, however, it became clear that the candidacy of Trápani was controversial to the extent of threatening the regime's stability (for example, the *progresistas* charged the Jesuit-educated Trápani with being an absolutist), and was thus set aside.

The way that France managed to prevail over British interests was shown in the second wedding of the *reales enlaces*: the *infanta* Luisa Fernanda was married to the Duke of Montpensier. Thus a new cause of discord emerged between France and Britain because, as had been agreed in 1845, this marriage would have been accepted only if Isabel was already married and had heirs. Balmes believed that the marriage between Luisa Fernanda and Montpensier had hardly brought any benefits to Spain: prompting the end of the Quadruple Alliance, it left Spain with 'the enmity of the world's most powerful nation' (Balmes 1846c, *EP*: 775). From the perspective of Donoso, who had a privileged viewpoint as the Queen Mother's confidant and who had close relations with the ambassadors of both Britain and France, the most pragmatic option needed to prevail. In a private letter to Agustín Muñoz, who had been raised to the rank of Duke of Riánsares in 1844, Donoso had expressed his choice in the following terms:

What is the real issue? The issue consists in nothing less than to declare ourselves the enemies of either England or France. [...] As an honest man, I decide in favour of France. [...] England will always, to a lesser or greater degree, protect the revolutionary interests in Spain. [...] France, on the contrary, is naturally inclined, at least as long as she is not forced to abandon her usual policy, to give her moral support to monarchical and conservative interests here (Donoso 1846a, OC II: 141–3).

When it came to justify such decision before the Cortes, in September 1846, Donoso had to address the concerns raised by the *puritano* Pastor Díaz on the international consequences of the queen's marriage. Donoso tried to dispel any fears among the deputies of the Cortes: 'Gentlemen, the conflict between France and England is present in the Iberian Peninsula, but also in the rest of the world, in Greece, in Constantinople, in Syria, in Egypt, in Africa' (Donoso 1846b, *OC* II: 158). At home, the marriage of Isabel II proved to be catastrophic: it led to sordid domestic scandal and a crisis in the Spanish court and government (Graham 1974: 72–4; Burdiel 2010: 181). What is most interesting, however, is the way in which these unexpected events challenged the *moderados*' ideas on the wielding of power, ideas which crystallised in the Constitution of 1845. The next section will analyse the role of Donoso in the process of constitutional reform, emphasising the challenges which the unhappy marriage of Isabel posed to the regime's viability.

III. Donoso & the Constitution of 1845

Political turmoil in nineteenth-century Spain can be related in one way or another to diverging views on sovereignty. This explains the importance given to constitutional texts as ways in which to crystallise a given set of power relations within Spanish society. The modern concept of sovereignty, understood as the right to rule regulated by a constitution, throws light on *who* were considered to be the rightful participants of the political game. In this sense, nothing reveals more accurately the *moderados*' world of nuances and toning down than the concept of sovereignty put forward in the Constitution of 1845. First and foremost, this constitution was a middle-of-the-ground solution: it did not accept the principle of popular sovereignty advanced by the *progresista* Constitution of 1837, and yet did not restore the almost untrammelled royal authority as prescribed in the Estatuto Real (Royal Statute) of 1834. In 1845, sovereignty was declared to rest with both Crown and Cortes. This ambiguity was, above all, a declaration of principles.

In late 1844, Donoso became the leading expert and secretary of the committee on constitutional reform, whose report laid the foundation stone for the Constitution of 1845 (Graham 1974: 54–8). This report, written by Donoso, clearly stated at the beginning: 'the constituent power resides only in the constituted power that, in Spain, is none other than the Cortes with the King' (Donoso 1844a, *OC* II: 74–5). This statement was highly significant. It implied that the text of the constitution would simply regulate what had already been a crucial feature in the history of Spain, namely the time-honoured relationship between the Crown and the Cortes (Sánchez Agesta 1978: 232). The insistence in the report upon the historical and internal constitution of Spain portrayed it as pre-dating the written constitution. Ultimately, this underpinned a key argument: that a constitutional monarchy existed in Spain well before liberalism had made its appearance. The monarch had always been the representative of the people. As a result, so the argument went, its authority did not need to be validated by the "revolution". This was an implicit reply to progressive and radical liberals who often claimed that Isabel II owed her throne to the people who had fought in her name against Carlism (Burdiel 2010: 184). For the *moderados*, it was thus vital to underpin the authority of the monarch in liberal terms but, at the same time, also to take it beyond liberalism. According to Pedro José Pidal, who thus argued in a speech before the Cortes in October 1844, the constitutional monarchy in Spain had venerable historical credentials:

In Spain, gentlemen, public power has always been expressed historically [...] in two great institutions, in two great legitimacies, and these are the Throne and the national assemblies. This is how I see it, gentlemen: in every epoch since the existence of the Spanish Monarchy has had a historical existence, I perceive the Throne and, next to it, I also distinguish an assembly, be it the Council, be it the Cortes, be it the Curia. The Throne and the Assembly; these are the two great poles around which the Spanish Monarchy revolves, and it is impossible for a secondary law, one that allocates power to these two great legitimacies, to be superior or equal to one of them (Diario 1844: 79).

The appeal to history was thus used to dismantle a particularly problematic concept, that of national sovereignty. When Pidal made it clear that, in terms of historical roots and durability, traditional institutions were superior to any legal code, he was not only trying to minimise the controversy which reforming the Constitution of 1837 naturally raised. The new concept of sovereignty put forward in 1845 implied the idea of a mutual agreement between the Crown and the Cortes, rather than of an explicit pact, updating and revising their traditional, long-standing relations. Historical tradition was turned into legal fact, under the assumption that the legitimacy of political power needed to be rooted in history, rather than in abstract principles. Here we find looming prominently the idea of national sovereignty or, in other words, the very fact that an assembly speaking in the name of the nation could become a constituent power. In short, the *moderados* sought to reinterpret the actual meaning of the liberal revolution in Spain – or, as Romeo affirms, to put forward a type of liberalism deprived of any revolutionary content (1998: 38–40).

In Spain, the concept of national sovereignty had made its first appearance in 1810, giving a *raison d'être* to the Cortes assembled in Cádiz. On his return to the throne, Fernando VII abolished the Constitution of 1812, declaring it void and null. Ultimately, the war which was later waged between the followers of Isabel and those of Don Carlos set the idea of constitutional monarchy against absolutism, national sovereignty against the divine right of kings. Yet, among the most cautious holders of liberal opinions, the idea of sovereignty was tempered by making the right to vote dependent upon property and education. This had been the case of Donoso and his 'sovereignty of reason', as expounded in his *Lecciones de derecho político constitucional [Lessons on Constitutional Political Law]* (1836–1837), a concept which would in practical terms give aristocratic privileges to the upper middle classes. As in this case, the influence of the French *doctrinaires* could still be appreciated a decade later: as both Crown and Cortes would come together as sources of authority and government, the concept of sovereignty of the Constitution of 1845 was presented as having reached a *juste milieu* between the monarchy and the people (Sánchez Agesta 1978: 234).

Within Spanish political thought, the idea of a 'historical constitution' can be traced from the late eighteenth to the late nineteenth century, that is, from Jovellanos to Cánovas del Castillo (Díez del Corral 1950: 503–504; Varela Suanzes 1995: 45–46). The distinguishing mark of this line of thought was the desire to preclude a situation in which a given government, especially one brought about by a revolution or any other accidental circumstance, could change *ex nihilo* the fundamental laws of Spain. Consequently, Jovellanos and the *moderados* shared a conscious desire to remove all the revolutionary implications associated with the idea of a constitution. In their view, a constitution needed to be a reflection of the fundamental laws of the kingdom and could not be *invented* by the deliberations of a constituent power, as had happened in France in 1789 or even in Spain with the Constitution of 1812, or so the argument went. It might be added, however, that this kind of historicist reading was not exclusive to thinkers with conservative or traditional leanings. Historicism had been an important component in early Spanish liberalism, that is, despite its having been a revolutionary rupture with the *ancien régime*. That had been the case of Agustín Argüelles and Francisco Martínez Marina who, keen on emphasising continuity with the past, claimed that the constitutional rights enshrined in 1812 were essentially a modern version of medieval freedoms (Pro 2019: 116).

To a certain extent, the emphasis of the *moderados* upon historic tradition was merely a façade. Their goals and their aims were in fact unequivocally modern. The Constitution of 1845 was not a revision of the ancient laws of the kingdom, but of the *progresista* Constitution of 1837. The starting point of this constitution had been the idea of national sovereignty and, in its foreword, this was taken as read: a nation that, being sovereign, undertook a revision of the constitution promulgated in Cádiz (Sánchez Agesta 1978: 278). In consequence, the monarch was supposed to simply accept the deliberations of the Cortes, as they were the supreme constituent power. The Constitution of 1837 had also strengthened local government, thus enshrining two of the institutions which had usually served as strongholds of progressive liberalism: the municipalities (*ayuntamientos*) with their popular election and the militias, local volunteer corps composed by non-professional soldiers (*milicias populares*). We might remember that in 1840, what became a highly contested law, deprived the municipalities of all their political functions. The municipalities had gained enormous *de facto* power during the First Carlist war, and were now turned into merely administrative institutions, headed by appointed delegates instead of by elected mayors (Burdiel 2010: 54–55). The uprisings staged in resistance to this law would, in turn, pave the way for the ascent of Espartero into power (Fradera 1996: 72).

By contrast, the Constitution of 1845 dissolved the militias and put forward a new concept of local administration. Local police forces were to be replaced by the federal Guardia Civil, created in 1844. Together with the army, this move responded less to the need to deal with foreign aggressors, and more with internal threats to public order (Pro 2019: 269–70). This led to what was a subtle but crucial difference between the two liberal families: for the progressives, the nation was the protector of natural individual rights, that is, their existence pre-dated the actual creation of the body politic; for the moderates, the State was the main guarantor of individual rights enshrined and defined by the law (Romeo 1998: 46–47). For the *moderados*, there could be no freedom above the law. The State, in their view, was the defender of public order, as well as the rightful arbiter of social conflict. As Alcalá Galiano argued in 1843, the actual source of the most dangerous tyrannies was not governments as such, but rather the 'exaggerated individualism' that led some to attempt the subversion of the social order (1843: 115–116). As Romeo concludes, Alcalá Galiano in eulogizing governmental repression, viewed mainly as a protective measure, implicitly paved the way for Donoso who, in the aftermath of the 1848 revolutions, would claim that a (governmental) dictatorship was a legitimate measure against revolution (Romeo 1998: 44). If we take into account Alcalá Galiano's view and its implications, we can see how the well-trodden argument that Donoso's later views on dictatorship were an aberration if not a personal eccentricity, is undermined. As I argue, Donoso took an already existing trend to new heights, and further blurred the line that separated the State from an ideally autonomous civil society.

Another crucial aspect of the Constitution of 1845 was that, decisively and strategically, it strengthened the position of the Crown. It endowed the monarch with an enhanced set of prerogatives: the express right to nominate ministers, withdraw royal confidence and require resignations, to dissolve the parliament and to call new elections, and veto new legislation (Payne 1978: 772). However, the underlying assumption of the Constitution of 1845 was that the *right* party would be able to control the monarch who, in turn, would have the upper hand in the political game (Burdiel 2010: 189). In everyday politics, as Marcuello minutely demonstrates, this meant that the Cortes were routinely maimed and even neutralised by the Crown (1986: 371–372; 2005: 26). The Constitution of 1845, it might be stressed, did not advocate a parliamentary monarchy in which the Crown assumed a neutral role, but rather a constitutional monarchy in which the Crown played an all-important political role. The days in which the Cortes were truly able to govern and exercise an executive power, as in the Constitution of 1812, were long over. The monarch was now able to designate governments at will, regardless of which party had the majority in the Cortes. In addition, a newly formed government could obtain from the monarch a decree that dissolved the Cortes, so that it could obtain a parliamentary majority anew. At the end of the day, this meant that it was much more important to have the backing of the Crown than to win the elections (Marcuello 1986: 369).

By gaining the general support of the queen, *moderados* were able consistently to exclude the *progresistas* from power; the latter, in turn, continued to rely upon extra-parliamentary means to achieve political influence. Yet this came at a high price, beginning with a recurrent instability. In the 34 years of Isabel II's constitutional reign (1833–1868), there were 34 presidents of the Council of Ministers, meaning that an average government lasted an average of nine months; in addition, the Cortes were more often closed than opened and in session, something that happened only 36% of the time (Pro 2019: 31; 2016: 37). Moreover, the Cortes were further damaged by the prevalence of electoral corruption which, without being exclusive to any party, nonetheless upset the accuracy of representation itself (Marcuello 2005: 5). The relative weakness of the Cortes, coupled with widespread electoral corruption, helps to disprove the contemporary view, common among traditionalists of all signs, from *vilumistas* to Carlistas, that Spain was on the verge of becoming a parliamentary regime, one in which the monarch was deprived from all functions of government – or, as it was often claimed, was a merely decorative figure that reigned but did not govern. In everyday politics, however, what was one of the key elements of the Constitutions of 1845, the desire to strengthen the Crown over the Cortes, led to problematic practical consequences, to the point of threatening the *moderados'* political hegemony.

In the first year of Isabel's effective reign (1847), a period in which she reigned without any interference from her mother and closest advisers such as Donoso, the balance of power actually shifted towards the *puritanos*, the left wing of the *moderados* (Burdiel 2010: 198–199). As mentioned earlier, the *puritanos* were a faction within the *moderado* party who were in favour of the reconciliation between all shades of liberalism (Castro 2011: 60–61). Isabel used the prerogatives she had been given in the new constitution to facilitate the rise of Joaquín Francisco Pacheco, friend of her favourite, General Serrano. The very existence of a royal favourite at this point shows how catastrophic the wedding between Isabel and Francisco de Asís had been. Their effective separation, by April 1847, became a well-known fact. At this time, Isabel also issued an amnesty that allowed for the return of several exiled *progresistas*. The growing concern which these events raised among mainstream *moderados* can be illustrated with the private correspondence of Donoso. In the spring of 1847, Donoso wrote thus to the Duke of Riánsares:

Conservative parties are strong when they can count on the throne: without its support, they are powerless. Will the moderate party proclaim the respect for the royal prerogative, as well as the preponderant influence that it should exercise in public affairs? If it proclaims this, it will be consistent with itself but, ultimately, it will lose itself and the nation, because the latter is the source of all our evils. But what if it proclaims the contrary principles? What if it seeks to control the Queen? To restrict her prerogatives? To limit her power and, in parallel, highlight that of the King? Then the moderate party will turn into a progressive one; but the progressive party is already there, and it knows how to do things, and will undoubtedly do them much better than we do (Letter of Donoso to Riánsares, April 29, 1847 cit. by Burdiel 2010: 189).

Using a habitual combination of legal and extra-legal means, the *moderados* were able to regain full control of the situation: the scandalous private life of the queen was used as a political weapon to discredit the Pacheco government, while the military authority of general Narváez was deployed in order to restore the power of the *moderados* over the monarchy (Burdiel 2010: 199; Sierra 2018: 34). As for the relations between the monarchy and the government, what is striking is the blurring between public and private, the institutional and the non-institutional. This phenomenon was closely related to the corruption prevalent in the *década moderada*, when power rested upon entrenched political and economic interests that were controlled by an influential minority. This elite, mostly composed of rich property owners, had increased its wealth either by the acquisition of properties that once belonged to the Church, or by (mis)using political posts as a means towards personal enrichment. The ensuing social disparity was mirrored in the electoral laws of March 1846, that granted a right to vote to only 0.8 % of the population – an amount elevated to 4.7 % in 1854, after a revolution marked a short-lived return of the *progresistas* into power (Pro 2019: 540–541). Despite the new liberal legal framework that affirmed the equality of all citizens before the law, and notwithstanding a substantial degree of social mobility, the means for integration into this elite continued to be based on the privilege of belonging either to a family or to a network of mutual solidarity (Cruz 1996: 2006).

Seen retrospectively, it is somewhat of a paradox that the agenda and interests of an elite could nevertheless serve as the foundation for a robust form of State (Pro 2007: 50). The genius of the *moderados*, according to Pro, was that what he refers to as their 'State project' implied a radical shift in priorities: a move away from the realm of politics, seen as synonymous of divisiveness and conflict, and to enter that of administration, viewed as means towards order and efficiency. As part of the *moderados'* ideal of an administrative State, parties and politicians were to be replaced by experts and scientists; ultimately, this was conceived of as a 'technocratic alternative' to both revolutionary liberalism and absolutist traditionalism (Pro 2019: 141). Interestingly, within Spanish universities, the earlier emphasis upon constitutional political law, as in the case of the lectures given by Donoso and Alcalá Galiano in the late 1830s, with its focus upon representative institutions and individual rights, was abandoned and replaced by an emphasis upon administrative law, thus reflecting the authoritarian and rationalist turn taken by the regime (Pro 2007: 46). In sum, the *moderados* made a decisive contribution to the construction of a strong State in Spain, capable of furthering economic growth and of providing it with vital nation-wide infrastructure (Pro 2019: 150). As will be seen in the next section, their project failed to convince Jaime Balmes who, despite sharing the *moderados*' desire to overcome both revolution and political factionalism, did not feel that it could really appeal to the majority of Spaniards.

IV. Balmes & the people of Spain

One of the most far-sighted criticisms of the contradictions of the *década moderada* would be made by Balmes. He believed that, notwithstanding their intention of becoming a national party, the *moderados* had attained nothing but the predominance of a single ideological line. Balmes' own project of conciliation between all Spaniards, via the symbolic union between Isabel II and the son of Don Carlos, only makes sense if we understand the profound social critique that went with it. Being outside the circle of power, Balmes made his main aim the vindication of the Spanish *people* – the dispossessed and the voiceless. He declared that a general sense of apathy stemmed directly from the Spanish political elite with their shortcomings. It was a matter of cause and effect: the way in which a minority exercised the practice of politics had led the majority to seek refuge in indifference and lack of concern:

...it should not seem strange that the Spanish people do not take as much interest in the new political forms as some would wish. If the Cortes are nothing more than an arena where ambition and other passions are unleashed, or, at most, a lyceum where a few illustrious orators show off their talents and erudition, so that that not a single drop of profit descends from such pomposities to the people, it is quite clear that all men who are not interested in becoming prominent would say to themselves: What is the use of all this? (Balmes 1840b, *OC* VI: 76)

Widespread political indifferentism could lead, Balmes warned, to a situation in which the government, instituted by law to address the needs of the majority, would in practice cater only to a minority (Balmes 1840b, *OC* VI: 76). Balmes put this argument forward in *Consideraciones políticas sobre la situación de España [Political Considerations on the Spanish Situation]* (1840), a series of reflections upon the meaning of revolution in both Spain and Europe. For Balmes, the term revolution stood for two separate, albeit intimately related phenomena: what appeared on the surface as a sudden episode of political unrest was, in reality, the expression of deeper social and economic changes.

Therefore, as Balmes suggested, the revolutionary transformations that had recently taken place in Spain were not to be regarded either as an anomaly or a fatality. In Spain, as in the whole of Europe, the great institutions of the *ancien régime* – the Church and the Crown – were being called into question. This idea of revolution, seen also as an irreversible and to some extent legitimate development, is what made Balmes conservative, as opposed to merely counter-revolutionary (Fradera 1996: 77). In fact, by publishing the *Consideraciones* in 1840, Balmes implicitly sought to enter into a dialogue with the *moderados*, thus hoping to influence what was a volatile political situation, and which was eventually decided in favour of Espartero and the *progresistas*. Although Balmes would have to wait a few years in order to try out the practical realisation of his ideas, the *Consideraciones* were nevertheless a decisive political statement, one that combined the descriptive with the prescriptive.

Not unlike the *moderados*, Balmes made an essential distinction as regards the tasks of government: politics was viewed as mere surface, and administration as its core. He criticised contemporary politicians not merely for being ambitious or self-interested, but for not going beyond the surface of Spain's problems. According to Balmes, they wasted most of their energies in political struggles, creating an atmosphere of divisiveness which was unlikely to lead to joint and serene solutions in matters of government. The remedy which Balmes proposed involved the following: the government needed to abstain from useless political infighting and concentrate instead on carrying out those 'practical and positive measures that could actually benefit that part of the people that works, pays, suffers and remains silent' (Balmes 1840b, *OC* VI: 89–90).

Every argument of significance that Balmes put forward in the *Consideraciones* was accompanied by an invocation of the needs of the Spanish people. The denunciation of Spain as a society ridden with inequality is what most distinguishes him from other contemporary thinkers. Interestingly, what he found most objectionable about the sale of ecclesiastical properties that began in 1836, is that it concentrated wealth further in the hands of a few, thus aggravating the precarious living conditions of the rural masses. This is what effectively happened, especially in the south of Spain (Rueda 1993: 22; Pro 2019: 241–242). Moreover, Balmes was aware of how the incipient economic modernisation of Spain was affecting the distribution of power in society. Writing from Catalonia, the region in which the effects of industrialization were most visible, Balmes felt entitled to write with concern about the rising fortunes of the industrial and commercial elite:

It is necessary to ignore society in order not to notice that, in its peculiar way, with more or less palliatives, feudalism still subsists, and that these great bankers, these wealthy owners of manufacturing establishments, have taken the place of the old nobility; and that, by the way, they do so with a glaring lack of the chivalrous spirit as well as of the generous impulses of their predecessors (Balmes 1840a, OC V: 738).

Using the adjective 'feudal' to describe social inequalities in Spain was, nevertheless, a piece of rhetoric. In fact, Balmes believed that Spanish society was essentially modern, meaning that – as in the rest of Europe – it showed in fact a break with the ancient privileges and rigid hierarchies of the past. The blurring of social classes was characteristic of modern societies; as a consequence, according to Balmes, these classes were now prone to anarchy (1840b, OC VI: 83). Yet Balmes was not interested in chastising these new developments, but in coming to terms with them. In particular, he was convinced that Catholicism could play a major role within modern societies, one of harmonising the multitude of disparate 'individual forces' within them. But what made Balmes unique, as Fradera sustains, is that he incorporated the modern idea of progress in his own thought, being aware – among other things – that industrialisation was a necessary development (1996: 59, 61). At this point, however, a modern capitalist development could be found only in limited areas in the north of Spain, especially Catalonia. According to a census in 1837, there were 12,222,000 inhabitants in Spain – of which 200,000 were classified as 'workers' (Tuñón de Lara 1973: 35, 50). What is notable is that, writing in times when industrialisation affected only a relatively small portion of the Spanish population, Balmes could nevertheless foresee the future impact of these changes:

This numerous population, created by industry, with no other means of subsistence but their arms, with no other guarantee of employing them but the factories, this multitude of men, no longer placed in the class of slaves as in the old republics, but declared by the law as equals to the most distinguished citizens; living with their families in misery, and yet enjoying an ample freedom to move places, to choose their profession, to change it, to acquire knowledge, to seek employment; with a lively desire to improve their condition, with a restlessness inspired by the very society in which they live, and yet confronted to ، sight of a few families swimming in opulence and riches, it is evident that, as time goes by, society might find itself in a terrible conundrum, so that it is necessary to make use of all means necessary to prevent such a scenario.

Balmes was convinced that, in order to avert social unrest, the Catalan elites ought to work together with the Catholic Church. Yet he did not close his eyes to the causal link that existed between capitalist development and social inequality and he was convinced that workers had in principle the right to organise themselves (Fradera 1996: 207–209). He also wrote about the socialist ideals of Charles Fourier, Robert Owen and Henri de Saint-Simon whose ideas, although he dismissed them on grounds on being a mere utopia, did have an influence in what was still only an incipient labour movement (Rodríguez 1998: 287–288; De Felipe and González 2020: 165). Ultimately, even if Balmes was remarkably receptive to the plight of the urban poor, he was mostly interested in vindicating those who – in his opinion – constituted Spain's neglected majority: the rural and small-town population. His views of those who counted as the quintessential Spanish people matched his idea of what a government should be, that is, an accurate reflection of those ideas and interests at play within society (Balmes 1840b: 63). If a government only served the interests of the few, so the argument went, it would necessarily rest upon shaky foundations.

In Spain, Balmes contended, political institutions were not stable or enduring because they had no real roots in society, that of the everyday man. To make things worse, the minority in power regarded the majority of Spaniards with contempt. When dealing with the whole of the Spanish nation, according to Balmes, the *moderados* seemed to follow this criterion: 'I respect your religion because I am aware that you are a fanatic; I will not give you more freedom than necessary, because you are brutal and would abuse it' (Balmes 1840b, *OC* VI: 70–1). This would explain, in Balmes' view, the *moderados'* lukewarm defence of the Church's privileges or their extreme caution when it came to extending political rights. Yet, Balmes stressed, those in power ought to respect the principles which the nation held in the utmost reverence: the monarchy and the Catholic religion. They also ought to acknowledge that the people, rather than the middle classes, was the incarnation of the religious and monarchic core of Spain.

This conviction explains Balmes' positive appreciation of Carlism, a movement which he believed was one that spoke on behalf of the most characteristic feelings of the Spanish people, its religious and monarchic loyalties. Yet Balmes' overall position bore similarities, but also very significant dissimilarities, with those known as Carlists. As Smith claims, Carlism was ultimately a revolt against the economic, social and political transformations brought by liberalism, beginning with the downgrading of the Church's position (2014: 40). Carlism was a heterogeneous and interclass movement whose banner 'God, King and Country' united both aristocrat and peasant at critical junctures (Canal 2000: 118). It was mainly present in the north of Spain (Aragón, Catalonia and the Basque Country), an area which had undergone profound social and economic changes since the beginning of the nineteenth century, thus exacerbating both cultural tensions and social dynamics. Early Carlism, as Lawrence argues, was 'a mix of radical royalists, absolutists and theocrats, prisoners of Spain's multiple pasts, and rivals in court and military politics' (2014: 20). The First Carlist War (1833–1840) amounted to a 'collective trauma' which killed between 2 and 4 percent of the 1833 population (2014: 224). When Balmes wrote the *Consideraciones*, Catalonia was far from being completely pacified; in fact, the confluence between the rejection of Isabel's marriage and other social grievances would lead to a new war in 1846–1849, the 'guerra de los Matiners' waged by the so-called 'montemolinistas' (Canal 2000: 128–9).

According to the Carlist world view, liberalism was inextricable from revolution. In turn, this was seen as resting upon the assumption that society could regulate itself, thus paying no heed to the authoritative dictates of both religion and tradition (Millán 2000: 24). For Carlists, social hierarchies – which culminated in an absolute monarch – were the foundation of political power and, therefore, were seen as being the fundamental laws of Spain. Such argumentation served to justify the rejection of the liberal State, seen as lacking any right to alter these allegedly perennial laws (Millán 2009: 268). Carlism thus became the vehicle of right-wing popular radicalism, once the 'healthy people' that had remained true to traditional values and was thus untouched by liberalism, were incited to rebel against the enemies of both Catholicism and the legitimate monarch (Millán 2009: 268). With support of the Church hierarchy, much of the peasantry in northern Spain, uprooted and impoverished through recent changes in land ownership, thus sought to 'settle scores with liberalism' (Barrio 2018: 262).

Balmes believed that, in all its drama and complexity, Carlism illustrated the gap between ideal and reality in Spanish politics. It was an expression of the estrangement which existed between the government and the population of Spain, something which he exemplified with what he thought was a relationship of cause and effect: 'the improvement of the cause of Don Carlos is always in direct proportion to the exaggerated ideas and degree of violence present in the measures taken by the government in Madrid' (Balmes 1840b: 45). In this sense, Balmes believed that the Spanish political elite had failed to accomplish a basic task: 'to govern properly, to make the people appreciate the benefits of the innovative systems. Has this been done?' (Balmes 1846b, *EP*: 754).

With the phrase 'innovative systems', Balmes basically referred to the introduction of both liberalism and representative government in Spain. He believed that the country had not been prepared for the political revolution that followed its War of Independence. In his view, it was only by virtue of an unprecedented confusion that a liberal-minded minority could make its ideas prevail. This, in a nutshell, was the nature of Spain's revolution according to Balmes: the situation in which a religious and monarchic nation had abruptly acquired a democratic Constitution, and yet without there having been any intervention of the Spanish people in the process (Balmes 1840b, *OC* VI: 38–9, 75). A similar account of new political developments in Spain can be found in many other traditionalist writers (Vélez 1818: I, 32; Alvarado 1825, III: 40–1). What makes Balmes both outstanding *and* modern is that, rather than looking back nostalgically to the past, he realised that these new developments should be acknowledged as a given, as a social fact. It was pointless, as the Carlists were trying to do, to present a staunch resistance against the 'new Spain' and its impulse towards change; it was equally pointless, as liberals tended to do, to briskly reject the 'old Spain' and its attachment to tradition. The construction of a real, national government in Spain would not be attained by removing either side of the equation, but rather by joining its extremes:

For whoever is to govern Spain, it is necessary to acknowledge that, besides the old Spain, the religious and monarchical Spain, the Spain of traditions, of quiet habits, of simple customs, of few necessities, of a peculiar character that distinguishes it from other European nations, there is also a new Spain, with its incredulity or indifference, its fondness for new political forms, its modern ideas in opposition to our traditions, its vivacity and movement, its customs imported from abroad, its necessities born of a refinement of culture, its love of pleasures, its eagerness for the development of material interests, its urge to imitate other nations, in particular France, its strong preference for a complete transformation that, erasing what remains of the truly Spanish character, might make us enter into that universal assimilation or fusion, towards which the world seems to be heading (Balmes 1845e, *EP*: 494).

The way in which Balmes planned to overcome the Scylla and Charybdis of Spanish politics had, *a posteriori*, some problematic aspects. For example, Balmes made it clear that the 'new Spain', despite its prominence and superior ability in proselytising its ideas, did not represent the majority of the nation (Balmes 1845e, *EP*: 494). In the future such an idea, when handled by less neutral critics, would be grossly simplified to the point of declaring the 'old Spain' superior and more righteous than the minority, simply on grounds of its numerical superiority (Larraz 1948: 17). Another problematic aspect of Balmes' arguments, insofar they could be too readily be invoked in support of maintaining the *status quo*, was the emphasis upon the exceptional character of the Spanish people. Interestingly, Balmes conceived of this *exceptionality* in reference to the relations between his country and Europe, as a way of overcoming the stereotypical image of Spain as an 'anomalous country' (Balmes 1840b, *OC* VI: 30).

So he presented the two main virtues of the Spanish people – its religious nature and its monarchic convictions – not only as being 'elements of preservation' within Spain, but also as advantages over the rest of Europe: 'in Spain, whose people are insulted by calling them barbarians, one does not find, as in England and France, assassins of kings [...]; impiety has not spread to the masses and the Spanish people in general are still believers' (Balmes 1840b, *OC* VI: 85–6). By shifting the discussion from anomalies to exceptions, as regards the Spanish people's virtues, Balmes implicitly blurred the line between what was due to moral superior qualities (essentialist argument) and what resulted from a given set of circumstances (historical argument). It is, of course, open to debate to what extent Balmes' idea of the Spanish people was an idealisation or an ideological construct – also put into the service of his own political agenda.

Balmes' reflections upon the people of Spain were in stark opposition with that cornerstone of the progressive liberals' politics: the idea of popular sovereignty. In the first place, Balmes held that universal suffrage would only aggravate the dangers and volatility within European politics (Balmes 1843b, *OC* VI: 348). He refused to acknowledge the link between the progressive party, as it often resorted to revolutionary politics, and the 'true people' of Spain who, in his view, remained faithful to tradition and were mostly engaged in agricultural labours, who were 'characteristically peaceful, calm and conservative' (Balmes 1844c, *OC* VI: 496–7). Progressive liberals, as Balmes concluded, were nothing but 'revolutionary and turbulent minorities' whose political creed clashed with Spain's constitution, as their reforming ideals were set against a naturally conservative institution: the monarchy. Interestingly, Balmes affirmed that a republic in Spain would be an 'extremely short-lived, miserable farce' (1844c, *OC* VI: 483–4, 498). His views on progressive liberalism were relatively close to those of Donoso who, in a contemporary speech in the Cortes, had advanced a similar argument:

The exalted [i.e. progressive] party does not acknowledge the deep foundations of the Spanish Monarchy and looks with disdain on the splendour of the Church. In other words, it represents nothing: neither European civilisation nor Spanish civilisation. It represents only one thing, and that is the democratic principle, and with that principle alone it has defeated us a thousand times. [...] Our task must be none other than to convert democracy from turbulent and revolutionary to peaceful and monarchical (Donoso 1844b, OC II: 92).

Yet Balmes and Donoso were not an exception to what was a rule among contemporary *moderados*: their critique of the progressive liberals was, ultimately, a 'view in negative' of what they thought about themselves (Pro 2006: 271). *Moderados*, because they saw themselves as being orderly, as well as staunchly religious and monarchic, often described their rivals as being anarchic, impious and disrespectful of the monarch. It might be stressed, however, that contemporary progressives did not support universal suffrage and, considering that most of its leaders belonged to the upper middle classes, were not always free of classist prejudices against the 'irrational populace' of both city and countryside (Pan Montojo 2006: 207). Nonetheless, the progressives viewed themselves as being the interpreters and intermediaries of the Spanish people and sought to preserve a higher degree of popular participation in regional and local politics on the assumption that this was the best antidote against revolution (Romeo 2006: 104–106; Romeo 1998: 54). Significantly, whereas moderates highlighted Catholicism and monarchy as the Spanish nation's defining themes, progressives tended to stress liberty and sovereignty as its leitmotifs (Romeo 2006: 109). Balmes felt at odds with the anti-paternalist and emancipatory language used by progressive liberals who, in addition, claimed that the Cortes ought to have more prerogatives than the Crown. According to Balmes, as well as to most moderates including Donoso, this could lead to what they viewed as a horror scenario, one in which the Spanish monarch would become a mere civil servant, endowed with symbolic rather than real and effective power (Pro 2006: 277). Although the much-feared 'parlamentarisation' of Spain, to use a contemporary expression, was far from being an acute danger, considering the actual erosion of the Cortes' power under the *moderados*, it did serve to trigger a defensive reaction among those who – like Balmes – believed that the monarchy was inseparable from Spain's national identity.

Balmes believed that Spain's political institutions, such as parties and constitutions, were merely the superficial expression of deeper forces. What really mattered, according to him, were the *social* institutions that throughout time had become the expression of the nation's ideas and traditions. He was concerned that the monarchy and the Church being put at the service of the parties' agenda, thus preventing their full realisation (Balmes 1840b, *OC* VI: 28, 52). The solution envisaged by Balmes thus involved a reversal of roles: they needed to put the political parties at the service of the social institutions of Spain. He believed that an alliance between the Carlists and the majority of *moderados* would provide a favourable setting for re-establishment of the fundamental laws of the Spanish monarchy as one that 'does not approve of the despotism of governments or individuals, nor to military, revolutionary or parliamentary despotism' (Balmes 1844e, *OC* VI: 703). In this scheme, the restoration of the king's full sovereignty would be translated into new limits for the Cortes, thought of in meritocratic rather than oligarchic terms: 'consisting not of governmental employees, not of adventurers, but [...] of the greatest and most select men of the country' (Balmes 1844e, *OC* VI: 703).

In mid-1844, Balmes published a series of articles on constitutional reform in the pages of *El Pensamiento de la Nación*. He summarised his views on the matter in two articles, putting forward an ideal of a minimalist constitution: '1. The King is sovereign; 2. The nation assembled in the Cortes levies taxes and intervenes in difficult business' (Balmes 1844d: *OC* VI: 629). Balmes believed that the monarchy was the guarantor of the country's national and political unity. Moreover, he defended the institution of the Cortes because, at least since the sixteenth century, an organ of national representation had existed in the greatest European monarchies – and not because he endorsed revolutionary theories (Balmes 1844d: *OC* VI: 627). He thus envisaged a bicameral system in which access to both a high and a low chamber was strongly restricted according to income. In a nutshell, Balmes sought to modernise the traditional alliance between Throne and Altar. However, according to González Cuevas, the practical realisation of Balmes' programme would have turned Spain into a veritable autocracy that, resting upon an coalition between conservative and traditional forces, might have led to the actual extinction of liberalism (González Cuevas 2000: 107–8).

This mistrust of liberalism seems justified by Balmes' association with the *vilumistas* who, throughout 1844, had publicised their authoritarian and even reactionary views on constitutional reform. Not unlike Balmes, the Marquis of Viluma was convinced that the monarch should exercise decisive control over the Cortes that, in turn, would be deprived of both its executive and legislative faculties (Marcuello 2013: 157–158). Elitist and corporative, Viluma's Cortes were a reflection of his own hierarchical view of society, starkly at odds with the individualist outlook of liberal political culture. According to Burdiel, Viluma's political project amounted to an 'involution' that would have practically turned the monarch into a despot (2010: 170). But why, one might ask, did Balmes put all his hopes in the *vilumistas* who, seen retrospectively, were little more than a small group of aristocrats and second-rate politicians, as well as a tiny minority among the moderates? According to Fradera, the trust placed by Balmes in the *vilumistas*, whom he believed capable of engineering a restoration of both Crown and Church within Spain, are also eloquent of his own preconceptions. Balmes consistently underestimated the appeal exercised by mainstream *moderados* among ex Carlists, but also the ability and even the willingness of the Catholic Church, then ideologically divided, as well as weakened by liberal legislation, to join his plans (Fradera 1996: 83–35, 234).

Balmes also sought to reformulate the (liberal) idea of national sovereignty. In his view, sovereignty, understood as the very foundation of political power, needed to be an accurate reflection of the interests and forces that prevailed in society (Balmes 1844d: OC VI: 623). In short, he never considered the nation to be necessarily synonymous with the State. This explains his mistrust of representative government in Spain that, ever since its introduction in the country, he thought had never been 'truly representative' (Balmes 1844d: OC VI: 634). In addition, Balmes was keen to highlight what he believed were the defects of parliamentary government: superficial discussions in the Cortes, electoral corruption, and lack of sound policies. Sovereignty, as Balmes seemingly concluded, could not be artificially created by means of elections, held in the name of an abstract Spanish people. As Millán suggests, Balmes' views on sovereignty were not dissimilar to those held by contemporary Carlist thinkers. That was the case of Magí Ferrer, a Mercedarian friar, who believed that society, and not the State, was the source of political power; in turn, if society was essentially autarchic, any government should be reduced to its minimum expression (Millán 2009: 269–271). However, it might be added that it was Ferrer who accused Balmes of following the heterodox steps of Lamennais (Fradera 1996: 35).

What ultimately distinguished Balmes from both the Carlists and the *vilumistas*, notwithstanding a shared traditional and hierarchical view of society, is that he clearly steered away from the past. However monarchical he was, Balmes did not dream of returning to the allegedly golden days of enlightened despotism. In fact, he was deeply concerned with setting limits to the power of Spain's political authorities, and thus favoured accountability over expediency. Balmes believed that only the restoration of the great social institutions of Spain (the monarchy, the Church and the people) could eventually lead the country towards peace and stability. And here the key word is *institutions*: rather than resorting to the sword of General Narváez, as the *moderados* often did, Balmes believed that it was necessary to 'strengthen civilian power in order to destroy military predominance' (Balmes 1846a, OC VII: 567). Moreover, as regards his staunch support of the throne, Balmes was less interested in supporting the monarch as such than in strengthening the cohesive role performed by the institution of the monarchy. He worked on the assumption that: 'in any country in the world, civil power is neither a single person, nor a single institution, but the result of the force of a group of social elements that concur at one point, what we might call a centre of gravity' (Balmes 1846a, OC VI: 570–1).

In this sense, Balmes' support of the union between Isabel and Montemolín, understood as a revitalization of the throne and as a symbolic gesture towards reconciliation, can be seen as just one of the ways of achieving what he believed was most necessary in Spain: the restoration of its great social institutions. Much more relevant in Balmes' ideas was the full restoration of Catholicism within Spanish politics and society. In other words, it meant the reconciliation between the Church and the *moderado* regime, as well as between the regime and the Holy See. The starting point of such reconciliation, coming to terms with the disentailment and massive sale of Church properties, was particularly uncomfortable. Yet the reconciliation involved much more than settling the animosities between the purchasers of former church lands and the clergy. Now that the Church had been deprived of a substantial part of its material wealth, the question was to decide on how religious practice ought to be maintained in the future.

As regards ecclesiastical matters, Balmes stood mostly at odds with the *moderados*. Unwilling to acknowledge the sale of Church properties as a *fait accompli*, he spoke of the need to have a financially independent Church, arguing that the current tax on worship and clergy (*culto y clero*) brought a heavy burden not only on the public treasury but on the people (Balmes 1844d: 705–6). The debates held in the mid-1840s on the maintenance of the clergy or the negotiations with the Holy See, mainly a debate on the role of the Church within Spain, saw Balmes pitted against Donoso. This is illustrative of how the differences between Balmes and Donoso went well beyond personality, or even political sympathies. As I will show in the next chapter, the key to understanding these differences lies at the very core of their thought: the relationship between Church and State, one characterised more by conflict and adjustments rather than by harmonious collaboration. If Donoso tilted the balance towards the State, Balmes leaned towards the Church.

Chapter 3: The Politics of Spanish Catholicism

Stating that Catholicism was the official State religion in Spain during most of the nineteenth century involves challenging a few preconceptions. Religious unity, the benevolent synonym of religious intolerance, is a good case in point. Despite presupposing an ideal of harmony and unanimity, religious unity in nineteenth-century Spain was maintained through complicated arrangements between religious and civil authorities. My interest in this chapter is to consider religious unity in terms of a living and continuous process and not merely as a status that, once it had been achieved, simply needed to be consecrated by a constitutional text. One cannot consider religion, whether as a set of values and beliefs, or as a social practice – or the two combined – without first looking at its institutional foundation. In contemporary Spain, faith was not seen as being a purely private affair, but as something inseparable from the public expression of worship, administered and sustained by the clergy. This explains the use of the expression *culto y clero* (worship and clergy) used repeatedly by contemporaries of Balmes and Donoso when referring to the role of the Catholic Church in Spain. In other words, faith was seen as inseparable from the institutional framework, as being a personal as well as a collective experience. In addition, thinking about the way in which a religious identity is given a practical expression, leads to a crucial issue: the interplay between religion and politics, as expressed in the relationship between Church and State.

In the first half of the nineteenth century, there was no fundamental dispute in Spain about the character of Catholicism constituting a supreme social value. However, in the 1830s and 1840s, relations between Church and State underwent a dramatic change. During this period, the Church became subordinated to the State; deprived of the greatest part of its material wealth, it now depended upon the government for its sustenance. The consequences of this shift for the Church towards financial and political dependence on the State were significant and sparked off a passionate debate on the impact which these new institutional arrangements would have. The crucial question was whether these would either hamper or enhance the practice of Catholicism in Spain. Balmes and Donoso gave a different answer to this fundamental question: although both were interested in affirming the Catholic identity of the Spanish people, they diverged when it came to thinking about how to put it into practice. This chapter explores the differences between them on a second and more profound level: their views on Church and State, and their respective roles in promoting Spain's national religion.

The differences between Balmes and Donoso will be illustrated in reference the ecclesiastical policy during the *década moderada* (1843–1854) as the government, avowedly committed to the cause of Catholicism, faced the challenge of dealing with both the Church and the interests of those who profited from the massive sale of ecclesiastical properties. When analysing the view of Donoso in this period, a special factor needs be taken into account: his religious conversion in 1847, when he turned 'from a perfunctory Christian into a zealot' (Graham 1974: 115). Despite a substantial change in tone and a renovated spirituality, it is striking that an essential feature of his thought about Spain's religious identity remained unaltered. Both before and after his conversion, Donoso constantly upheld the role of religion as an aid to governance. This meant that he viewed the Church as an instrument at the service of the State. The second part of this equation, the State, would in fact come to have a more prominent position in his later writings. Foreshadowing the authoritarian drift of twentieth-century Catholicism, Donoso was the first Spanish author to posit the State – and not only the Church – as an actual means towards the 'salvation' of society (Colom 2006: 11).

Whereas Donoso tended to support the role of the State in religious matters, Balmes upheld the independence of the Church's mission, thus tracing a clear line between religion and politics. He would become an advocate of a type of freedom associated to religion, that of the right of the Church and of the clergy to be free from unwarranted government interference (Steinel 1971: 76). This plea was particularly relevant in the late 1830s and 1840s, when the government was introducing drastic changes in the Church's internal organization. Balmes believed that not only was the independence of the Church being compromised, but also that Spain's Catholic identity was at risk. Yet he was willing to act according to the new times, his strategy being to defend both the Church and Catholicism with modern weapons (press and parliamentary politics), while emphasising the need to fill in the vacuums left by successive waves of ecclesiastical legislation. In sum, Balmes put forward a distinctive 'Catholic modernity', conceived of as an alternative to a to a purely 'liberal modernity', with the aim of harmonising – via a comprehensive nationalistic discourse – the interests of both Church and State (García Cárcel 2013: 425). The viability of Balmes' project, as will be seen, would be strongly compromised by developments taking place both outside and inside the Catholic Church, in Spain as well as in Europe.

I. Old and new trends in Church-State relations

It has been argued that, in the nineteenth century, religion became a divisive factor rather than the unifying force it had been in Spanish history until the end of the *ancien régime* (Connelly 1983: 145). Recent scholarship, however, has emphasised how the ecclesiastical policy of liberal governments, especially in the mid-1830s and early 1840s, could be often understood as anticlerical – but *not* as anti-religious. For the first generation of Spanish liberals, it was a matter of fact that Catholicism provided a moral framework, as well as a solid foundation for the organisation of society (Portillo 2000: 460). In the next decades, Spanish governing elites consistently defended a type of State that was not only overtly Catholic, but also intolerant of other religions. According to Alonso, we need to acknowledge that these elites acted out of 'deeply-felt convictions', and not merely out of calculation or conformity (2017: 59). In fact, what the nineteenth-century liberals had in common with the *ilustrados*, the late eighteenth-century enlightened elite, was the assumption that, since religion was a powerful political instrument, the Church ought to be used as a means to further State moves aimed at modernising the country (Smith and Gardner 2017: 14).

At the same time, however, the institutional framework underpinning the sustained influence of Catholicism in Spain underwent a profound transformation, ushered in by the liberal revolution that – both in theory and practice – changed the *ultima ratio* of politics and power relations within Spain. In a nutshell, the Catholic Church ceased to be simply the auxiliary of the monarchy, as it had been during the *ancien régime*, and became subordinated to the liberal State. During the 1830s, the issues at stake went far beyond earlier measures concerning the reform of the clergy, such as a much-resented reduction in the size of the regular orders during the Liberal Triennium (1820–1823) or even the government's customary expedient of resorting to the Church's wealth in case of need. The 1830s saw a complete redefinition of the economic structure of the Spanish Church, notwithstanding its zeal for autonomy and despite the condemnations issued by the Pope. The massive sale of ecclesiastical properties following on from the laws of *desamortización* (disentailment), deprived the Church of its traditional sources of income. As a result, it became dependent upon the liberal State for its maintenance, a process by which the clergy implicitly acquired the status of State employees (Pro 2019: 346).

Yet this was not achieved without hesitation and controversy. After all, the two families of Spanish liberalism, *progresistas* and *moderados*, always stood at odds on how fast change should occur, on how far the changes should go. Discussing the changes on Church-State relations brought about by liberal legislation, Balmes was to some degree justified when he argued that 'the only difference between the progressives and a certain faction of the moderates is that the former say: "Do it quickly and by any means", and the latter say: "Do the same thing slowly and by gentle means"' (Balmes 1845b: OC VII, 117). This matches what Fradera affirms, that the moderados carried out an 'institutionalization of the [liberal] revolution' between the mid-1840s and mid-1850s (Fradera 1996: 239). Although they acted in a more conciliatory manner, one that was conservative but decidedly not counter-revolutionary, they turned both the Church and Catholicism into an *instrumentum regni* (Alonso 2017b: 139). Before entering into the details of how the Church became subordinated to the liberal State, it is important to bear in mind that this cannot be read as a 'teleological tale of inevitable decline' (De la Cueva 2018: 276). Although this period was experienced by the Church as being in a veritable existential crisis, that crisis also paved the way for its accommodation – in however an imperfect and complicated manner – with the new ideas and institutions associated to liberalism, and did not outlaw future revivals in the second half of the nineteenth-century.

In a first instance, both the governments of the moderates Francisco Martínez de la Rosa (January 1834 to June 1835) and José María Queipo de Llano, Count of Toreno (June to September 1835) addressed the issue of Church reform in a gradual way. A royal commission, the Real Junta Eclesiástica, was then appointed to study the question of the regular orders. However, any provision for ecclesiastical change based merely upon the

THE POLITICS OF SPANISH CATHOLICISM 115

reform of the orders satisfied no one, given that it was perceived to be 'either too much or too little' (Callahan 1984a: 150). This caution about change can be mostly explained by looking at the context, one of civil war. This was a period of polarisation in which Carlism, a movement wholly identified with the Church and infused with theocratic ideology, coexisted with bursts of violent anti-clericalism. Such was the case with the slaughter of friars (*matanza de frailes*) on July 17, 1834, a day in which the rioting of angry crowds in the streets of Madrid led to the murder of seventy-eight Jesuits, Franciscans, Dominicans and Mercedarians; it was followed by the burning of convents in Zaragoza, Reus and Barcelona during the spring and summer of 1835 (Moliner 1998: 78). Yet the cautious way in which ecclesiastical reform was handled was also the result of miscalculation: the extent to which the Church could contribute to a Carlist victory was overestimated, whereas the strength of a new generation of liberal *progresistas* was underestimated (Callahan 1984a: 151).

The ascent of the *progresistas* took place in mid 1835, in a context of instability and agitation, when Juan Álvarez Mendizábal rose into power. His programme involved obliterating the vestiges of Old Regime privilege that his predecessors had tried to eliminate through a slow legislative process (Burdiel 2010: 49). In October 11, 1835, a decree suppressed all but a few of Spain's monasteries. In February 19, 1836, a decree ordered the sale at public auction of their properties to benefit the public treasury. In March 8, 1836, a decree suppressed virtually all religious communities of men – their properties would go on sale – and imposed a reduction in the feminine orders. Later, the government of José María Calatrava (1836–1837) openly punished clerics who were political dissidents and established absolute control of the finances of the secular clergy, declaring its properties to be 'national'. The tithe was abolished in a decree of July 29, 1837; very significantly, this decree also stipulated that the government would pay the salaries of the clergy from now onwards (Callahan 1984: 162–3).

The immediate aims of the radical liberals were to alleviate fiscal penury and to finance the war against the Carlists, while consolidating both Spain's constitutional regime and the throne of Isabel II (Moliner 1998: 95; Pro 2019: 28). Ultimately, the massive transfer of property away from the "dead hands" of the Church was supposed to encourage both a circulation of wealth and a more efficient exploitation of land, at the same time as creating a body of property owners whose interests were linked to the survival of the liberal State (Cárcel Orti 1976: 306; Callahan 1984a: 160–1). As Callahan notes, the sales of Church property in the 1830s were only the first part of an extensive process that would continue until 1860, eventually including the property of both secular clergy and charitable institutions, and municipal common lands. These measures had profound consequences for the Church, especially as they deeply affected its internal organization. The vacuum left by the male religious orders could not easily be filled by an ill-prepared secular clergy who now faced an increased burden; moreover, the drastic fall in clerical incomes impaired the Church's traditional charitable and educational activities. By 1860, the number of clerics and nuns in Spain had dwindled to 63,000 from more than 148,000 in 1797 (De la Cueva 2018: 277). The Church's state of weakness and direction of its own affairs was further hampered by the rupture between the liberal State and the Papacy (February 1836), which prevented the appointment of new bishops to replace those who had either died or fled into exile – by 1840 only 11 of the kingdom's 60 dioceses were being administered by their bishops (Callahan 1984a: 161–4, 179).

Yet liberal legislation, though strongly anti-clerical, was not necessarily anti-religious. Regardless of the obvious attack on the privileges of the clergy as a class, it did not neglect an important issue. If the practice of Catholicism were to be sustained, new institutional arrangements had to be made. After all, both enemies and friends of Church reform alike agreed that a Catholic State ought to provide the means both for worship and upkeep of the Church's ministers (Revuelta 1996: 331). The reforms were therefore followed by a discussion on the *means* to ensure the financial and material support of the clergy. There were the traditional means: tithes and landed property; but there were also the means proposed by the new liberal legislation: salaries and pensions. Despite the fact that reforms were directed towards management and governance, rather than belief, the Church deeply resented the interference of the State in its internal and domestic affairs, disposing of its properties and deciding on its organisation. Clerics such as Balmes thus claimed that reforms did not only affect the institutional aspects of religion, but that they put an obstacle to the dissemination of religious belief.

These complications were, however, not new. To some degree the nineteenth-century liberal State was continuing the *regalismo* that had been practised by the eighteenth-century Bourbon monarchs of Spain. *Regalismo* is a term that refers to the desire to create a clerical establishment that will favour the objectives of government policy. It also refers to the assertion of the government's rights to interfere in ecclesiastical affairs, especially in a way that would limit the influence exercised by the Pope within the Spanish Church (Callahan 1980: 200–1). There was a further complication which was brought about by the liberal legislation on ecclesiastic matters: the relationship of Spain with the Papacy. It must be stressed that the Spanish Church was not autonomous and crucial measures such as the appointment of bishops, the reform of the clergy or the creation of new dioceses could not be undertaken without the approval of the Pope.

The complication provided by the need to have the Pope's approval became particularly evident during the regency of General Espartero (1841–1843). This period saw one of the most daring attempts made by the State to deal single-handedly with the Church, that is, without taking the Pope into account. Espartero's aim was to create a Church that would serve the purposes of liberalism and he took the following measures: the ecclesiastical map was redrawn and a schedule was established of salaries for all clergymen, both high and low in the hierarchy; additionally, a law of 2 September 1841 ordered the sale of properties of the secular clergy, with the proceeds to service the national debt (Callahan 1984a: 167–8; Pro 2019: 349). The links with the Pope Gregory XVI were neglected, and Espartero entertained plans for a civil constitution of the clergy or even a schismatic national church (Payne 1978: 86; Fradera 1996: 127–128). Yet Espartero counted on the support of a minority of liberal and progressive clerics, who acted under the conviction that ecclesiastical reform could be brought about by an alliance between Constitution and Altar (Callahan 1984a: 172; Valverde 1979: 496). Their plans were met with hostility by a pro-Roman majority of clergymen who believed that reform should be the result of a diplomatic agreement between the State and the Papacy. Thanks to their having organised a spontaneous campaign of civil disobedience against the government, the Church was able to regain a sense of agency, thus overcoming the attitude of 'fatalistic resignation' that had shown regarding the disentailment and sale of its properties during the 1830s (Callahan 1984a: 169–70).

During the 1840s, the Church moved towards a more realistic and sober appreciation of the drastic changes that had taken place in Spain. It was still in a vulnerable position and its state of disarray prevented it from presenting a strong front against the State's ecclesiastical policies. For the most farsighted clergymen it became evident that the Church needed to come to terms with the present, its new ideas and institutions, since it was impossible to restore the privileges of the past (Revuelta 1996: 339). In their view, the Church had to reconcile itself with the liberal state; more importantly, it needed to learn to use the tools of liberalism, ranging from the periodical press to discussions in the Cortes, for its own benefit (Callahan 1984a: 174–6). The writings of Balmes, which signalled the emergence of a truly effective Catholic press, symbolised this new realism. According to Fradera, Balmes became the thinker 'after the deluge' which, for the Church, had been both the liberal revolution and the regency of Espartero (1996: 286). In the pages of *El Pensamiento de la Nación*, Balmes thus exhorted his readers to make use of modern means in order to pursue the traditional goals of Catholicism:

Such is the spirit of the age, such is the way in which material means are considered, such is the importance which discussion in the press has acquired, and such are the other expedients which have been adopted to influence public opinion and the course of government, that we Catholics must not allow ourselves to lose this beautiful position which we have gained. It is necessary that by all the means at our disposal we should try to keep up with the century, and that, without allowing ourselves to be infected by what is bad in it, we should absorb from it what is good; if weapons of force have been used up, we still have others of much better quality: the vigour of the intellect and the energy of the will. The press in all its forms, associations, either permanent or temporary, firm expositions, temperate and decorous protests, in a word, intellectual light and the energy of moral sentiments, these are the weapons of our century (Balmes 1844b: 446).

Yet Balmes was not so ready to acknowledge the loss of the Church's privileged status and properties, which had customarily enabled the Church to carry out a prominent social and economic role. Without clinging blindly to the past, Balmes constantly affirmed that the Church ought to be able to act on its own initiative, its activities guaranteed with appropriate means of action – that is, with its own financial means. Yet he refused to flag up the Church as being at the service of a political party, nor did he confine its actions to the realm of governmental policy. Balmes' trademark in contemporary debates became his insistence upon the independence of the Church, that is, from government encroachment *and* from partisan politics, whether Carlist or liberal:

Let the religious men of Spain be convinced of this: they should not identify cause of Eternity with any temporal cause, and when they give support to any legitimate and decorous alliance, it should always be one that preserves the independence demanded by their principles. We will repeat here what we have already said on other occasions: It is not politics that must save religion, it is religion that must save politics; the future of religion does not depend on government, the future of government depends on religion; society must not regenerate religion, it is religion that must regenerate society (Balmes 1844b, OC VI: 446).

THE POLITICS OF SPANISH CATHOLICISM 119

It is legitimate to ask whether Balmes was justified or not, especially taking into account the Church-State relations during the *década moderada* (1843–1854). When the *moderados* were settled in power it opened the way for making more concessions to the Church, however cautiously, as these moves were likely to arouse the hostility of the *progresistas* and a substantial deal of controversy within *moderado* politicians, whose views on Church-State relations were far from being beyond dispute. Yet in the summer of 1844, the sale of the property of secular clergy was suspended; in April 1845, the government ordered the return of all property as yet unsold (Payne 1984: 189; Burdiel 2010: 236). The Constitution of 1845 would firmly uphold the Catholic character of the Spanish nation in its article 11. Moreover, already in mid-1844 a special representative had been sent to negotiate an agreement with Pope Gregory XVI who still had not recognised Isabel II as Spain's legitimate monarch (Rosenblatt 1976: 592–3).

Yet the *moderados'* relationship with the Church was, above all, a marriage of convenience. In their dealings with the Church, while keeping the previous trend of subordination, the *moderados* added a new dimension, that of the manipulation of both religion and Church, for the sake of governance and social consensus (Fradera 2003: 273). Being able to co-exist with the Church proved to be useful for a regime that, despite its avowed religiosity, was nevertheless keen on preserving the gains made from the destruction of the old social order. It was therefore determined to regard the previous sales of ecclesiastical properties as a *fait accompli* (Comellas 1971: 297–8). The debates held between 1844 and 1845 in the Cortes led to the redefinition of Church-State relations along *moderado* lines. As will be discussed in the next section, these debates gave rise to one of the few occasions in which the disagreement between Balmes and Donoso was expressed in an open and public way.

Finally, we should emphasize the exceptional character of the decade of the 1840s. The Church's institutional weakness brought about an unintended result, that of producing, if only among distinguished clergymen, a considerable degree of ideological flexibility (Fradera 2003: 305). Balmes was the most consummate example of this attitude of relative open-mindedness, characterised by the willingness to enter into a dialogue with those regarded as antagonists. For a Church that was facing impoverishment and disarray, having an accommodation with the *moderados* was an attractive way of restoring its privileged relationship with the civil authorities. Once the Concordat of 1851 secured its privileges, the Church of the 1850s and 1860s would be characterised by its attitude of defensiveness and disapproval, of righteousness and immobility. A related phenomenon would be the disappearance, towards the middle of the century, of what had been an influential minority within the Church, that of liberal and progressive clergymen (Valverde 1979: 496). It is therefore important to bear in mind that the writings of Balmes and Donoso discussed in this chapter were written *before* the Concordat of 1851, a 'stern bastion of Catholic unity' that secured the Church's position and established governmental responsibility for that position (Rosenblatt 1976: 600–1).

II. Balmes *versus* Donoso (1844–1845)

The writing which gave Balmes access to the realm of Spanish national politics was *Observaciones sociales, políticas y económicas sobre los bienes del clero [Social, Political, and Economic Observations on Clerical Property]* (1840). When Balmes published it, the regular clergy had already been suppressed and its properties put on sale, following the measures taken in 1836–1837. The tithe had also been abolished, while the fate of the properties of the secular clergy, having been declared to be the property of the nation, remained uncertain. Balmes raised a number of objections to these measures, pragmatic in character, and the way that he did it showed him complying with what he labelled as the 'scientific taste of the century': selecting a fact and then making observations which would demonstrate the political, social and economic relations between this fact and its context (Balmes 1840a: 677).

Initially, Balmes justified the existence of the clergy's properties by affirming that the possession of wealth and estates were inseparable from the Church's role as an 'organising and civilising association'; its ability to act and to exercise its influence upon society depended upon 'a combination of moral and physical means' (1840a: 690, 703). Constantly stressing that only the ownership of property could guarantee the independence and stability of any class or group within society, Balmes illustrated a paradox present in the controversies on Church property. The supporters of the secularization of this property usually deployed 'spiritual' arguments, centring upon the need to make the Church revert to a supposed primitive purity and simplicity; by contrast, apologists for the Church usually emphasised 'practical' aspects, arguing that property was an essential tool for the accomplishment of its spiritual ends (Revuelta 1996: 335).

So Balmes would pursue the traditional line of defence of Church property, but he added a new aspect: the stress upon context, both of historical antecedents and of present needs. In order to justify the importance of the Church for society, Balmes praised the role played by the Catholic Church in salvaging European civilisation after the fall of Rome, an argument which had already been brilliantly expounded by Guizot (1828: 39, 96–7). More importantly, in the *Observaciones* (1840), Balmes gave an eloquent historical account of the role of the Church within Spain. Moving easily from the rhetorical to the pragmatic, he called into question the ecclesiastical policy of the government. He denied that clergymen would be regarded as a kind of public employees from now onwards, but he (rightly) doubted the public treasury's ability to cover the expenses related to religion (Balmes 1840a: 727–8). Balmes believed that 265 million *reales* were needed to provide for ecclesiastical salaries and to maintain churches and seminaries (Balmes 1840a: 727–30). By contrast, the annual budget for *culto y clero* would be 153 million *reales* in 1851 and 124 million *reales* in 1855 (Callahan 1984a: 191, 201). Regardless of how ambitious Balmes' calculations were, the point remains that the State would be unable to cover the expenses associated to the Church only with the income derived of the sale of ecclesiastical properties. Making up for this deficit in Church finances would be a challenge for future governments, while the sale of the properties was still going on. In September 1841, the sale of the holdings of the secular clergy was authorized; three years later, when this process was brought to a halt, 62 % of these properties had been sold. As Callahan puts it, these sales 'broke the back of the imposing structure of ecclesiastical wealth that had sustained the Church for centuries' (1984a: 168).

Despite striving for the restoration of the Church's pre-eminent position, Balmes urged the Spanish clergy to remain free from any association with political parties and firmly stated: 'religious ideas will not owe their triumph to political schemes' (Balmes 1843a, *OC* VI: 282–3). He thus rejected a scenario where religious matters became subordinate to the political game, one in which the Church might turn into a mere appendage of the State. What makes his argument problematic is that in his writings *religious matters* often stand for two different things: on the one hand, religion; on the other, the institutional Church. One might argue that Balmes did not consider that it was necessary to make this distinction. However, even if his main aim was to affirm the independence of the Church, he strongly believed that the State owed the Church not only respect but a privileged relationship:

What we demand [from the government] is very little: that it does not destroy. That it should respect the sacred nature of conscience, following in this regard the very principle of freedom; that it should respect the rights of the clergy as it respects those of other citizens; not to allow the establishment of chairs of impiety or other anti-Catholic sects in universities and other educational establishments; that it should not allow the press to pervert or corrupt; and the rest will take care of itself, for the work of God does not need the weak hand of man (Balmes 1840b: OC VI: 87).

The duties that Balmes thought the government should observe in relation to religion obviously involved an active role, that of protecting the Church. He questioned the views of those who believed that the future of Catholicism in Spain depended solely upon the restoration of absolutism. Carlism had lost the battle and yet 'religion is preserved and makes its powerful voice resound and conquers part of its lost territory' (Balmes 1844b, *OC* VI: 444). Showing a considerable degree of ideological flexibility, Balmes constantly stressed that Catholicism in Spain – in terms of its strength and influence – was ultimately independent of government support regardless of whatever shape or form this government might take. Despite his occasional diatribes against progressive liberals, Balmes thus implied that collaboration between the Church and a liberal, representative regime was possible.

The Church, according to Balmes, needed to overcome the shock caused by liberal legislation, adapt to it, and find ways of blossoming again. This was demonstrated in an incident concerning the budget allowed for the Church in 1844–5. Writing in the pages of *El Pensamiento de la Nación [The Thought of the Nation]*, Balmes urged the government to stop the sale of clerical holdings and insisted upon the need to re-establish relations with the Holy See. As explained in the previous chapter, Balmes had been cultivating a relationship with the Marquis of Viluma, the unofficial leader of a small political faction located at the right wing of the *moderados*. At the beginning of the 1840s, Balmes made the acquaintance of several of the so-called *vilumistas*, since they had similar views on how to achieve reconciliation of all Spaniards. The wished-for reconciliation of Balmes and the *vilumistas* involved two goals, equally important: the marriage between Isabel II and Montemolín, *plus* the restoration of the Church's privileged position. The possibility of carrying out these goals, in collaboration with the *vilumistas*, prompted Balmes to move from Barcelona to Madrid, where he became the editor of *El Pensamiento de la Nación*, a newspaper in which he expanded and justified his ideas. Nonetheless, Viluma's attempts at influencing policy-making in favour of the Church failed miserably.

On 21 December 1844 the actual part of the national budget allocated to the Church was decided in a session of the Cortes. The minister of the Treasury, Alejandro Mon, had calculated a budget of 159 million *reales* for expenses associated with religious worship, corresponding to the following year (1845). The group associated with Viluma tried to take advantage of the occasion – a mere discussion of the budget – in order to make a decisive move: salvaging the Church's properties. So the *vilumistas* tried to introduce an amendment to Mon's proposal, which involved putting an end to the sale of the holdings of the regular clergy, while returning the property as yet unsold to both the secular clergy and to nuns (Balmes 1845a, OC VI:1043). But they did so in a hasty way, prompting the anger of minister Mon, who then publicly accused them of proceeding in a 'sneaky way' (Urbina 1939:127). Offended by the crude epithet, a group of twenty deputies, including Viluma, resigned from the Cortes as a sign of disagreement with the regime's ecclesiastical policy. A month later, in January 1845, Viluma issued a manifesto in which he suggested, among other things, depriving the Cortes of the 'revolutionary right' to levy taxes (Castro 2011: 47).

From the perspective of Balmes, the whole episode of December 1844 seemed scandalous. He reacted passionately to the whole incident and used it as an excuse to voice his disagreements with the regime. He argued that the attitude of Mon, shared by a majority of *moderados*, expressed the unwillingness to enter into dialogue with diverging opinions. The result, a political situation characterised by its 'exclusivity and narrow-mindedness', prompted Balmes to question: 'where is representative government?' (Balmes 1844h, OC VI: 1040; Balmes 1845b, OC VI: 1054). As for the question of Church-State relations, Balmes vented his anger against a particular brand of *moderados*:

... those who have been protesting for many years against the outrages and spoils of the revolution, who have been protesting against the sale of clerical property, and who, nevertheless, have been more quick to sell it than the progressives themselves; those who have been considering the necessity of a reconciliation with the Holy See, and who, in order to pave the way to that reconciliation, have continued to despoil the Church in a scandalous manner (Balmes 1844e, OC VI: 701–2).

Finally, used the strongest words to discredit the *moderados*' ecclesiastic policy:

...you want the sad glory of consummating what the revolution began. Congratulations, acquire that dismal glory, but at least do not call yourselves repairers, nor zealous for the

124 THE POLITICS OF SPANISH CATHOLICISM

lustre of religion, nor conservatives; unless it is supposed to mean conservatives of the conquests of the revolution, as one newspaper frankly put it. Be frank and we shall know with whom we are dealing (Balmes 1845a, OC VI: 1046).

Balmes' criticism of the *moderados* was centred upon their incoherence. In this he anticipated what became the classic description of the party, penned by the conservative scholar Marcelino Menéndez y Pelayo in the late 1880s. According to this author, the problem of the *moderado* party was that, despite appealing to a minority of sincere Catholics, it was mostly populated by 'former Volterians' who had tempered their political views but not their religious ones. Their fear of both anarchy and the populace had rendered them cautious, suggested Menéndez, but not free from impious thoughts, or of a persistent 'hatred against Rome' (1948, VI: 217). Rather than taking this judgement at a face value, it is worth stressing how the *moderados* were caught between the past and the present. Theirs was a modern conservatism; a conservatism within liberalism.

The *moderados'* reaffirmation of traditional religiosity took place in the context of the liberal revolution, in which the ending of the hierarchical society of the past was signalled. This would be brought about not only by new political and institutional developments but also by the renewal of the structure of landed property (Tomás y Valiente 1978: 15). As Botti claims, the ultimate objective of the disentailment and sale of ecclesiastical properties was not to exclude the Church from the economic system, but to force it to adapt to the new economic circumstances (2008: 81). This was reflected in the overall co-existence, within the *moderado* regime, of elements such as economic modernization, political elitism and traditional religiousness. The *moderados* thus illustrate what Payne calls the halfway nature of nineteenth-century liberalism in Spain, given that 'the first liberals soon became the new conservatives and sought the same institutional supports that had sustained their predecessors in the old regime' (Payne 1984: 97). More recently, Pro has demonstrated how the sale of Church properties was crucial for the underpinning of the construction of the liberal State in the 1830s, given that it financed the incipient creation of both a federal army and a national civil administration, while strengthening the regime's social base (2019: 241–242). At the same time, however, the *moderados* realised that in Spain social consensus could not be disentangled either from Catholicism or from the institutional Church, with the result that a degree of compromise in Church-State relations was necessary. And it was Donoso, speaking in the Cortes in early 1845, who would eloquently illustrate the approach of the *moderados* to ecclesiastical policy: on the one hand, it justified the loss of the Church's properties and privileges through the process of *desamortización*; on the other, it was determined to use the Church as a bastion of social order.

In two speeches, delivered in January and March 1845, Donoso viewed the disentailment and subsequent sale of ecclesiastical properties as being 'a revolutionary fact, already embodied in the civilisation of peoples, and therefore unalterable' (Donoso 1845b, *OC* II: 106). This was related to his idea of revolution: new political, social and economic developments in history which brought about both positive and negative consequences. Revolutions were thus bound to have a double significance: 'civilisation and crimes; that is, a providential as well as a satanic doing' (Donoso 1845a, *OC* II: 94). Among the new trends which could justify the sale of Church properties, Donoso insisted upon the economic aspects. The clergy would not simply regain its independence by becoming a property-owner again: landed property was losing importance in the face of the increasing relevance of both industry and commerce – a development which, during the *década moderada*, was still restricted to few areas in Catalonia and the province of Biscay (Donoso 1845a, *OC* II: 99; Cruz 2000: 274–275).

'The State has to be secular', affirmed Donoso in one of these speeches, adding that 'those who want to turn it into an ecclesiastical or a military entity are promoting barbarism' (Donoso 1845a, *OC* II: 96–7). Notwithstanding this statement, he did not question the status of Catholicism as the official religion of the State. His argument was that the State must be free from the interference of the Church in *temporal* matters; but at the same time he believed that the Church must be free from the interference of the State in *spiritual* matters. Underlying this discussion was something that had been one of the key debates of eighteenth-century Catholicism: deciding on what fell within the scope of either the civil or the religious authorities, thus about tracing a clear line between their respective spheres of influence (Fradera 2003: 263). Implicit in Donoso's argument was the uncontested right of the State to manage the temporal (i.e. institutional) matters of the Church including, of course, ecclesiastical properties. This implied focus in turn raised the question of how to maintain the independence of the Church. Donoso did not believe that the new arrangements would result in a situation of dependence for the Church; actually, he in fact argued in the Cortes that the budget on ecclesiastical matters should acquire a more or less permanent status, instead of being debated every year. But Donoso's plea that members of the clergy should be treated 'as rightful creditors, and not as salaried creditors' (Donoso 1845a, *OC* II: 100) did not alter the essential imbalance of the *moderados*' Church-State equation. Even if the clergy's social importance was acknowledged, it was felt that it should be deprived of the means (i.e. properties) which would allow it to set out an independent political course:

We will be religious when we aim to provide the subsistence of the clergy and at the same time the independence of the Church. Neither will we give less to the clergy, because to give it less would be to throw it into the path of impiety, nor will we give it more, because to give it more would be to throw it into the path of reaction (Donoso 1845a, OC II: 105).

Donoso emphasised the need to reach a balanced view on the issue of ecclesiastical properties, because it had led to a 'inevitable war between the clergy and the State' (Donoso 1845a, *OC* II: 100). He likened his views to those he referred to as 'impartial men'. Such men were characterised by 'a certain natural propensity to bring all things to the point of compromise, to compare the means with the ends, the purposes with the results' (Donoso 1845b, *OC* II: 111). Here his implied point was that such men, whose aim was the conciliation of all interests, were none other than the *moderados*. They were men who perceived the advantages of having a collaborative Church at their side. This was because, as Donoso put it, perfection was to be found in 'the union of Empire and Church', a collaboration that meant moving away from the extremes represented by both 'regalists and ultramontanes', keen on affirming the supremacy of either the State or the Papacy in matters concerning Church government (Donoso 1845b, *OC* II: 120).

It could be argued that Donoso did everything he could to minimise the fact that the Church was now dependent upon the State. He even resorted to sweeping arguments on how the subservience of the Church to the State was essentially anti-Catholic. He argued that affirming the independence of national Churches at the expense of the Pope's authority led to Jansenism, and even in the long run to Protestantism, creating a situation in which national churches were directly under the control of the monarch (Donoso 1845b, *OC* II: 117–9). Yet Donoso, in the two speeches that he delivered in January and March 1845 in the Cortes, concluded that the recent sales of ecclesiastical properties, carried out without the consent of either the Spanish Church or the Papacy, were an irreversible fact.

Donoso's two speeches were sharply criticised by Balmes, who wrote from the pages of *El Pensamiento de la Nación*. It is important to stress that this is practically the only instance in which Balmes interacted directly with

THE POLITICS OF SPANISH CATHOLICISM 127

Donoso's writings and vice versa. The main disagreement between the two men centred on Church property – in Spain and in general. In order to discredit Donoso's arguments on this matter, Balmes targeted both his logic and his literary style. In March, Donoso had argued that the properties of the Church did not have the inviolable character that individual property ownership was believed to have. He claimed that every political assembly in the world had diverging views on Church property, and yet not one them would call individual property rights into question: 'this proves that the former is a question, while the latter is a truth that lies in the consciousness of human beings' (Donoso 1845b, *OC* II: 108).

Balmes strongly disagreed:

Mr. Donoso's reasoning boils down to the following: 'There is uniformity of opinion, therefore truth is certain; at the very least there is doubt'. This reasoning is sophistic. [...] The fact that a truth has been disputed, the fact that there has been a diversity of opinions about it, does not mean that it is not true, and is a very certain truth. [...] Diversity of opinions is not, therefore, a good criterion to make truth or certainty waver (Balmes 1845c; OC VII: 121).

When the deep social impact of the disentailment laws came under debate, Donoso argued the following, throwing responsibility onto the Cortes:

I believe that errors are the patrimony of humankind, but I believe that crimes belong to individuals only. I believe that none of the many assemblies that deliberate in public are capable of committing a crime, just as humankind cannot be labelled as criminal; I simply do not believe in collective crimes. It is such a sad thing to believe that these were crimes committed by individuals! [...] Many interests have been created [by the sale of Church properties], and the greatest of crimes is to disturb these newly-created interests (Donoso 1845b, OC II: 109).

Balmes, when commenting on this speech, made direct and negative remarks about Donoso's style, with personal comment on his character as politician and as man of letters:

Mr. Donoso, by casting assemblies and nations outside the moral order, exempting them from all crime, has attacked not only reason, but poetry. And this, in a poet... He deserves it. Was he unaware that he was getting too close to the material interests created by the revolution, and that the proximity of injustice burns the wings of genius? (Balmes 1845c, OC VII: 125).

What Balmes found most objectionable is that Donoso often put his rhetoric to what was, as Balmes saw it, a bad use, employing beautiful and elevated language to justify political aims that were far from being lofty. Commenting upon Donoso's literary style, Balmes additionally came close to suggesting that rhetorical profusion was often a sign of intellectual vacuity:

He cannot present his thoughts naked; he needs to cloak them in magnificent robes. He is so fond of the magnificence and splendour of form that he often forgets the background; if the prestigious castle rises to gigantic dimensions, it does not matter if it lacks the foundation of reality. [...] Mr Donoso does not know how to deal with an idea, however great he supposes it to be, if it is on its own: he needs another that contrasts symmetrically. He does not want objects to reach the eye in a straight line, but to pass through a multiplied reflection: it is as if he were arranging a combination of mirrors to increase the illusion. Nobody listens to Mr Donoso's speeches to be convinced, but to enjoy their beauty, their originality, which is at times somewhat strange (Balmes 1845c; OC VII: 119–20).

It is important to set these detailed (and not very pleasant) disagreements between Balmes and Donoso in the context of a much broader picture, namely the negotiations between Spain and the Papacy. In mid-1844, a diplomatic agent had been sent to Rome to negotiate with Gregory XVI with the following task: to secure papal recognition of Isabel II as the kingdom's legitimate sovereign and of the royal prerogatives in the appointment of bishops. This task was also taking into account the fact that the government had made gestures that were conciliatory to Rome, such as the suspension of the sale of the property of the secular clergy and of the female orders (Payne 1984: 189; Rosenblatt 1976: 593). The *quid pro quo* of these negotiations, a bargaining about *desamortización* being suspended in order to get Isabel II recognised by the Pope, was heavily criticised by Balmes. In fact, he believed that the ecclesiastical properties were being used as a bargain chip with the Pope, as if implicitly saying: 'Either you give me what I have taken, or I will not give you back what is left over' (Balmes 1845a: 1044). From the perspective of Donoso, what appeared as worrying was that many were ready to shun a compromise, as if the past could be easily overturned: 'The reactionaries say: "Then everything must be returned to the clergy"; the revolutionaries say: "Then nothing must be returned to the clergy". The impartial also draw their consequences: "Then it is necessary to return to the clergy whatever we can"'. (Donoso 1845b, OC II: 111). By January 1845, an agreement (*convenio*) had already been worked out with the Papacy and was being discussed in Madrid. The agreement met the State's original demands; however, a new provision authorizing the re-establishment of male religious orders at an 'opportune' time aroused controversy not only in the cabinet, but also amidst *progresista* and even *moderado* newspapers, who resented the fact that the agreement

THE POLITICS OF SPANISH CATHOLICISM 129

had been negotiated secretly and without paying heed to the Cortes (Callahan 1984a: 190).

In April 1845, a limited agreement was reached between Spain and Rome, including papal recognition of Isabel II and the sale of church property that had taken place since 1834. In the same month, the Cortes voted in favour of a proposal to return unsold properties to the Church; in reality, the government was giving up little of material value as the most productive church land had been sold between 1842 and 1844 although it had 'gained tremendously in propaganda value' (Rosenblatt 1976: 591–2, 595). Balmes, who had constantly upheld the irregularities within the process of disentailment, which he considered to be fundamentally unjust, gave in to the Pope's decision to recognise Isabel and to accept a form of *status quo* on the sale of church property.

Balmes' acquiescence here was not easy for him, as it had a direct impact upon his own political ventures. As explained in the previous chapter, during the years 1844–1846, Balmes campaigned in favour of the marriage between Isabel and the son of Don Carlos, as a way of achieving reconciliation between all Spaniards. In April 1845, he realised that the papal acknowledgement of Isabel's legitimacy cast a shadow of doubt on the cause of Carlism, and further undermined the rights of Don Carlos (and his descendants) to the Spanish throne. Addressing followers and non-followers from the pages *El Pensamiento de la Nación*, Balmes emphasised how his political ventures had always obeyed an all-encompassing national interest rather to a narrow dynastic one:

We have never considered the question of the marriage (between Isabel and the Count of Montemolín) as a lever for reaction; and we have never wished that the arrangement of ecclesiastical matters should be prolonged so that their delay would contribute to the marriage: this was because we could not subordinate the religious to the political; because we could not put the temporal before the spiritual (Balmes 1845d, OC VII: 134).

But the agreement of April 1845 did not lead to a final agreement between Rome and the Spanish State, that is, to a Concordat. It actually brought about a 'wave of public wrath' in both the press and the Cortes. In particular, the faction of the *puritanos* affirmed that the Spanish State was giving up more of its rights than the Church (Rosenblatt 1976: 595, 598). By early 1846, the cabinet of Narváez decided to drop the agreement. A definitive settlement between Spain and Rome would not be reached until 1851, when a series of new circumstances facilitated the acceptance of a Concordat in Spain: not only was there a new Pope (Pius IX) who was more sympathetic towards Spanish affairs but also the revolutions of 1848 had by this time swept through the whole of Europe, a context which favoured the return to order and traditional religion.

III. Balmes: updating Spanish Catholicism

Balmes updated and modernised the traditional tenets of Spanish Catholicism, and thus ensuring their survival and growth in new circumstances. In this section, I will build my case on Álvarez Junco, who argues that Catholicism only became truly modern once it came to terms with the idea of nation (2007: 381). This is what Balmes did in Spain. His idea of Spain as a Catholic nation, in which traditional goals would be pursued through modern means, is one that sets him apart from previous conservative thinkers – from fray Diego de Cádiz to Rafael de Vélez. These thinkers, according to Álvarez Junco, had enthusiastically embraced the idea that the Catholic religion was fundamental to the Spanish identity. But they had been staunch opponents of the (liberal) idea of a nation because it derived political power from a secular source. The legitimacy of the liberal nation, in the view of these thinkers, seemed to require no religious validation, given that the liberal concept of sovereignty was grounded upon the political community itself and not upon the authority of divinely-appointed monarchs. Following the line of sixteenth-century scholasticism, Balmes had argued that political power, notwithstanding the fact that it had God as its ultimate source, had its roots in the community. But Balmes put forward a distinctively Catholic idea of the Spanish nation, and resorted to the past in order to demonstrate that Spain was historically linked with Catholicism. The end product of Balmes' line of thought was Catholic nationalism which can be summed up as having been 'the reformulation of a pre-revolutionary identity in the language and mentality of modernity' (Villalonga 2014: 331).

The image of Spain as a fundamentally Catholic nation that Balmes advanced had two clear limitations. Firstly, it was a cultural imperative which implied that Spain ought to develop in a *certain* direction, in order to be fully coherent with what was supposed to be its core value (religious identity). Secondly, the practical realisation of this idea, given that Catholic Spain was both a political and a religious project, required the collaboration of the Church, the monarchy... and the liberal State. From this we have the idea that Balmes laid the foundations for modern National-Catholicism,

THE POLITICS OF SPANISH CATHOLICISM 131

that is, the union of nation, Catholicism and State that was first essayed in the dictatorship of Primo de Rivera (1923–1930) and came to fruition under the regime of General Francisco Franco (1939–1977) (De la Cueva 2018: 286). The underlying assumption is that Balmes' traditionalist and organic view paved the way for the twentieth-century alliance between a corporative State and the Church (Colom 2011: 191). Yet it must be stressed that Balmes did not regard the nation and the State as being identical entities; more significantly, his critique of the liberal State centred upon a key contention: that it did not stood for the interests and concerns of the whole Spanish nation. The fact remains that in Spain in the 1840s, Balmes' voice was a lone one. His ideas did not lead to a powerful political movement, especially not to one that could challenge the ideological hegemony of the *moderados* for whom religion was also a key political issue. His two main political projects (the marriage of Isabel II to Montemolín, and the restoration of the Church's property) proved to be either too unrealistic or too divisive and came to nothing – at least during his brief life. Yet these were political aims, and rather specific. On the other hand, there were Balmes' intellectual constructs that posited a pre-eminent role of the Church in Spain, as well as assuming an innate religiosity of the Spanish people, that endured and had later impact. These constructs were later *activated*, and their potential unlocked by successive re-appropriations (and also simplifications) of his work. Throughout this section, in order to understand the persistence of these intellectual constructs, I will analyse how and in which context Balmes created them.

It is also important to emphasise that Balmes developed these ideas in a period when the Spanish Church was in a weak and vulnerable position. The breach between Church and State would only be partially remedied by the Concordat of 1851, brought about by exceptional circumstances – and this of course occurred after the death of Balmes in 1848. Yet the fact that Balmes wrote in what were difficult times for the Church, makes it even more interesting to consider what his main contribution to Spanish thought was: the idea of Spain as Catholic nation, one in which national identity was seen hand-in-hand with Catholicism. As a priest and believer, Balmes was totally convinced of the Church's superiority – at least in spiritual terms, if not material ones. Yet he did not write from a position of arrogant confidence. Rather he sought to enter into dialogue (orthodoxy permitting) with the new liberal mentality, while giving renewed strength to traditional Catholicism. Most significant was the way in which Balmes expressed the *raison d'être* of religion in this new context and how it sprang from an attitude of relative open-mindedness that was far from being shared by the conservative majority of the Spanish clergy. In this sense, Balmes was more a complication than an exception to the rule that, throughout the nineteenth century, the Spanish Church as a whole was characterised by a 'homogeneous ideology which left no room for dissent' and by its simplistic attitude towards social questions, one in which loss of religious belief was seen as the cause of all problems (Shubert 1990: 155–6).

In *Cartas a un escéptico en materia de religión* [*Letters to a Sceptic in Religious Matters*] (1846), Balmes orchestrated a dialogue between Catholicism and modern philosophy. In these letters, Balmes dwelt upon the concerns of his addressee, an unnamed young man who felt hampered by Catholicism, which he perceived as being an obstacle to both his freedom to think and to act (Huerta de Soto 2021: 551). Mirroring his own intellectual journey, Balmes devoted several pages to describe a series of personal encounters with contemporary philosophers. He was aware that, among Spain's cultured elite, the attention once enjoyed by 'sensualist' authors such as Antoine Destutt de Tracy, Étienne de Condillac and John Locke was rapidly shifting to 'spiritualist' ones, that is, to Immanuel Kant, Johann Gottlieb Fichte, Friedrich Wilhelm Schelling, Georg Wilhelm Hegel and Victor Cousin (Balmes 1880: 134). In contrast to the prevailing opinion, Balmes believed that the German philosophers now in vogue were 'unworthy heirs' to his beloved Gottfried Wilhelm Leibniz. In his view, Leibniz was truly worthy of praise for his philosophical and scientific works, as well as for having shown – from a Protestant perspective – an appreciation of Catholicism (Balmes 1880: 51).

What Balmes found disquieting in authors such as Kant and Schelling was what he believed was their underlying assumption: that there was no reality beyond our thoughts, no religion beyond human reason. If taken to its ultimate consequence, as Balmes argued, this assumption might lead one to negate God's character as a superior entity, distinct from his creation, and to whom mankind was accountable (Balmes 1880: 134). What Balmes found most irritating, however, was the 'jargon' employed by Hegel, who seemingly demanded from his readers that they should not only forego their common thoughts, but their common sense too (Balmes 1880: 139–140). It might be argued however that, in *Letters to a Sceptic*, Balmes was less moved by a desire to disqualify his ideological adversaries, than to demonstrate that Catholicism could be intellectually progressive too, and thus coexist with modern philosophical enquiries. Interestingly, Balmes' quotations in this work revealed him, however inadvertently, as a reader of the *Revue de deux mondes*, a French periodical popular among Spanish liberals (Balmes 1880: 140). Full of confidence in the future, Balmes concluded that religion would not be replaced by philosophy, but rather continue to provide society with a solid moral foundation (Balmes 1880: 177–178, 290).

It was the pursuit of a similar goal, positing Catholicism as essentially commonsensical, that had prompted Balmes to write *El criterio [On Discernment]* in the course of 1843. This treatise on the art of thinking, his most famous work in our time, was written in a didactic prose and in a hybrid manner, in which theoretical considerations went hand-in-hand with fictional parables. In it Balmes put forward an idea of religion as essentially reasonable, that is, as an aid to human reason. Starting from the assumption that human beings were essentially good, Balmes spoke of the need to train and to educate the powers of reason, as well as to temper the passions with the help of religion, which was seen as the source of morality (Balmes 1845 g: 186, 190). Significantly, Balmes also hoped to raise awareness of how our behaviour was moulded by context, as well as by irrational elements. *El criterio* thus recounted, among other things, the anecdote of Don Marcelino whose political convictions changed according to his moods and egotistical concerns, so that one day he would defend absolutism and another support representative government (Balmes 1845 g: 122–124). Characteristically, Balmes had a wide audience in mind, so that *El Criterio* sought to address the concerns of the everyday man, offering insights on how to run a business or how to read a newspaper critically (Balmes 1845 g: 47–49, 154–155).

Balmes' position was unique in the degree to which, as Fradera puts it, he was able to cross with ease the boundaries that divided the Catholic intelligentsia from upper middle-class intellectuals (2003: 109). He therefore describes *El criterio* as 'the most bourgeois' of the religious works written in Catalonia during the nineteenth century (Fradera 1996: 309). After all, it was in Catalonia that the political and economic transformation of Spain was most deeply experienced; in the specific case of the middle classes, the social changes brought about by trade and industrialization were reflected in new forms of interaction between Catholicism and the new liberal culture. In the 1840s, Balmes symbolised the curiosity and awareness towards these new developments, not only in terms of the impact of philosophy and science upon religion, but also of the impact within the clerical establishment.

When writing on the role of the Catholic Church in Spain, Balmes referred to the Church as being both a religious institution and a tool for social reform. In his view, the Church was, together with the monarchy, the greatest of all Spanish 'social institutions'. As such, they supported the country's lifestyle and traditions, so that neither 'could be overturned or altered without the social state itself being affected by the change' (Balmes 1842b, *OC* V: 495). In like manner, social institutions were the foundation stone upon which 'political and administrative institutions' rested. Here Balmes implied that both governments and constitutional texts had to acknowledge the importance of Catholicism and thus were bound to protect the Church. In addition, Balmes sounded a note of warning, suggesting that a consistent practice of Catholicism would keep Spain free from deep social turmoil. Throughout the writings of Balmes, we find a recurring idea: that Catholicism could be related to a specific set of political virtues (order, obedience and authority), all conducive to social harmony and political stability. These political virtues, halfway between social control and social cohesion, were particularly useful in times of change. Balmes thus referred as follows to the ideal relationship between Catholicism and representative government:

If the popular element was to take part in the government, it was necessary that, given its growing influence, it should be tempered by some principle that would be above political forms and vicissitudes; that is to say, it was then that the gentle and strong restraint of religion was most needed, [so that] it would not abuse its power and precipitate itself, with the usual impetus, into excesses and outrages (Balmes, n.d., OC VIII: 487).

This argument, a reflection on politics made within a religious framework, led Balmes to the assertion that great institutions *and* great ideas – the Church & Catholicism, in this case – were the necessary fabric of good government and historical development:

It has already been observed that a government cannot govern alone: and is government able to stand alone if not supported by robust institutions which, linked with great and vigorous ideas that extend throughout the nation and form a broad, well-established, firm base on which the basis of government can be securely established? And do we find this in Spain? (Balmes 1840a, OC V: 744–5).

Nowhere was this more true than in Spain, Balmes would argue, where Catholicism had been the backbone of the country's history and the key cultural ingredient of its identity. In this, he illustrated one of the most persistent political myths of nineteenth-century Spain, the conviction that the *sine qua non* condition of social stability was – above all – religious unity (Álvarez Junco 2007: 328). This conviction allowed Balmes to insist upon the *exceptional* – rather than the anomalous – situation of Spain within Europe:

The Catholic religion is the most fertile element of regeneration found in the heart of the Spanish nation. [...] We do not simply rely on general considerations about the salutary influence of Catholicism on the civilisation of peoples, but we also take particular circumstances into account the, characteristic of Spain, and that place her in a position that cannot be compared to that of other European nations in any way (Balmes 1842c, OC VI: 185).

In the context of Europe, Balmes argued, this close relationship between Catholicism and the State did not work to Spain's detriment nor was its religious unity a disadvantage for its future development as a nation. This distinguished him from forward-looking Spaniards for whom Europe had been an 'abiding fixation', one that carried the promise of a new way of life that would enable them to overcome their backwardness, and for whom the Church had had a negative impact on the country's intellectual life (Kamen 2008a: 142, 153). Yet Balmes conceived of the idea of Spain as a Catholic nation in strictly positive terms, especially within a European context. So instead of speaking of Spain's exclusive commitment to Catholicism in terms of an *aberration* within Europe, Balmes referred to it as an *advantage* that distinguished Spain from other European countries:

There is among us an element of well-being which, if it is exploited as it should be, could produce immense advantages for us: I am speaking of religious unity. [...] Has enough thought been given to the fact that such is the state of modern societies and so many are the dissolving forces, that maybe even the first politicians of Europe envy us this happiness, this element of preservation? (Balmes 1840b, OC VI: 79).

The recipe for Spain's continued success, in terms of a stable national identity, seemed to be clear: any religion other than Catholicism should not be tolerated. Balmes affirmed that the Catholic principle in Spain was 'strong, exclusive, energetic, incapable of yielding ground to any of his opponents' and therefore should be 'observed and respected to the fullest extent of the word' (Balmes 1840b, OC VI: 72–3). This ideal of religious unity had an inescapable political counterpart, as it called not only for the collaboration between Church and State in order to maintain the exclusive position of Catholicism within Spain and to ensure that other religions (i.e. Protestantism) could not be practised. Yet Balmes approved of religious tolerance in countries where it satisfied a social necessity, as it did in England or the United States where there was already significant religious pluralism (Steinel 1971: 73–4). When it came to Spain, however, Balmes was strongly intolerant of faiths other than Catholicism, as for him it was the cement that bound Spain into a unified nation. Rather than believing that a basic agreement in matters of faith could actually help overcome the numerous disagreements over politics, Balmes highlighted the role of Catholicism as an element of social cohesion (Balmes 1840b, *OC* VI: 87).

For Balmes the role of Catholicism in Spain was underpinned by what he saw as the staunch religious nature of the Spanish people whose faith had remained unaltered by the country's recent political vicissitudes. The confidence which Balmes felt in this conviction led him to affirm: 'a lack of belief has no real or scientific existence for us' (Balmes 1844b, *OC* VII: 443) curiously aiming to give his argument an air of respectability drawn from the world of science. Balmes believed that this (religious) unity could be turned into a political consensus, and suggested that Spain's political elite had been neglecting or wasting this valuable opportunity. Here it is difficult to say if Balmes was being practical in his emphasis upon the political capital afforded by religion, or unrealistic by supposing a conflict-free relationship between Church and State. Yet he claimed the right to speak on behalf of the majority of Spaniards, whom he described as follows:

The Spanish people, that is to say, that part which is guided only by the inspirations it receives from current events, can be divided into two great groups, namely that of those who live in the capitals which saw the importation, at one blow, not of civilisation but rather of foreign culture. [...] The other, much larger group, is scattered in the countryside and villages, and inhabits second-order towns that, due to their situation and other circumstances, are not much subject to the influence of the capitals, and their number might even include the people who live in the main towns of Spain, meaning those who have not been involved in the spirit of innovation and who, with more or less modifications, keep to the old customs and habits (Balmes 1842c, *OC* VI: 188–9).

The most problematic aspect of this argument is the sharp divide that Balmes traced between the 'innovative spirit' and 'foreign culture', on the one hand; and the 'national traditions' and 'ancient practices and customs', on the other. This is the one aspect of Balmes' thought that might seem to bring him close to late eighteenth-century reactionaries, whose interpretation of Spanish history centred on the conflict between the Spanish tradition and foreign ideas, which were seen as being revolutionary, heterodox and anti-Spanish (Herrero 1971: 15–6; Álvarez Junco 1997: 336). But Balmes was writing from a different frame of mind, one which went beyond the eighteenth-century reactionaries' usual response to political change and cultural modernity, and whose basic response to the intellectual feat of the Enlightenment was that of the customary Inquisition (Herrero 1971: 180).

Although different in tone and purpose from that of eighteenth-century reactionaries, the antagonism sketched out by Balmes between (assuring) Spanish traditions and (threatening) foreign ideas remains problematic. This is because it was a binary framework, one in which the categories of friend and enemy were too easily set in opposition. Nonetheless, it must be stressed that neither 'Spanish traditions' nor the 'foreign ideas' were unquestionable, self-evident categories – and as shown in previous chapters, the matter how to put the country's Catholic identity into practice was (and would remain) a controversial issue. The very definition of Spanishness, of what constituted the nation's core values and when had these reached their zenith, depended upon a political agenda. When it came to the writing of national history during the nineteenth century, liberals and conservatives would be roughly divided according to their different interpretation of what had been Spain's *golden age*, that is, when, as they saw it, national qualities and traditions had not yet been affected by pernicious foreign influences. In general, historical accounts tended to follow a narrative scheme of paradise, fall and redemption (García Cárcel 2013: 402). By contrast, liberal-minded historians tended to see the Middle Ages, with its regional laws and ancient liberties, as a sort of golden age that came to an end with the ascent into power of the Hapsburg monarchs, thus suggesting that Spain's future happiness lay in the affirmation of national sovereignty and individual rights. For conservative-minded historians, the end of paradise was precipitated by advent of the Bourbons, with their love of foreign enlightened ideas, so that future happiness lay in a return to local monarchic and Catholic traditions (Álvarez Junco 2007: 431).

The ideal of national unity (achieved through religious orthodoxy) upheld by Balmes had in common with contemporary historiography the disjunction between 'national history' and 'national project', one that resulted in an inability to look forward (Jover 1991: 165–6). The writings of Spain's greatest historians during the reign of Isabel II (1833–1868) were characterised by an absence of utopian views, and by a lack of imagination when it came to envisaging the future (García Cárcel 2013: 647). Their nationalism was retrospective, given that it was formulated to defend the continuation of the *status quo* and to uphold an interpretation of the past. Balmes' treatment of the religious faith of the Spanish people was eloquent about a similar inability to imagine the future. He affirmed that the people had proven impervious to 'impious' readings because 'that part of the Spanish people we have in mind *does not read*, and therefore cannot be misled by books' (Balmes 1842c,

OC VI: 189). What would happen if, as was foreseen, Spanish society became increasingly urban, literate and educated?

We should, however, avoid jumping to conclusions, and imagine that Balmes believed that illiteracy was essential for being a good Catholic. In fact, one of the most interesting passages in *Cartas a un escéptico en materias de religión [Letters to a Sceptic in Religious Matters]*, is where he gave an account of the groundwork of his faith. Recalling his youth, Balmes described how his submission to both faith and the authority of the Church had been a rational process, rather than the result of ignorance or intellectual conformity. If he had at one time argued 'down with scientific authority', it was because he had come to the conviction that science did not provide utter certainty and could not give a comprehensive answer to all problems (Balmes 1880: 6–8). Similarly, he refused to accept the idea that an exceptionally intelligent man was essentially different from the mass of the people. In fact, he claimed, the genius of such men lay in their ability to collect ideas that, in the same way as 'ripe fruit', had come into being from within the masses (Balmes 1880: 61–63). It is important not to lose sight of the crucial fact that Balmes was trying to set up a dialogue between Catholicism and the new liberal culture and constantly insisted upon the need to improve education in Spain, both for the general population, and for the clergy who would act as their pastors. This remains valid even if we consider further developments in Spanish traditionalism which became increasingly open to the modernisation of the country, namely to industrial developments within a capitalistic framework. At the same time, however, it would consistently reject every critique to its ideal of religious and cultural unity (Colom 2006: 48; Louzao 2013: 76).

From the vantage point of hindsight, it is possible to question the very idea of a Catholic Spain by analysing not the quantity but the *quality* of religious faith. As Henry Kamen put it, the question to resolve was not 'whether Spain was Catholic, but whether it was Christian' (2008: 79). In fact, between the sixteenth and nineteenth centuries, religion in Spain comprised a series of social practices rather than a system of faith, so that actions were more important than beliefs (Vilar 1994: 28; Kamen 2008: 76–7). Elements such as the ignorance of both clergy and laity, the superficial knowledge that the people had of Christianity, anomalies in belief and practice, lack of exceptional devotion to the faith, etc. led Kamen to conclude that Spain as a Catholic nation had been nothing but a 'myth'. It was created in a spirit of cultural self-defence during the mid-nineteenth century, when the 'advancing forces' of materialism and unbelief were perceived as threats for the moral convictions of the Spaniards, in the context of the overall social and economic changes brought by liberalism (Kamen 2008b: 81–2). Judging from the fragmentary evidence available, in mid-nineteenth century Spain a decline in religious practice – or 'dechristianization' – was already in progress in urban centres, large or small, affected by a developing economy, while contrasts were already appearing between districts affected by economic change and peasant areas that continued to observe traditional practices (Callahan 1984b: 165; Vilar 1994: 27–28). In the times of Balmes and Donoso, the changes in the practice of religion, however minimal or incipient, were enough to add a sense of urgency to their writings on the relationship between Spain and Catholicism.

Whatever the doubts that might be cast on the quality of faith of the Spanish people, there was nonetheless an energetic and enthusiastic promotion of the 'symbolic representation' of Spain's religious identity (Shubert 1990: 205). The point here is that there was an overwhelming presence of religion (and the Church) in public debate not only in nineteenth-century Spain, but also in contemporary Catholic societies in Western Europe. Thus not only in Spain, but also in France and Italy, new and modern strategies employed in the promotion of Catholicism prompted a situation in which the tensions between Church and State became an 'all-encompassing ideological and political struggle' (Clark 2003: 11, 46). The consequences of the prominence of religion, even its omnipresence, in the nineteenth-century European public sphere have been analysed by Turner who, writing on Victorian England, argues that 'expansive, intensified religion' is more likely to lead to inner crises and personal conflict. In this context, the individual's conflict is prompted less by 'dissolvent, sceptical literature than from a Christian faith that had become *overbearingly intense* on the personal and vocational levels and shamelessly embittered on the political, educational, and social scenes' (1990: 9).

IV. The impact of conversion on Donoso's thought

A perfect illustration of the overbearingly intense character of faith in the nineteenth-century Spain would be the conversion of Donoso in 1847 to a more committed and rigorous Catholic practice. His conversion, and the way in which he expressed his renewed commitment to religious belief, was symptomatic of a trend towards both orthodoxy and intransigence within Spanish Catholicism. It can be argued that, once it reached a *modus vivendi* with liberalism, the Spanish Church could concentrate its efforts at restoring its links with the Papacy, thus gaining a more acute sense of its role beyond Spain. The account of Donoso's conversion, along with the analysis of several developments within European Catholicism as a whole, will throw light on why the conciliatory and relatively flexible Catholic views of someone like Balmes were soon to become a thing of the past.

Donoso had always been a Catholic. But in 1847 he realised that he had practised Catholicism in a perfunctory and half-hearted way: 'my faith was sterile, because it neither governed my thoughts, nor inspired my speeches, nor guided my actions' (Donoso 1849c, *OC* II: 342). His conversion to a more deeply-felt Catholicism was mostly inspired by the death of his pious brother Pedro in June of that same year. This religious experience would have a major impact on the political ideas of the *converted* Donoso, as they became subject to a new and urgent imperative: to bridge the gap between faith and political practice. Of particular importance after his religious conversion in 1847, was that trends that were already present in his thought became more significant. Most obvious was his distrust of human reason, coupled with an increased appreciation of faith and a desire to fit historical events into a providential framework; less obvious was his intention of turning religion into a political instrument, as the only way in which to avoid revolutionary turmoil. Foreshadowing later developments in his thought, Donoso wrote of the dangers posed not only by the supposed shortcomings of liberalism, but also by the rise of socialism.

Unwilling to draw a line between religion and politics, Donoso gradually engaged in a catastrophist stance following the traditional line of divine punishment. In other words, he turned his profession of faith into a political creed, one which believed that the moral corruption of society, living in conflict with Christian principles, was conducive to political disaster. Here the logic was the same as the one by which a morally corrupt individual would be seen as constructing his own damnation. A key issue, present in all of his post-1847 writings is that Donoso sought – albeit not always with clarity – to give a sure guide on how to avert political disaster. He stressed the need to restore the influence of Catholicism in public life, and in this leaned towards a gradual and *institutional* solution. But also, in relation to cases deemed urgent enough to require immediate action, he favoured an expedient and *extra-legal* solution. The best example of the latter was his 'Discurso sobre la dictadura [Speech on dictatorship]' (January 1849) in which Donoso justified dictatorship to the Spanish Cortes as a legitimate means to put a radical end to both political revolution and moral anarchy. This speech, written in the aftermath of the European Revolutions of 1848, made Donoso suddenly famous in Europe (Graham 1974: 116). This topic will be further discussed in the next chapter. At this point, however, one should note that there is a constant in Donoso's thought: he privileged the role of the State, broadly understood as political authorities, in bridging the gap between religious ideals and political realities. This had been true in the case of the promotion of Spain's religious identity by the *moderado* State; now, in the context of post-revolutionary Europe, Donoso would constantly invoke the figure of a dictator or, if on the wings of a less passionate rhetorical burst, that of a Christian prince.

The idea that history could be studied in terms of the faithfulness of the people towards God gave rise to a series of unpublished and unfinished *Estudios sobre la historia [Historical Studies]* (1847–1848), which had been originally prepared as lectures on European history for Isabel II. This text illustrates a slight change in Donoso's style of writing, especially when touching religious or theological issues, namely that he conveys a strong hint of self-persuasion mixed with a desire to conform to religious orthodoxy. In the introductory notes to the *Estudios*, Donoso affirmed that history was 'the revelation of those immutable and inflexible laws by which God governs the moral world that He created' (1847–8, OC II: 227). The intention of placing himself within a providential narrative is clear from the beginning, in that he took as his models the Bible, Augustine's *De civitate Dei* (426) and Bossuet's *Discourse sur l'histoire universelle (1681)*. His own table of contents, beginning with the 'History of early times', included the Creation, Original Sin, the story of Cain and Abel, and the Flood. It also included an ambitious overview of universal history, in which the Church appeared as the principal protagonist. It dealt with the history of the peoples of Israel, Greece, Rome and the Middle Ages, and ended with a section significantly titled 'Historia de la descomposición y fraccionamiento de la República cristiana' [History of the fall and partition of the Christian republic] spanning from the Reformation to the French Revolution. However, Donoso only wrote part of it, a few chapters dwelling on the primitive times of mankind, from a biblical point of view.

In these unfinished sketches, Donoso emphasised an interpretation of the Christian message as constituting a safeguard of social order given that it strongly disapproved of both 'the insurrections of peoples against the authority of princes, and those of princes against the liberty of men' (Donoso 1847–8, OC II: 229). He had already described Christianity as being a 'complete civilisation', compared to the 'imperfect culture' of Antiquity (Donoso

1838b, *OC* II: 654–5). In later writings, he would insist upon the superiority of Christianity, as reflected in its views on social organization. A truly Christian government, Donoso affirmed, would establish a relationship of reciprocity between rulers and subjects that was grounded upon the (Christian) idea of human dignity and equality of all men. This was an argument that traditionalist and conservative-minded writers such as Donoso would make constantly. In so doing, they were responding to the desire either to maintain the *status quo* or even to guide social change, and thus tried to dismantle the revolutionary language of freedom and equality, arguing that these had always been Christian postulates and not the achievements of the French Revolution.

More significantly, in these historical sketches, Donoso established for the first time a link between secular liberalism and socialism and conceived of them both as absolutely in opposition to Christianity (Graham 1974: 132). This argument stemmed from his rejection of the idea of an indefinite, ever-ascending progress in human history, as was famously heralded by Condorcet's *Sketch for a Historical Picture of the Progress of the Human Mind* (1793). Donoso's own idea of progress which consisted in the 'slow and progressive materialisation of truth in the world' (1847–8, *OC* II: 242), deliberately excluded revolutionary change. According to Donoso, there be no utopian thought outside the Christian framework: even perfection was something that belonged to God alone. According to Donoso, the only solution to the current problematic situation of Europe, that is, to its overall social and political restlessness, was a moral and spiritual awakening. Other means, such as the political reforms espoused by the 'liberal school' or the social and economic change invoked by the 'socialist school', along with social and economic reform, along with visions of heaven on earth, were deemed to be not only insufficient but dangerous. We can see here how Donoso, using religious imagery, expressed his first crucial criticism of both liberals, especially the radical-progressive variety, and socialists, in particular those who spoke of revolution:

According to this law, that of so-called perfectibility and progress, men began by living a rough and savage life; then they pursued a hard-working life of hunting; then a nomadic and pastoral life; then a settled and quiet life, until they reached the state and position in which we see them today, one which will be polished and improved until the beautiful ideal of absolute perfection is realised on this lowly earth. / This is the origin of all those voracious and senseless aspirations of turbulent men, as well as of all those dazzling utopias which deafen the world like hollow and resounding cymbals. The liberal school, composed of sluggish workers, has taken for itself the task of polishing governments. The socialist schools, composed of fearless and indefatigable workers, knowing that the kingdom of God is suffering, have resolved to break into it, to take it by storm. When that great day rises, everything will be transfigured on earth, and in heaven, and in hell... (Donoso 1847–8; *OC* II: 270).

The irony is that Donoso's thought was not free from utopian elements, that is, free of a vision of the City of God on earth, and this again, stemmed from the unwillingness of Donoso to draw a line between religion and politics. All these ideas would reach their fullest expression in the *Ensayo sobre el catolicismo, el liberalismo y el socialismo [Essay on Catholicism, Liberalism and Socialism]* (1851), still the best known of Donoso's writings and the cornerstone of his reputation as a European thinker. The intellectual path that led to its writing is evident in his rejection in the *Estudios* of the secularization of society which, as he argued, would necessarily lead to it breaking its links with the institutional Church (1847–8, *OC* II: 274). The problematic parallel drawn between society and individuals is shown in this passage, where they are treated as if they had identical religious obligations:

Except through submission to the Church there is no salvation for human societies, just except through submission to God there is no salvation for man. And just as God and the Church are one and the same thing, so society and man are one and the same thing. [...] From this arises a most notable difference between society and man; [...] the individual, made for eternity, usually receives here below neither the punishment nor the reward that his actions deserve; society, however, made for the present time, necessarily receives therein the reward it deserved for being saintly, or the punishment it called down upon itself for having been sinful (Donoso 1847–8; *OC* II: 275).

This passage is a clear illustration of the discourse of divine punishment which increasingly characterised Donoso's writings after 1847. One of its most problematic aspects is the idea that societies inescapably receive the punishment for their sins, problematic because it effectually diminishes the intellectual content of Donoso's statements about the desirability of religious revival, not least because it bypasses individual agency. The final outcome of his writing here is that he seems to make threats which have an emotional charge, rather than persuade with rational arguments. This aspect of Donoso's writing shows some lack of novelty on his part of Donoso in that he seems simply to be carrying forward the apocalyptic predictions of eighteenth-century reactionaries. Nonetheless, he did give a modern flavour to topics such as the 'unleashing of the passions' which was thought to be inseparable from impious and revolutionary ideas (Herrero 1971: 35–7,

109, 167; Acle Aguirre 2012: 162–163). Similarly, he would blend ancient and modern narratives, as in the speech on the Bible that he delivered in 1848 to mark his entrance into the Real Academia Española. On that occasion, he compared Jews and Spaniards as history's greatest chosen peoples, thus predestined to be the representatives of true religion in their respective ages (Donoso 1845a, *OC* II: 98).

In Donoso's conversion, the man of politics and the religious individual had come together. In other words, his conversion became a public profession of faith. Successive appointments and honours would implicitly put him into the quandary of how to reconcile his new religious commitment with the political and literary prestige that he had won in previous decades. This involved redefining his relationship to the *moderado* party, as well as to long-time friends. Donoso parted ways with Mendizábal and Alcalá Galiano in the early and late 1830s respectively, and with Sartorius and Ríos Rosas in the mid-1840s and even with Narváez in the late 1840s (Garrido Muro 2015: 56). After his conversion, Donoso took an increasingly stringent view of morality and worldly pleasures, so that he felt out of favour within the so-called *camarilla*, the powerful clique headed by Muñoz and María Cristina (Burdiel 2010: 220). The fact that Donoso later opted for a diplomatic career has been interpreted as a result of his ideological estrangement from the *moderado* elite, and hence expressed a desire to put a physical distance between him and Spain. However, as I will argue, Donoso did not lose his ability to influence Spanish political debates. More significantly, he became influential beyond Spain and, in the process, gained a European reputation.

A key example of Donoso's religious fervour when shown in political matters is his 'Discurso sobre la situación de España' [Speech on the situation of Spain], delivered in the Spanish Cortes on 30 December 1850. Donoso spoke with renewed confidence now. In the aftermath of the European revolutions of 1848, his ideas had acquired an international reach and thus turned him into a symbol of the new spirit of defense against revolutionary turmoil. His speech on Spain became part of an unintended trilogy: the speech of December 1850 would be preceded by a 'Speech on dictatorship' (January 1849) and a 'Speech on the general situation of Europe' (January 1850), all of which will be discussed in the next chapter. After spending a year as ambassador in Berlin (1849), Donoso was able to distance himself from the *moderados*, at least symbolically. As mentioned before, his relative aloofness regarding Spanish affairs, as well as his increasing involvement with European ones, would char-

THE POLITICS OF SPANISH CATHOLICISM   145

acterise the last stage of his public life, and he served as Spanish ambassador in Paris from 1851 to his death in 1853 (Kennedy 1952: 523).

Donoso's speech on Spain (1850) was not, as has often been argued, a symbol of his rupture with the *moderados* in general. In reality, it was a fierce indictment against the current government, then headed by General Narváez – who allegedly perceived Donoso's speech to be like a 'shot in the back' (Graham 1974: 223, 229). He directed his critique against the very foundations of the regime, repeatedly emphasising what he believed to be its main flaw: *corruption*. The year 1850 had been one of economic recovery for Spain, but also of irresponsible expenditure and increased administrative corruption. In addition to this, there had been notorious irregularities in the elections that year (Comellas 1970: 279–80; Graham 1974: 222–3). The corruption of the moment, according to Donoso, was evident in an artificial kind of social mobility, one which represented the triumph of individual ambition over the common good, and in which the desire to rise was more important than actual achievements: 'no one is happy in his place; all aspire to rise, and to rise, not in order to rise, but in order to enjoy' (Donoso 1850d, OC II: 483). It is important to note that the key towards the full understanding of this speech is to be found in its draft. Therefore, what Donoso meant by corruption is better understood in passages that did not make it from the draft to the definitive version that was read aloud. Here is an example:

Corruption cannot be cured by industries or by reforms; it can be cured by the restoration of the great Catholic institutions, which the revolution has thrown to the ground, and which it is up to you to raise up. The most corrupt and corrupting character of this society is the middle class, which we represent, gentlemen.... (Donoso 1850d, OC II: 483).

It can be argued that, thanks to his long-time collaboration with Muñoz and the Queen Mother, Donoso was perfectly qualified to judge the extent of corruption existing within the Spanish political and economic establishment. Yet he went far beyond condemning the materialism and capitalist greed present in the country's elite. Insofar as it singled out the middle classes, broadly regarded as the embodiment of the new liberal political culture, Donoso's speech was dubbed by Graham as an 'antiliberal blast' (1974: 223). This was further reflected in his condemnation of newspapers, an emblem of the liberal freedom of both expression and press. There is a passage in the speech in which Donoso used religious language to mock the Spanish press and practice of journalism: 'each one reads the newspaper of his opinions; that is to say, each Spaniard is busy talking to himself'; because, after all, 'a newspaper is the voice of a party that is always telling itself: Holy, holy, holy' (Donoso 1850d, *OC* II: 487).

What Donoso objected to was not the modernization of the country, as reflected in the growing network of rail-roads or incipient industrialization, but the fact that the country had seemingly lost its moral compass. Hence, in December 1850, he raised what he believed to be the fundamental question to his fellow deputies in the Cortes: 'whether society is safer and stronger when it rests upon the material order or upon the moral order, upon virtue or upon industry' (Donoso 1850d, *OC* II: 491). The reply given by Donoso to this question, in which he elaborated on the parallel drawn between the salvation of individuals and that of society, emphasised the need to keep a balance between soul and body, between material progress and moral improvement (Donoso 1850d, *OC* II: 481). Otherwise, nothing but a sad destiny awaited Spain:

...I still affirm and assure that all its power will come spectacularly to an end if this nation remains corrupt in its feelings and perverted in its ideas; I still say that this society, so opulent, so splendid, so great, will be given over to extermination, for there has never been a lack of exterminating angels for corrupt peoples (Donoso 1850d, OC II: 490).

In the case of Donoso, the use of religious imagery when describing political upheavals may be interpreted as a kind of rhetorical simplification used in order to make more vivid and maybe more readily graspable the threat represented by modern developments. Socialism is a good case in point. Addressing the Spanish Cortes in 1850, Donoso dramatically recalled how the revolution in 1848 had prompted the fall of Louis Philippe of Orléans, the 'Citizen King' of France. The true explanation of Louis Philippe's downfall was, according to Donoso, that material prosperity during his reign had led to France's moral corruption – socialist ideas were seen as part of this corruption – and to ultimate disaster. In this context he referred to the 24th of February, the day on which Louis Philippe was forced to abdicate, as 'the day of the great deliverance, the day of the great anathemas'; moreover, when trying to look for reasons behind the upheaval, Donoso spoke of the 'socialist phalanxes' and the 'republican deluge' (Donoso 1850d, *OC* II: 491).

Fuelling his speech with religious imagery, Donoso now led his audience to imagine what would happen if socialism also made its appearance in Spain. The situation was ripe for it to happen, he warned. Almost every condition was already present in Spain – 'corruption, error, industrial fever' –, something which was aggravated by a local condition, the tendency to exaggerate things, due to the fact that 'our blood, which, as well as being Spanish, is also African' (Donoso 1850d, OC II: 491). But Donoso also viewed socialism as a reflection of a more complex social problem, the distribution of wealth within society. The solution given by Donoso to this problem, though analysed at length, was in the end deceptively simple: it was the need to give alms:

Socialism owes its existence to a problem, which in human terms is insoluble. What is at stake is how to ensure the most equitable distribution of wealth within society. This is a problem which no system of political economy has ever solved. The system of the political economists of ancient times led to monopoly by means of restrictions. The system of liberal political economists will arrive at the same monopoly through freedom, through free competition, which fatally and inevitably produces the same monopoly. Finally, the communist system leads to the same monopoly by means of universal confiscation, depositing all public wealth in the hands of the state. This problem, however, has been solved by Catholicism. Catholicism has found its solution in charity. In vain do the philosophers weary themselves; in vain do the socialists toil; without alms, without charity, there is not, and cannot be an equitable distribution of wealth. Only God was worthy to solve this problem, which is the problem of Humanity and of History (Donoso 1850d, OC II: 492).

With a twist in rhetoric and argumentation, Donoso thus emphasised an idea that had been a constant in his thought: that the Church needed to be the foundation of both governance and social consensus in Spain. His view of the Spanish Church was close to an idealized one when he spoke of its social function, 'to serve as a mediator between the poor and the rich', and its historical role: 'Spain has been a nation made by the Church, formed by the Church for the poor; the poor in Spain have been kings' (Donoso 1850d, OC II: 493). This idealised and somewhat vague vision allowed Donoso to bypass the Spanish Church's own claims (i.e. independence from government inference, the line followed by Balmes) and also the question of its institutional reform. Donoso might have nostalgically raised the question of 'which beggar did not have a piece of bread when a convent was open?' but the fact remains that liberal policy, including the ecclesiastical policy of the *moderados*, had consistently reduced the Church to the performance of pastoral functions (Callahan 1984a: 178–9). In other words, the liberal State had taken over the Church's traditional charitable activities, especially as regards poor relief. What we see here is how the newly converted Donoso was now questioning the way that clerical charity was being transformed into a system of public assistance. These issues were made particularly urgent by Donoso's pessimistic insistence upon future class war and revolt by socialistic masses.

It would be more precise to say, however, that what Donoso feared most was the secularization of Spanish society – something that, following the logic of his own argument, would open the door to revolution. He thus urged the government to realise the manifold benefits that would result from a close partnership with the Church. As shown in the sweeping conclusion of his speech in December 1850, he spoke from a position of assumed moral authority: 'I do not simply represent the nation; [...] I represent tradition' (Donoso 1850d, *OC* II: 497). In a way, Donoso thus situated himself on a higher plane of discussion than did Balmes in *El Pensamiento de la Nación [The Thought of the Nation]*. This is a feature that would develop increasingly, as Donoso started thinking about Catholicism more in European terms than in purely Spanish ones, to the extent that his ideas on religion in Spain became a mere extrapolation of his general argument on Europe.

Donoso's speech in December 1850 was powerful and successful enough to bring down the government headed by Narváez, then succeeded by Juan Bravo Murillo, Treasury Minister and a conservative-leaning *moderado* – as well as long-time friend of Donoso. In early 1851, Bravo Murillo formed a cabinet that complied with the wishes of the party's unofficial leadership, that is, of both Muñoz and María Cristina (Burdiel 2010: 232–233). The link between Bravo Murillo and Donoso is worth stressing, insofar as both had a similar perception of where liberalism had seemingly gone wrong. In contrast to the idea that Donoso became an isolated eccentric (Garrido Muro 2015: 56), Burdiel demonstrates how decisive his influence was in the project of constitutional reform submitted by Bravo Murillo to the Cortes in 1851 (2011: 237). It was guided by a twofold aim, that of putting an end both to corruption and to the chronic instability that was seen as inseparable from parliamentary politics. Hence we have the markedly 'authoritarian' character of Bravo Murillo's projected reform, insofar as it sought to strengthen the role of civil administration, as well as to strengthen the power of the Crown to the detriment of the Cortes (Burdiel 2010: 238). Notwithstanding the enthusiastic support of the *vilumistas*, the reform was strongly rejected by the core of the *moderados*, who even entered into an alliance of convenience with progressive and radical liberals to hinder its approval.

The government of Bravo Murillo did succeed however in one key endeavour: settling relations with the Papacy. After more than 6 years of negotiations, a Concordat was signed between Spain and the Holy See on March 16, 1851. This was the attempt of the *moderados* to heal the breach between Church and State that had been opened up by liberal legislation. The significance of the Concordat of 1851 is still a matter of debate. According to Rosenblatt, the Concordat proved to be less favourable to Spain than the abortive earlier *Convenio* (1845), in the sense that it went far beyond establishing governmental responsibility for the Church's position. The Concordat stipulated that instruction in both public and private schools had to conform to Catholic doctrine. This destroyed the overall state control of education that had been carefully worked out between 1845 and 1850. Although open to broad interpretation, there was an article that stipulated an eventual re-establishment of religious orders in Spain (Rosenblatt 1976: 600). In Callahan's view, concessions made by the *moderado* State to the Church were neither substantial nor costly: the State's willingness to support the Church financially was only a 'restatement of intentions' made by every liberal ministry since 1834, while the papal recognition in the Concordat of the Crown's traditional patronage rights gave the State significant leverage in its relations with the Church (1984a: 191). According to Comellas, the main benefit of the Concordat was that it provided a legal framework that allowed the Church to function normally for the first time since 1834, while it paved the way for addressing vital issues such as the demarcation of new dioceses and the improvement of clerical education at the seminaries (1970: 300). Finally, in Payne's view, the price to pay for this reconciliation with the Church was nevertheless an 'increasingly clerical cast to conservative politics' that further widened the split between moderate and progressive liberals (1978: 774).

To make the Church compatible with the conditions created by the liberal revolution was, according to Pro, the main goal achieved by the Concordat in 1851. The institutional network of the whole Spanish Church became thus permeated by the 'reforming ethos' of liberalism: it was modernised and rationalised and, in the process, it came to be aligned to both the political goals and the administrative structure of the Spanish State (Pro 2019: 368–369). Hence the plethora of new regulations that were issued throughout the year 1852. The end result of both the Concordat and this secondary legislation, according to Pro, was that the Spanish Church became a truly 'national church'. The underlying logic of this process was that, insofar as the Church provided a public service, the 'nation' was entitled to choose not only the bishops, as had been traditionally the case, but also every priest parish priest who would receive a salary from the State (Pro 2019: 374).

It therefore makes sense to think also about the Concordat from the Spanish Church's point of view. We need to see it as standing for the acceptance of secularisation in a purely material sense, given that Pius IX recognised all the sales of ecclesiastical property until then. Secondly, it symbolised an absolute rejection of secularisation within the individual realm of thought and conscience, and within the public realm of education and politics (Revuelta 1996: 353; Revuelta 2002: 165–166). Yet even if one agrees that the State took the upper hand in the Concordat, the fact that remains that the concomitant affirmation of religious unity in Spain created, in the immediate term and in the long run, a lot of expectations within the official Church. It came to believe that the State should act similarly in the fields of religious dissent, education, social customs and censorship, thus leading the country to a 'new age of piety and morality' (Callahan 1984a: 192–3). The opportunities that the Concordat offered to the Church in terms of social influence, now that the confessional character of the State had been reaffirmed, would be seized by a new political group: the *neocatólicos* (Maier 2003: 100). After all, Donoso had referred to the Concordat as an 'excellent starting point' (González Cuevas 2000: 727). Believers in the close relationship between religious and political unity, the *neocatólicos* emerged as a distinctive group during the biennium dominated by the progressive liberals or Progressive Biennium (1854–1856). During these two years of rule by the progressive liberals, the Church saw the sale of most of its remaining property. The *neocatólicos* (neo-Catholics or new Catholics) would jump into national politics during the 1860s with figures such as Cándido Nocedal, Gumersindo Laverde and Juan Manuel Ortí y Lara. Their ideological debt to Donoso Cortés was especially noticeable in their belief in the need for the unity of action between politics and religion, and also in their strategy of trying to influence Isabel II while rejecting any link with Carlism (Canal 2000: 154).

In conclusion, the institutional reorganization of the Church after 1851 paved the way for a return to a position of doctrinal intransigence on the part of conservative opinion, ecclesiastical and pro-clerical alike. The 1840s therefore had proved to be an exceptional decade, as the very urgency of the task of guaranteeing the Church's survival and coherence as an institution, forced a minimum of flexibility on it. In a renewed position of confidence, the 1850s and 1860s would see the Spanish Church fighting for the predominance of its cultural values in a more aggressive, less conciliatory spirit. In the next chapter, these developments will be linked with those taking place within European Catholicism. I will show how an exceptional historical moment in Europe – the short-lived liberalism of Pius IX, brought to an end by the Revolutions of 1848 – allowed Balmes and Donoso to acquire a European reputation. This will be another illustration of the profound differences that exist between them, given that, despite a common interest in supporting the cause of Catholic Europe, their respective messages were qualitatively different. If Donoso gave new ammunition to the Catholics' fear of modernity, Balmes foreshadowed the later development of social Catholicism.

Chapter 4: Spain and Catholic Europe

It is clear that, as the place of the Church within society came increasingly under question, the dilemmas faced by nineteenth-century Spain were actually shared by the rest of Catholic Europe. These dilemmas had two facets: an institutional one, because during this period a marked conflict between Church and State became evident, one in which practical problems such as the provision of education and social welfare became contentious issues; and an ideological one, which went deeper than the attack on ecclesiastical privileges and properties, and in which religion was increasingly set against modern philosophy and science. But the balance between the institutional and the ideological aspects was an uneasy one. It is true that political discourses such as liberalism, nationalism and socialism, especially as they implied both change and a break with the past, were usually accompanied by a strong anticlerical stance. Yet the possibility of adapting religion to these new discourses was also a task envisaged by men who were favourable to the cause of the Church. With varying degrees of flexibility, this would be the case of Balmes and Donoso in Spain, but also of Charles Montalembert and Louis Veuillot in France, Ignaz von Döllinger and Wilhelm Emmanuel von Ketteler in Germany, and Vincenzo Gioberti and Antonio Rosmini in Italy (Villalonga 2014: 321–322). As a result, the Catholic Church found new ways to reinvigorate itself in the public sphere, and was thus able to combine 'traditional self-understanding with the tools of modern mass mobilisation' (Schaefer 2014: 271).

The beginning of the pontificate of Pius IX in the summer of 1846 marked a turning point for the future of Catholicism in Europe. The first actions of Pius IX stood out for their less intransigent approach, when compared with those of his predecessor, Gregory XVI (1831–1846). Both his sympathies towards the movement of Italian unification and his reforms of the Papal

States' government brought into view the image of a 'liberal' Pope. It was a powerful image, containing as it did the promise that traditional Catholicism could be successfully adapted to social and political change. The Pope's alleged liberalism led to a series of controversies, as it affected not only his position as head of the Papal States but also of Catholic Christendom. As was the case elsewhere in Europe, the figure of Pius IX awakened hopes and debates in Spain. Only months apart from one another, Balmes and Donoso wrote extensively on what they believed would be the consequences of this new pontificate for both Spain and Europe.

Until now we have seen how Balmes and Donoso both, albeit in dissimilar ways and through different institutional arrangements, believed that Catholicism ought to be the foundation of Spanish identity. This chapter will now explore the European dimension of how Balmes and Donoso expressed their faith, and how Europe figured in their arguments. They wrote with a European rather than a merely Spanish audience in mind, thus showing an acute awareness of events taking place in Rome, Paris, London and Berlin. They were thus raising their voices not as Spaniards but as Catholics, that is, as members of a transnational community of faith, one in which local and global events were inextricably combined. In 1847, Donoso celebrated the Pope for being representative of 'Catholic civilisation' in Europe, in that he held a balance between obedience and authority, capable of keeping social unrest at bay. Writing shortly afterwards, Balmes welcomed the reforms of Pius IX with this phrase: 'The Pope and I have crossed paths' and wrote about the need to make an alliance between Catholicism and the positive aspects of the 'modern spirit' (Casanovas 1948: 530). But these convictions would be soon challenged as the revolutionary wave swept Europe in 1848.

Balmes and Donoso were quick to acknowledge the significance of the European Revolutions of 1848. They realised that these revolutions resulted not only from poverty, economic crisis and rising social tensions; but also that revolutionary turmoil was fuelled by nationalist and socialist discourses, which included demands for greater political participation and reforms (von Strandmann 2000: 1–4). Yet Balmes and Donoso drew significantly different conclusions, especially from the revolution that broke out in Paris in February 1848. Balmes was not necessarily sympathetic to the cause of French revolutionaries; but he did insist upon the need to address social tensions, rather than merely to repress them, especially the legitimate demands of workers. His premature death in July 1848 prevented Balmes from taking these points of view further. It is still open to speculation what his reaction might have been to the Pope's forced exile from Rome in November 1848, followed by the creation of a Roman Republic in early 1849. The fact remains that Balmes' message of conciliation and moderate reform, alongside the Pope's short-lived liberalism, would soon sink into oblivion and give way to a religious, almost apocalyptic interpretation of the events.

This shift of focus was illustrated by Donoso, on whom the Revolutions of 1848 left a crucial imprint, leading to the radicalisation of his ideas. Preferring order over liberty, Donoso defended the legitimacy of dictatorship as an emergency measure against revolutionary turmoil – and thus gave support to the heavy hand of General Narváez, who crushed all signs of rebellion both inside and outside Madrid. Moreover, Donoso's previous critique of the shortcomings of representative government then turned into a profound indictment of liberalism, now judged to be a weak barrier against the challenges posed by socialism. A series of speeches before the Spanish Cortes and especially his *Ensayo sobre el catolicismo, el liberalismo y el socialismo [Essay on Catholicism, liberalism and socialism]* (1851) gave Donoso a European reputation, partly sustained by the fact that he lived in Paris during the last years of his life, which like that of Balmes, was also brief. In coherence with previous writings, Donoso now argued that the defence of Catholic ideals necessarily supposed an active involvement in politics. This conviction marked Donoso's relationship with French Catholics, from the liberal Montalembert to the intransigent Veuillot, and led him to give active support to the *coup d'état* of Napoleon III. At the end of this chapter, I will discuss Donoso's legacy in both Spain and Europe, taking into account the fact that he heralded both the movement of the *neocatólicos* in the Spain from the mid-1850s onwards and the *Syllabus errorum* (1864) – the Pope's condemnation of modern, secular society.

I. Balmes, Donoso and a liberal Pope

Exactly a fortnight after the death of Pope Gregory XIV in June 1846, cardinal Giovanni Maria Mastai-Ferretti became Pius IX. His unusually fast election – the concordat lasted only two days – marked the beginning of the longest pontificate in Church history until then, lasting thirty-two years. This pontificate began on a series of positive notes, ranging from a generous amnesty for political prisoners decreed in July 1846 to an effort at improving the outdated aspects of the Papal State's administration, reflected both in practical reforms and in the appointment of open-minded prelates as collaborators. These gestures, however limited, led to the creation of the myth of a liberal Pope. In Italy, this myth acted a catalyst to the expectations of change that were the common denominator of a variety of progressive opinions, those of former opponents of the Church, Catholics won over to modern ideas, and the patriotic clergy (Aubert 1981: 59). As a result, a group of intellectuals known as the Neoguelfs, such as Antonio Rosmini, lent support to the idea that the Pope should lead the creation of a federal Italian State, thus delivering Italy from Austria, in that many Italian states were at that point under Austrian rule (Sperber 1994: 93–94; Villalonga 2014: 321). These expectations created the idea that the Pope was not only a reformer, but was also a major player in international politics, one viewed as 'the single most important opponent of Austria and its reactionary chancellor, Metternich' (Matsumoto-Best 2003: 173). The popularity of the Pope outside Italy also reached a peak, and expectations of what he might do were equally high. As Chadwick notes, change was sought not only in papal policy but in the papacy itself. Pius IX was not only expected to lead the movement towards the creation of a free Italian confederation, but also to bless those Catholics in Europe who wanted to bring together faith and liberalism (Chadwick 1998: 64). An eloquent description of this mood – especially of its sense of high expectations – was given by Balmes at the end of 1847:

At such a sudden and profound change, in the very centre of Italy, and promoted by a Pope, the whole Italian peninsula is moved; strong heartbeats are felt right to the extremities; from Calabria to Venice and Turin enthusiastic cheers resound to the Pope and to the independence of Italy; in the uprisings the cry of the rioters is: Long live Pius IX; and the hymn of Pius IX is a hymn of liberty. [...] In the meantime, European diplomacy is in motion; all the political regions are agitated; all the liberal, religious and impious newspapers declare themselves strongly for the Pope, as if the word ultramontanism were to become synonymous with progress and liberty (Balmes 1847b: OC VII: 949–50).

In the long run, the character of Pius IX as rallying point for these expectations would be unsustainable, because it gravely compromised his position of being *both* the ruler of the Papal States and the head of the Catholic Church. Hopes of what Pius IX might do proved to be based on a misconception about what he really intended to achieve (Matsumoto-Best 2003: 173). If the Pope sympathised with Italian patriotism and resented the intervention of Austria in Italian affairs, such feelings would ultimately be subordinated to his role as head of all Christians, given that taking an active part in the struggle for Italian unification would eventually entail waging war against Austria, whose subjects were also the Pope's 'spiritual sons' (Aubert 1981: 61–2). Similarly, any attempts at increasing the political participation of laymen in the Papal State would find a clear limit in the religious character of the Papal government, given that its *raison d'être* was – after all – of an ecclesiastical nature.

Pius IX never intended to turn his domains into a modern constitutional state. In fact, the encyclical *Qui Pluribus [On Faith and Religion]*, issued in November 1846, contained a rejection of the key tenets of liberalism, in that it referred negatively to 'the free license to think, speak and write' although this went virtually unnoticed (Chadwick 1998: 68). The reference was set within a framework of 'ecclesiastic paternalism' that Pius IX allowed for freedom of press and assembly in the Papal States, along with the formation of a council of twenty-four notables in October 1847 (Aubert 1981: 60). A lay element would be introduced into the government of the Papal States in January 1848, while the fall of Louis Philippe in France prompted the approval of a constitution – *Statuto* – in March (Aubert 1981: 58–60). Pius IX's decisions were, however, more and more the result of external pressure and less of his free will, so the line between reform on the one hand and concessions on the other that looked like weaknesses was thus blurred (Chadwick 1998: 67).

In Spain, the very idea of a liberal Pope was discussed vehemently by both Balmes and Donoso. Their reactions show that ultimately the crux of contemporary debates in Catholic Europe was a discussion about the legitimacy of employing Catholicism as a tool for social and political *transformation*. This was a possibility that was often contrasted with the option perceived as that of greatest safety, namely that of turning Catholicism into a guarantee for the *conservation* of a status quo which was judged to be preferable to any revolutionary alternative. The position of Balmes and Donoso in this debate is particularly interesting, because of their conscious desire to propose arguments which could be valid for the whole of the Catholic world.

Within months of one another, Balmes and Donoso wrote about the significance of the reforms undertaken by Pius IX: a series of four articles by Donoso appeared in *El Faro* in September 1847, while a pamphlet by Balmes entitled *Pío IX* was published in December of that year. Meditating upon this coincidence two years later, after the death of Balmes, Donoso made the following reflections: 'Providence had placed us in opposite political parties, although, shortly before his death, religion inspired us with the same things. [...] Balmes and I said the same things, articulated the same judgements and formulated the same opinions' (Donoso 1849c, *OC* II: 343). As a detailed analysis of their texts on Pius IX will show, however, that was not necessarily the case.

As a starting point, it can be argued that both Balmes and Donoso would have agreed with many of the statements put forward by the encyclical *Qui pluribus* (1846), which had made reference to a current war, the greatest ever, being carried against Catholicism. It spoke negatively of the so-called 'philosophers' who had turned their backs on religious dogma and were now asserting the self-sufficiency of human reason, thus implying that Catholic doctrines ran counter to the well-being of society, entailing the persecution of the Church and the widespread deterioration of morals. In sum, the Pontiff had spoken of a 'great crisis of religion', a diagnosis which Donoso and Balmes wholeheartedly embraced. Yet they envisaged different ways out of this situation. They did not necessarily want to preserve the same values against the onslaught of the modern spirit. Their support of the Pope, however passionate, was not unconditional, given that it underpinned a particular view on the future of Catholicism.

In his articles on 'Pío IX', Donoso began by stressing the role of the Pope as the head of Christendom. This assertion was crucial if one considers that Donoso thought the following concepts to be practically synonymous: Europe, Christianity, civilisation and the Papacy. He argued that Popes were endowed with a providential task, because they had been given their place by God in order to solve the great social and religious problems of humanity. In the case of Pius IX his mission was to show to a world which had struggled in vain to solve its problems by resorting either to monarchies or to revolutions, that there was a viable way out of the dilemma, which was the 'Catholic solution' (Donoso 1847; *OC* II: 198). In addition, according to Donoso, the Pope needed to demonstrate how deceitful philosophy was. Donoso extended the Pope's negative appraisal of rationalist, modern philosophy, taking the view that such philosophy ought not simply to be rejected, but had to be unmasked: it was founded upon the appropriation and distortion of what he thought were simply divine truths. Donoso believed that all fundamental ideas of modern civilisation had derived not from philosophy but from God's revelation: 'fraternity' was effectively a re-expression of the concept of the unity of the human race as displayed in the book of Genesis, and true 'liberty' was to be found in the Christian concept of free will (Donoso 1847, *OC* II: 199).

In modern times, Donoso affirmed, only Catholicism could provide humanity with a framework in which the liberty of those who ruled and those who obeyed could coexist peacefully. This conviction was grounded in a historical argument, based on the features which distinguished ancient from modern societies (Donoso 1847, *OC* II: 199–201). According to Donoso, the peoples of Antiquity had been characteristically theocratic: their inability to distinguish between political and religious authority had led to the deification of the State. The omnipotence of the State, given that its power extended over both the body and soul of the members of the political community, was thus capable of annihilating the individual. In his view, societies only reached the status of being modern when the political and the religious became different from one another, mutually independent powers. The concept of authority within a society was, in his view, modelled on the image of man, divided in body and soul: the prince was exclusively concerned with containing and restraining the bodies of those in the nation, whereas the Church primarily claimed control over the intimate realm of human consciousness (Donoso 1847, *OC* II: 204–5). This separation of head and body, princely authority over the body and religious authority over the mind or soul was, he affirmed, something that triumphed over the earlier 'tyrannical omnipotence' of the State. It was also, so the argument went, superior to the tyranny that still survived in contemporary Protestant states in which rulers were simultaneously political and religious authorities (Donoso 1847, *OC* II: 204).

Whether or not Donoso was strictly accurate in the historical detail of his account, he was making a crucial point when he argued that the 'mutual independence' of Church and State had to be regarded as a historical fact (1847, *OC* II: 204). A superficial analysis of this statement gives the impression that Donoso was close to defending the idea of 'a free Church in a free State', namely the separation of Church and State. But he did not advance a secular or non-confessional definition of a State, nor did he clarify what the independence of the State from the Church meant, for example, in financial terms. Donoso's views on the 'independence of the Church' served a clear purpose, however, that of severing the Church from any pre-established link with the Old Regime as embodied in the absolute monarchy. In the present democratic age, he argued, the Papacy would be making a serious mistake if it were to link the cause of Catholicism to the decadent monarchies of Europe (Donoso 1847, *OC* II: 211–2).

Beyond his grandiloquent and all-encompassing historical accounts, Donoso's articles on Pius IX can be summarised as following: epochs and empires had risen and fallen, and the Church had successfully adapted to changing circumstances – including liberal and representative forms of government. What greatly diminished the flexibility of this argument, however, was his insistence upon the duty of obedience, which for him related to the divine origin of political authority. He specifically considered 'Catholic liberty' to be completely different to 'revolutionary liberty' – which, in his opinion, necessarily led to the empowerment of a few demagogic agitators and to the enslavement of the people (Donoso 1847, *OC* II: 216). Donoso thus asserted the superiority of the Catholic version of liberty insofar as, in his view, it withstood the danger of political tyranny. At the same time, however, he came close to saying that the authority of the State was holy:

When the people in Catholic societies obey the supreme authority, they are obeying only God, who has thus willed His authority to be represented in the State and to be a holy and august thing. *Omnis potestas a Deo* [*All power comes from God*]. (Donoso 1847, *OC* II: 203).

Contrasting with Donoso's arguments for a State that, because of its embedded Catholic authority, would be a protection against against revolution, Balmes proposed no distinctively Catholic solution to end the troubles of an agitated age. His stance can be thus summarised in a crucial sentence of his pamphlet *Pío IX*: 'Do you want to avoid revolutions? Make evolutions' (Balmes 1847b, *OC* VII: 997). Balmes wrote *Pío IX* after a three-month stay in Paris, fascinated by the French political situation and especially by the news that arrived in Paris about the events then happening in Rome (Casanovas 1948: 523). In fact, a profound knowledge of current European politics would be one of the key characteristics of Balmes's *Pío IX*. His analysis of the reforms undertaken by the Pope was thus made from a European perspective, as shown in his accurate description of the conflicts of interest that ran through the cause of Italian unification. So rather than labelling the Pope's reforms as concessions, Balmes advanced the idea that they were a necessary and healthy updating of local administration, intended to work towards the creation of a common 'public spirit' which would allow the Papal States to overcome European social and political vicissitudes and avert the need of resorting to foreign aid (Balmes 1847b, *OC* VII: 969). He also expressed the conviction that it was essential to maintain the *temporal* sovereignty of Pius IX, not only as the head of Christianity but also as a king with a throne, in order to avoid a scenario which might include the Pope's captivity or exile. But if Balmes was interested in upholding the independence of the Pope's role, he was nevertheless also open to the cause of Italian unification, expressing his understanding of the Italians' mistrust of Austrian intervention in their own affairs.

The topic of the liberal Pope, one who possessed a reforming outlook, allowed Balmes to emphasise how necessary it was to establish an alliance between Catholicism and 'whatever good there is in the modern spirit' (1847b, OC VII: 971). This alliance became the international projection of the symbolic marriage between old and new that Balmes thought was vital for Spain. As discussed in the second chapter, the debates on the marriage of Isabel II (1844–1846) had provided Balmes with an occasion to preach the reconciliation of diverging ideas and world-views within Spain. Now, the ascent to power of Pius IX allowed him to write in European terms, stressing the need to turn what was a dramatic process of change, as shown in the recent political upheavals of Europe, into a 'peaceful transformation' (Balmes 1847b, OC VII: 971). Balmes illustrated how this might happen with a discussion on the relationship between religion and forms of government. He was aware that, just as Spain had done at the turn of the century, several European countries were seeking to make a transition from absolute monarchy to representative forms of government. According to him, this shift towards regimes which favoured higher degrees of political freedom was not only a generalised trend but – more importantly – was a positive one:

> To insist that the system of Austria or Russia is the only hope of society, is to hopelessly condemn the human race; for the world is not going the way of Metternich or of Nicholas. [...] The whole of America is covered with republics. In Europe, several forms of political freedom can be found in Portugal, Spain, France, Belgium, Holland, Great Britain, Sweden, Switzerland, as well as in many parts of the German Confederation, including Prussia itself (Balmes 1847b, OC VII: 976)

Balmes plainly stated that Catholicism should not be associated with any specific form of government. Every political regime, he argued, had its advantages and disadvantages when it came to furthering the cause of religion. It was erroneous to believe that an increased political freedom could harm the cause of religion, and equally wrong to suppose that nothing but a close alliance between Throne and Altar would sustain it (Balmes 1847, OC VII: 978–9). His reasoning shows him moving on a step from Donoso's emphasis upon the Church's ability to adapt to changing circumstances for the past eighteen centuries – a number relished by Catholic commentators. Balmes' point was to associate the Church not only with the idea of *conservation* but also with the possibility of *transformation*, stressing that Christianity itself had been 'a great reform' and that the Church had been 'always a reformer' (Balmes 1847b, *OC* VII: 999–1000). In his view, the Pope had an urgent task to perform: he had to show that, in modern and civilized societies, the divorce between religion and progress was not inevitable. It is essential to see that Balmes conceived of progress in both material and intellectual terms. In the most meaningful passage of his *Pío IX* he would thus describe the mission of the Pope:

... to make, in due time, the necessary reforms, showing that the spirit of present times is not to be feared, thus attracting all noble spirits, persuading them that there is nothing in religion that is opposed to good order in administration, to material progress, to the development of intelligence, to the exercise of political liberty; that among the human forms that expire and fall into decay, the Catholic religion is not to be counted; and that it, with its dogmas, its morals, its hierarchy, its authority, can remain unharmed in the midst of all empires' vicissitudes; that it can plant the cross on the palace of the Caesars as well as on the popular assemblies; that it can anoint a monarch under the vaults of a Gothic temple, or bless an iron road; that it can be heroic under the armour of a crusader or beneath the humble headdress of a Sister of Charity; that it can defend a king against the hosts of Napoleon, or republican liberty on the banners of the *Sonderbund* (Balmes 1847b, *OC* VII: 980–1).

This statement on the vitality of religion in a world of modern republics and shiny rail roads was accompanied by a series of meditations on the actual future of Catholicism. Like many of his well-informed contemporaries, Balmes was aware that the balance of power in Europe – and even the world – was shifting in favour of a small number of great powers: Russia, Britain and even the United States, countries which were not intrinsically friendly to the cause of Catholicism. Balmes was not speaking purely out of prejudice when referring to Protestant countries. He praised the Catholic Relief Act (1829) which opened the door to the full political participation of Catholics in Britain, while referring in positive terms to religious tolerance in the United States (Balmes 1847b, *OC* VII: 979). At the same time, he insisted upon labelling both Russia and Britain as 'anti-Catholic powers', thus expressing his sympathies towards Catholic struggle in Ireland while lamenting the repression of Catholics in both Russia and Poland (1847b, *OC* VII: 1000).

Unlike Donoso, Balmes did not make a saintly virtue out of obedience to the State. According to Balmes, it was perfectly right for the Pope to encourage the peoples to be obedient to their political authorities but, at the same time, acknowledged the danger of expecting too much from them. Maybe with Spain in mind, Balmes added that the Pope would do wrong if he thought that these authorities were necessarily the most trustworthy allies of Catholicism, because sometimes they were neither willing nor capable of defending the Church (Balmes 1847b, *OC* VII: 1000). Also unlike Donoso, who was willing to resort to extreme measures in order to contain revolutionary turmoil, Balmes expressed his distrust of the 'earthly powers'. He therefore stressed that it was not only dangerous to follow blindly the cries of 'liberty' and 'fraternity', but also to embrace uncritically the causes of 'social order' and 'conservation', because they might hide the grim interests of sheer despotism:

... it is a matter of acknowledging that, at the same time as the names of liberty and progress very often express licence and ruin, words such as authority and legal preservation can stand for oppression and exploitation too. [...] Anarchy is a horrible thing, but despotism is certainly not beautiful; the spectacle of a destructive revolution at work might be off-putting, yet it is also comparable to the repugnant picture created by an oppressive authority (Balmes 1847b, *OC* VII: 1001).

The main biographers of Balmes coincide in stating that his *Pío IX* was widely read, arousing a significant degree of controversy. In Spain, Balmes was accused of entertaining high ambitions, such as that of becoming a cardinal, and of having pronounced inopportune and premature judgements – earning him, once more, the nickname of 'Spanish Lamennais' (Casanovas 1949: 533–5). It might be added that Lamennais, famous for his social critique and progressive stance, was indeed a very popular figure among Spanish republicans and radical liberals (Barnosell 2012: 45). Suggesting that negative reactions against Balmes were mostly limited to Spain, Casanovas points out how quickly *Pío IX* was either reproduced or praised by the French Catholic press (*L'Univers*, *L'Ami de la Religion* and *Le Correspondant*) and also refers to the laudatory comments made by Monsignore Brunelli, apostolic delegate in Spain (Casanovas 1948: 537–8). In addition, Cardinal Ferretti, Apostolic Secretary of State, sent a note in January 1848 to Balmes asking for his opinion on the 'right of nationhood'. In Italy, the works of Balmes were also influential among Catholic nationalists in Italy, such as the group of intellectuals known as Neoguelfs, who were keen on seeing the Pope as head of a national unification movement (Villalonga 2014: 321). Yet one of the most comprehensive critiques of Balmes, *Reflexiones sobre los principios políticos emitidos por el presbítero Jaime Balmes* [*Reflections on the political principles issued by the presbyter Jaime Balmes*] by Tomás Mateo (1848), shows that the reception of *Pío IX* in Spain was neither blindly negative nor free from complexity.

Mateo's critique centred upon the conviction that the ideas of Balmes on sovereignty were an invitation to the 'tyranny of the many' (Mateo 1848: 8). His examples ranged from one of the key tenets of *El Pensamiento de la Nación* [*The Thought of the Nation*] – 'political power should represent power relations in society' – to the positive appraisal of representative governments made by Balmes in *Pío IX*. Mateo believed that the 'system' put forward by Balmes had a dangerous weakness: it derived the legitimacy of the government from popular consent, thus making it dependent upon 'the fickle opinions of men' (Mateo 1848: 17–20) – women, after all, were not able to vote in Spain until 1933. In his view, the conservation of social order was inseparable from a categorical affirmation of the government's right to rule, seen as grounded upon what he regarded as the divine origin of authority. Mateo was not necessarily a belated supporter of absolutism, as his sympathies for the work of a Carlist philosopher, *Leyes fundamentales de la monarquía española* [*Fundamental laws of the Spanish monarchy*] (1843) by fray Magí Ferrer, might suggest (Mateo 1848: 46–7). Insisting upon the need to endow society with truly sovereign and expedient governments, Mateo's attitude was reminiscent of Donoso's earlier critique of the French *doctrinaires*. In the late 1830s, Donoso had criticised them for being unable to reconcile the demands coming from both the people and the monarchy. As the argument went, this sort of conciliatory liberalism was unable to provide a sure guide to follow if circumstances brought about a choice between order and freedom. In 1848, according to Donoso, revolution would bring precisely that choice to the fore.

II. A turning point: 1848

The Revolutions of 1848 signalled the erosion of the idea of Europe which, in the aftermath of the Napoleonic Wars, had been consecrated in the Congress of Vienna (1815). It had been characterised by a conservative social ideal, based upon the monarchy as a 'ruling institution' and the churches as 'guardians of cultural values', and by the attempt to contain liberal and national forces within Europe (Evans 2000: 11). Two powers had been entrusted with maintaining international order, Russia and Britain, while the balance in central Europe was thus secured by a German Bund or Confederation and a loose aggregation of Italian states, both presided over by the Austrian Empire (Evans 2000: 12, 19). The post-Napoleonic Europe of balance-of-power politics and active international diplomacy was personified in Clemens Metternich, foreign minister and chief advisor of the Austrian emperor Francis I, who believed that reform led ineluctably to revolution. Commenting upon the rapid and almost unexpected way in which the revolution had spread throughout Europe, Balmes made an ironic reference to a phrase by Metternich: 'After me, the deluge' – who actually repeated what Louis XV, the French eighteenth-century monarch, once said (Mould 2011: 43). Nonetheless, Balmes referred to this phrase not only as an indication of Metternich's personal arrogance, but also as one that offered an unintended moral lesson for the conservatives of Europe, given that the Prussian chancellor's fall from power in March 1848 proved that 'stubbornly to avoid transformation is to hasten death' (Balmes 1848, *OC* VII: 1050–1).

In the revolutions of 1848, two main forces were at work: on the one hand, a party of movement split into a moderate, constitutional monarchist and a radical, republican democratic wing; on the other, a party of order that stood for religious and dynastic loyalty, as well as for military authority and reliance on the State (Sperber 1994: 240–245, 249; Peyrou 2015: 93–94). In February 1848, the outbreak of revolution in France became the trigger for the escalation of tensions in the Hapsburg Empire, Italy, Germany and Spain. Taking regional variations into account, revolutionary turmoil had several common themes, soon to be echoed all over Europe: widespread opposition to the *anciens régimes*, desire for greater political participation, emphasis upon the need for social reforms, and the assertion of national self-determination (von Strandmann 2000: 3–5). In 1848, the very idea of revolution underwent a change in both theme and protagonist: it was no longer the political revolution once strived for by the educated middle classes, but was now also the social revolution spearheaded by the lower middle classes and the incipient working classes. Although unsuccessful in the short term, the 1848 revolutions made democratic ideas respectable again, thus positing a more inclusive vision of citizenship and a concept of the people as 'redeeming and regenerating force' (Thomson 2017: 99).

France remained as the crucial example of the 'cumulative effect of social dislocation and radical thought' (Evans 2000: 17). The February revolution put an end to the reign of the Orleans monarchy of Louis Philippe (1830–1848) and gave way to the creation of a republic which, in principle, was aimed at addressing the workers' grievances – a category that, at this specific period in time, stood more for artisans than for industrial workers in a modern sense. The true novelty of what became known as France's Second Republic (1848–1852) was to be found in the meaning then acquired by the word republic. As contemporaries put it, it needed to be a 'democratic and social republic', one in which every Frenchman would have the right to vote, but also to work. The underlying, crucial assumption was that workers should be regarded as full-right citizens too, even though, in France, only 5 percent of the population, composed of adult male property owners, was allowed to vote (Lida 2000: 327–328; Sperber 1994: 70). Among radical thinkers, a political revolution was viewed merely as a first step in the right direction, that is, it was to lead to a thorough social and economic reorganization that would rectify the capitalistic exploitation of labour. This was the case of communists like Pierre-Joseph Proudhon and Étienne Cabet, who took forward the postulates of their socialist predecessors such as Saint-Simon and Fourier. Even if the spread and appeal of their ideas was confined to urban areas, they did contribute to create a widespread fear that was related, among other things, to the eventual abolition of private property (Sperber 1994: 82–83).

These events found an acute observer in Balmes. He was able to perceive that, strictly speaking, the revolution of 1848 in France was not a fight against monarchy and nobility, but rather a questioning of the privileges of the wealthy bourgeoisie which had prospered under Louis Philippe – a king whose legitimacy, Balmes commented, did not rest upon tradition but rather upon the July Revolution (1830). What was being ventured in France, according to Balmes, were not only new forms of government (he added that he entertained serious doubts on the viability of the French republic) but the possibility of improving the imbalances in the relationship between capital and labour. Writing between March and April 1848, Balmes wrote the following on the recent events in France:

What has fallen is not a throne of fourteen centuries, but a monstrosity born among the barricades; there are no privileged classes who uphold ancient rights based on principles of justice, but a group of rich people who wish to retain their property and whose claims to influence in public affairs are based on theories, not traditions. There is no struggle against the nobility and the clergy, and for this reason their members are not persecuted; there is a struggle, however, against the aristocracy of gold based on the name of liberty and on the impulse given by political economy, and for this reason attacked in its arrogance with what is called the organisation of labour, which in its turn is also organised on the impulse of new economic doctrines and the theories of liberty (Balmes 1848, *OC* VII: 1037).

This passage is part of the very last of Balmes's writings, a series titled 'República Francesa' [French Republic] which, according to Casanovas, ought to be regarded as his political will – although it only became known in 1850, when it appeared published in a volume of *Escritos póstumos* (Balmes

1848: *OC*, VII: 1025–6). Balmes died on the 9th of July 1848, after a month of agony spent in his native Vic. We can only speculate about what his reaction would have been to the increasing conservative turn taken by the French Republic, due to the sharp divide that existed between the working classes and the bourgeoisie. This was reflected in the disturbances of the June Days, when the insurrection of Paris workers, partly triggered by the closing of the state-run workshops, was harshly repressed, with a death toll of 1,500 plus 11,000 imprisoned (Lida 2000: 327–328). The June Days gave encouragement to those who advocated the use of violence against revolution (von Strandmann 2000: 7). Moreover, the fear of revolution prompted the Orleanist bourgeoisie to make common cause with the Church in order to maintain order and to defend property. They would convince the French Church for the next twenty years that religion, morality and the traditional social order were in danger, thus prompting the return of the Church to a conservative stance (Aubert 1981: 66–7). The fear of socialism opened the door to all sort of compromises, including an alliance between conservatives and liberals against the extreme left (Sperber 1994: 77). This attitude paved the way for the rise of Louis Napoleon Bonaparte. Elected as president of the Second Republic in December 1848, a *coup d'état* three years later would be the first step in turning him into Napoleon III, head of the Second French Empire (1851–1871). The plebiscite that ratified his conversion into emperor was interpreted thus by the publicist Veuillot who, followed by the majority of French Catholics, argued: 'There is no choice between Bonaparte as Emperor and the socialistic republic' (Aubert 1981: 68).

For a long time, it was assumed that Spain did not have a revolution of 1848 but rather a series of failed uprisings, centred upon Madrid on 26 March and on 7 May, and echoed in Seville on the 13 May (Cabeza 1981: 11). The uprisings were staged by a relatively loose coalition of progressive liberals who, wanting to provoke a crisis that would enable them to return to power, were aided by an incipient political movement, that of republicans and democrats. They wanted to replace the monarchy of Isabel II with a regime similar to the French one, but their democratic and republican ideals were not French in origin. As Barnosell insists, these ideals arose from the Spanish liberal tradition that, originally embodied in the Constitution of 1812, had posited equal citizen rights for all men (2012: 52). This republican ideal was not necessarily anti-monarchic, as Lida argues, but stood mainly for the idea of a *res publica*, that is, a government based upon a more inclusive idea of citizenship, including the right to work and to associate (2000: 332). Ultimately, what made

Spain truly exceptional in 1848 was not the lack of real revolutionaries capable of staging a real revolution. As García de Paso demonstrates, it was the fact that the Spanish government took repressive and counter-revolutionary measures earlier than its European counterparts – at least three months in advance – thus preventing the emergence of a coherent, far-reaching movement (2016: 205).

As soon as the news of the February revolution in Paris arrived in Spain, the government's premier, General Narváez, rushed to obtain the approval of the Cortes to a series of emergency measures (March 15, 1848) that would facilitate the government's expedient action. Enhancing the role of the army as guarantor of order, General Narváez assembled the highest military authorities in Madrid, and sent an army of 50,000 men to protect the frontier in the Pyrenees. After the urban riots in March, in the framework of a legally sanctioned dictatorship, there was a quick transition from preventative to repressive measures: the Cortes were closed down and citizens' constitutional rights were suspended, thus allowing the government to proceed with executions, deportations and military operations against revolutionaries (Cabeza 1981: 140–2; Comellas 1970: 265, 270; Evans 2000: 21). The revolutionaries were forced to change their strategy, moving from the city to the countryside, where they formed urban guerrillas and went as far establishing an alliance of convenience with Carlists in April 1848 against the national army (García de Paso 2016: 196–197; Cabeza 1981: 102).

The greatest beneficiary of the 1848 in Spain was General Narváez, who then earned a European reputation: from Paris to St. Petersburg, he became known as 'hero of the anti-revolution' (García de Paso 2016: 198). The 'exemplarity' of Spain in 1848 was confirmed by Austria, Prussia and the Kingdom of Piedmont-Sardinia, countries that finally gave their official diplomatic recognition to Isabel II. This paved the way for Spain's direct involvement with the problems then affecting Catholic Europe, as shown in its active efforts to restore the Pope to Rome, which, in turn, would earn Narváez the Pope's blessing too. In November 1848, the revolutionary events in the Papal States had forced Pius IX to flee and take refuge in Gaeta, a seaport 120 km from Rome. This was the culmination of a long chain of events.

The popularity of Pius IX had been greatly affected when, in April 1848, he refused to join the Piedmontese government's war against Austria. On that occasion, the Pope did not hide his sympathies for the Italian demands but, to the disappointment of the progressives and supporters of unification, he justified his refusal to intervene militarily on grounds of Christian neutrality, given that Austrians were also part of his spiritual flock (Aubert 1981: 61–2). Discontent, economic crisis, political assassinations, all came to a head by the end of the year. After the murder of Pellegrino Rossi, papal premier and liberal *doctrinaire*, the revolutionaries besieged Pius IX in the Quirinal Palace, demanding a constituent assembly and war on Austria, thus prompting the Pope's flight. Soon after, in January 1849, a republic was proclaimed in Rome. Coordinating efforts in the so-called conference of Gaeta, a joint military intervention by Austria, Spain, Naples and France put an end to the Roman republic and allowed for the Pope's return by September 1849. Spain's role was particularly active, and General Narváez sent an army of no fewer than 8000 men, although their part in the events was obscured by the leading role of the French armies in the liberation of Rome (Cabeza 1981: 145–7). Pius IX would not forget Spain's gesture, one which led to the recognition of Isabel II and smoothed the path for signing of the Concordat in 1851 (Comellas 1970: 250–1).

Other than being based upon his domestic and international policy, the European fame of General Narváez owed much to the fact that the legitimacy of his actions had been eloquently justified – and even glorified – in a speech that Donoso gave in the Cortes in January 1849 (Orozco 2010: 303). On that occasion, Donoso straightforwardly stated that 'dictatorship is, in certain circumstances, such as the present ones, a legitimate government' (Donoso 1849d, *OC* II: 307). Given that General Narváez was already ruling in a semi-dictatorial manner, Donoso spoke in defiance of the progressive liberals' claim that government should be based on the law only. In his view, the salvation of society was the *ultima ratio* of legality: 'when legality is enough to save society, then there should be legality; when this is not enough, then dictatorship' (Donoso 1849d, *OC* II: 306). Donoso spoke with the assumption that the Spanish upper and middle classes would accept the expedient of dictatorship if revolution was to be kept from spreading to Spain: a sheet of support for the queen and government with 60,000 signatures, collected on the initiative of the Spanish Grandees, had confirmed the desire of the ruling classes to maintain the status quo (Comellas 1970: 269–70). According to Donoso, there were important lessons to be drawn from recent events in Europe. To stave off revolutions, he argued, governmental resistance was more effective that liberal concessions such as those made by the Pope; in his view, Louis Philippe had fallen by not resisting and Pius IX, by giving in to the voices of reform (Graham 1974: 148–9). The causes of revolutions were not to be found in social inequality or economic hardship, he concluded, but rather

170 SPAIN AND CATHOLIC EUROPE

in a spirit of rebellion created by agitators who were keen to stir the masses' envy of the wealth of the bourgeoisie:

Revolutions are diseases of rich peoples; revolutions are diseases of free peoples. [...] No, gentlemen; the germ of revolutions is found neither in slavery nor in misery; the germ of revolutions is to be found in the over-excited desires of the multitude, because of the intervention of tribunes who exploit them for their own profit. *And you will be like the rich*: see here the formula of socialist revolutions against the middle classes. *And you will be like the nobles*: see here the formula of the revolutions of the middle classes against the noble ones. *And you will be like the kings*: see here the formula of the noble classes against the kings. Finally, gentlemen, *and you will be like gods*: see there the formula of the first rebellion of man against God (Donoso 1849d, *OC* II: 311–2).

The rhetorical power of Donoso's speech on dictatorship lies partly in its boldness, because Donoso spoke unabashedly about what was a tremendously charged word, namely dictatorship, and used it not only as a description of Spain's current political situation but as a proposed remedy for revolution. The other source of rhetorical power was the range of similes that Donoso established between religion and politics, beginning with the idea that modern revolutions could be regarded as repercussions of original sin, considered as the belief in the self-sufficiency of the human reason that led to the overturning of tradition and hierarchy. Moreover, Donoso even played with the idea that God was also capable of acting dictatorially when performing a miracle, because He was momentarily breaking the divine laws of the universe (Donoso 1849d, *OC* II: 309). In the same way that miracles were short-lived interruptions of a regular and divine *order*, Donoso believed that dictatorship was an exceptional (if legitimate) means of government. The problem is that he also affirmed that, due to the revolutionary *disorder*, dictatorship had become the inescapable fate of European societies.

The most distinctive feature of Donoso, when we think of him as a counter-revolutionary philosopher, was his insistence upon the idea that the time had come to make a crucial decision. In January 1849, he exclaimed passionately: 'Liberty is over!' In post-1848 Europe, he affirmed, it was no longer possible to choose between order and liberty. Yet the alternatives envisaged by him were tragically narrow. In his view, the only choice left was between the disorder of the revolutionaries and the order of the government; in other words, between two kinds of dictatorships, as in this oft-quoted passage: 'it is a question of choosing between the dictatorship of insurrection and the dictatorship of government; [...] between the dictatorship of the dagger and the dictatorship of the sword: I choose the dictatorship of the sword because it is nobler' (Donoso 1849d, *OC* II: 322–3).

This pre-eminent role given to choice, along with an almost blind faith in the righteousness of the *sword* (the State, the army, the government, the status quo), came to be a central feature in Donoso's later writings. His works culminated in a lifelong search for a political theory based upon certainty. And so, in the last years of his life, Donoso undertook his most ambitious attempt ever at taming the revolution. His attempt stemmed from his awareness, shared by his contemporaries, that the term revolution was undergoing a crucial change of meaning. 'Political revolution' was a thing of the past; nowadays, what was now at stake was 'social revolution' – described as a 'multi-faceted monster' by the moderate liberal Nicomedes Pastor Díaz, in his lectures on socialism at the Ateneo of Madrid in 1848–1849 (1867: 11). Writing from Catalonia, Roca i Cornet, a former collaborator of Balmes, offered his readers an overview of contemporary European thought, and concluded that the supreme danger came from the 'revolutionary school' that preached universal suffrage, thus positing a 'sovereignty of the ignorant' as embodied in the uncivilized and uneducated masses (Roca y Cornet 1847: 268, 282).

Yet Donoso would exceed his contemporaries in his painting of the horrors that allegedly would ensue if a socialist revolution – or, to use his term, a 'dictatorship of the dagger' – would ever take place in Europe (Donoso 1849d, *OC* II: 322–3). Speaking in the Cortes in January 1849, Donoso prophesied a tragic future for a world which was inexorably marching towards 'the emergence of a despotism, the most gigantic and devastating in the memory of mankind' (Donoso 1849d, *OC* II: 316). Following a line of thought that would culminate in his *Ensayo sobre el catolicismo, el liberalismo y el socialismo [Essay on Catholicism, liberalism and socialism]* (1851), Donoso spoke against the threat represented by socialists, whom he believed to be 'bloody and revengeful men'. Significantly, he established a link between socialist ideas, allegedly leading nowhere but to tyranny and an increased level of repression, and the new means of surveillance and control that, in an era of improved communications, were now available to governments. He suggested that modern technology favoured the centralisation of power in the hands of governments, thus putting individual liberties in peril:

Governments have said: 'In order to repress, a million arms are not enough for me; in order to repress, a million eyes are not enough; in order to repress, a million ears are not enough; we need more: we need the privilege of being everywhere at the same time' [...] Gentlemen, the way is paved for a gigantic, colossal, universal, immense tyrant: everything is ready for it; [...] there is no longer any physical resistance, because with steamships and iron roads there are no frontiers; there is no physical resistance, because with the electric telegraph there are no more distances, and there is no moral resistance, because all spirits are divided and all patriotisms are dead (Donoso 1849d, *OC* II: 318–9).

A natural first objection to raise is that Donoso seemed to have ruled out the fact that it was also possible to employ these means in the pursuit of conservative, or even counter-revolutionary goals. Yet Donoso was careful to stress that the only real alternative to either revolution or dictatorship was a religious and moral reawakening of the people (Graham 1974: 149). This was further justified by the assumption that, in a given society, a high degree of religious observance could be correlated with a high degree of governability, because 'when the religious thermometer is reading low, the political thermometer, political repression, tyranny, reads high' (Donoso 1849d, *OC* II: 316). There is yet another problematic assumption made by Donoso, further proving that the endorsement of dictatorship is still the most controversial aspect of his thought: he believed that a given society could be legitimately saved from anarchy by means of the 'dictatorship of the sabre'. Putting it differently, his programme for political reconstruction and moral regeneration depended upon 'an initial show of force' (Graham 1974: 5–6).

In January 1850, a 'Discurso sobre la situación de Europa' [Speech on the situation of Europe], delivered by Donoso in the Spanish Cortes, gave a further impulse to his fame and reputation across the continent. This justifies Graham's assessment that Donoso was to the European revolutions of 1848 what Edmund Burke and Joseph de Maistre had been to the French Revolution of 1789 (Graham 1974: 3). His 'Speech on dictatorship' had been translated into French and German, turning him into the spokesman of European reaction. Now, his speech on Europe was described by Metternich as 'a masterpiece in the sphere of principles', while also receiving the attention and praise of Louis Napoleon of France, Frederick William IV of Prussia and Nicholas I of Russia (Graham 1974: 158). To some degree, Donoso's authoritative judgement on European affairs was the result of his period as ambassador of Spain in Berlin, from February to November 1849 (Schmitt 2006: 82). After having experienced the interplay of European politics at a closer range, Donoso was able to develop his views on the threat represented by socialism and more specifically by Russia. This also allowed him to insist upon the 'exemplarity' of Spain when compared to the rest of revolution-ridden Europe; moreover, conveniently forgetting the chronic troubles of the reign of Isabel II, he claimed: 'Spain, gentlemen, is to Europe what an oasis to the Sahara desert' (Donoso 1850a, *OC* II: 455). Nevertheless, in a private letter written in June 1849, Donoso had urged General Narváez to consider further stringent measures in order to keep revolution out of Spain: cultural autarky, *cordon sanitaire* and a bigger army (Urigüen 1986: 91).

Donoso's speech on Europe centred upon a crucial question: how to defeat socialism. He criticised the Spanish deputies for acting under the illusion that economic reforms were an effective way to prevent the outbreak of revolution. To put economics ahead of political, social and religious problems would not defeat socialism, which he characterised as an 'economic sect' and 'offspring of political economy', but only contribute to its further spread (Donoso 1850a, *OC* II: 454). This emphasis on materialism, which characterised the remedies proposed both by socialists and their opponents, was in stark opposition to what Donoso believed to be the only solution for Europe: a moral and religious renaissance, a return to the Catholic values that preached charity to the rich and resignation to the poor. The root of Europe's problems was to be found in the disappearance of the idea of authority, both in a human and a divine sense (Donoso 1850a, *OC* II: 457). Obedience to God and obedience to the monarch, according to Donoso, were practically the same thing. At the same time he stressed that lack of religiosity and 'heretic' political innovations came hand in hand, thus explaining the links that he traced between republicanism and pantheism, between revolution and atheism. These complicated categories, based upon a series of 'affirmations' and 'denials', were ultimately designed to prove that governments were free of blame:

> Evil is not to be found in governments, but in the governed; evil lies in the fact that the governed have become ungovernable (Donoso 1850a, OC II: 457).

The cataclysm was imminent, warned Donoso. And, for the first time, he called attention to what he believed was a frightening scenario: the union between socialism and Russian politics which, in turn, would lead to the triumph of socialist revolution and the domination of Europe by a vast Russian state. In hindsight, a phrase such as 'I think that a revolution is more likely to happen in Saint Petersburg than in London', that Donoso pronounced as early as 1850, earned him the reputation of being prophetic and of having predicted the Russian revolution of 1917 (Schmitt 2006: 98). The remedy he then proposed seems, also in retrospect, less realistic. He stressed the need to return to a conservative Concert of Europe, headed by Britain who, very importantly, needed to then abandon its pro-liberal foreign policy and embrace a monarchic-conservative one (Donoso 1850a, *OC* II: 463). This would not be enough, however, if Britain refused to make use of the only doctrine capable of counteracting both revolution and socialism: Catholicism. In saying this, Donoso was not wholly misguided: on the one hand, he was aware of the pro-Catholic efforts carried out in Britain by cardinals John Henry Newman and Nicholas Wiseman; on the other, his desire was to strike a sensitive chord in both listeners and readers, namely the belief that Europe, with all its past and future greatness, depended upon its Christian character, origin and purpose.

Yet one of the most provocative aspects of Donoso's speech on Europe would be, precisely, his choice of two figures – the priest and the soldier – as being the personification of what he believed to be the most valuable aspects of European civilisation: both were to embody a spirit of self-sacrifice, charity and obedience to lawful authority. In other words, Donoso not only believed that both Church and army were the greatest representatives of Christian civilisation; he affirmed that the salvation of Europe was actually in their hands:

> Now (and here is the solution to this great problem), the ideas of the inviolability of authority, of the sanctity of obedience and the divinity of sacrifice, these ideas are not to be found in today's civil society: they are found in the temples where the just and merciful God is worshipped, and in the barracks where the strong God, the God of battles, is worshipped under the symbols of glory. That is why [...] the Church and the army [...] are the two representatives of European civilisation (Donoso 1850a, *OC* II: 465).

The substantial controversy aroused by Donoso's views was centred in Paris. *L'Univers*, the Catholic newspaper edited by the ultramontane Louis Veuillot, distributed fourteen thousand copies of Donoso's speech. His views, as expressed in this speech, were challenged by the Russian philosopher Alexander Herzen, writing from *La Voix du Peuple*, edited by the socialist Pierre-Joseph Proudhon (Graham 1974: 158–9). Thanks to the fact that it was denounced to the police, Herzen's article acquired a sudden popularity and its forty thousand copies were sold overnight (Herzen 1851: 152). Amidst the chorus of praise given to Donoso by Catholic and royalist journals, Herzen raised a sharply discordant voice. He agreed with Donoso's diagnosis, concerning a Europe which had lost its way and was on the verge of cataclysm; nonetheless, he strongly disagreed with the proposed remedy – 'religion *réchauffé*' – adding that 'to sacrifice others and be self-sacrificing on their behalf is too easy to be a virtue' (Herzen 1851: 152–4, 158).

Herzen affirmed that, in believing passionately that only a return to Catholic faith would save Europe from disaster, Donoso had overlooked the possibility of individuals choosing *not* to believe. Thus Herzen strongly objected Donoso's choice of the priest and soldier as a means of salvation, because 'the last representative of intellectual slavery unites himself with the last representative of physical coercion' (Herzen 1851: 158–9). Moreover, Herzen played with an idea that would trigger the adverse reaction of the police: if the point was to uphold the existing governments at all costs, the hangman was superior to the priest and the soldier because 'he kills in cold blood, with calculation, without danger to himself, like the law, in the name of society and order' (Herzen 1851: 160). Whereas Donoso was interested in correcting and improving the old order, Herzen rejected it completely, 'as the early Christians renounced the Roman world' (Herzen 1851: 156). In so doing, Herzen confirmed what Donoso found it impossible to accept: the way that socialists often portrayed themselves as true followers of Christ. Dismantling the claims of those who thought like Herzen would be the objective of his last and still most famous work: the *Ensayo sobre el catolicismo, el liberalismo y el socialismo* [*Essay on Catholicism, liberalism and socialism*] (1851).

III. An essay on pessimism

Evil was innate in man, and not in institutions – in a nutshell, this is the argument of Donoso's *Ensayo sobre el catolicismo, el liberalismo y el socialismo* (1851). The *Ensayo* can thus be regarded as an eloquent example of the 'anthropological pessimism' which characterises the conservative outlook, especially in its most radical varieties (González Cuevas 2000: 32). The foundation stone of Donoso's argumentation was that human nature, damaged by original sin, was not only incapable of reaching perfection but was in constant need of divine guidance. Donoso argued with the intention of questioning the dreams of progress and social justice envisaged respectively by liberals and socialists. He would also question the core of their argument, that evil was not to be found in man but in political and social institutions that had to be reformed, replaced or overthrown. In contrast with liberals and socialists, Donoso believed that evil had to be eradicated from the heart of man before it could actually be extirpated from society and the state. By confronting fully his liberal and socialist opponents, Donoso's ultimate aim was to insist upon the idea that only a return to religion could prevent the ruin of modern society.

The Donoso of the *Ensayo* is the one that usually appears in the histories of European political thought. Yet the origin of this, his only book, was more random and unexpected than is generally acknowledged by a long tradition of scholarship, eager to reduce the whole of Donoso's thought to a coherent whole. It was Veuillot who encouraged Donoso to write the *Ensayo*, in Paris in 1849. It would be part of his *Bibliothèque Nouvelle* of Christian apologetics, conceived of as a 'pamphlet series for simple souls' (Graham 1974: 270–1; Donoso 1850b, *OC* II: 472). While keeping the dogmatic and combative tone that Veuillot required, Donoso was hard put to resist the temptation of addressing a more intellectual audience in this book, written in just four months, between April and August 1850. The *Ensayo* became the vehicle of an ambitious undertaking: in it he set out to prove that, in modern times, theology could still be regarded as the science of everything. In order to support this conviction, Donoso put forward an interpretation of history according to strict Christian lines, one in which peace and prosperity were directly correlated to peoples' faithfulness towards religion and – very importantly – to the prominent public presence of the Church. His unwillingness to admit the validity of solutions that contradicted his own, either by endorsing a secular view of human affairs or confining religion to a private realm, gave a controversial character to the *Ensayo*, based on its inflexibility and lack of nuance. It left its readers with the impression that it was a disproportionate diatribe against liberals and socialists, and against all things modern (Graham 1974: 293). Yet its powers of persuasion should not be underestimated, partly because of its simplifications, conveniently exaggerated, but mainly because of the appeal exercised by the strongly autobiographical character of the *Ensayo*. Donoso wrote with both the impatient fire of a recent convert and the lifelong convictions of an experienced politician.

The links between the *Ensayo* and French Catholicism, further strengthened by Donoso's appointment as ambassador in Paris (1851–1853), contribute to give this book a foreign air, and it has led some critics to suppose it to be mere gloss of De Maistre's ideas rather than a further development of the 'Spanish *tradition*' (Baralt 1860, II: 15). Attributing the boldness of Donoso's arguments in the *Ensayo* to elements such as origin, nationality or even intellectual influence, obscures the key fact that his thought did not become unexpectedly radical. After all, it had been the Donoso's support of dictatorship that gave an abrupt ending ten years earlier to his *Lecciones de derecho político constitucional [Lessons on Constitutional Political Law]* (1836–1837). A decade later, the experience of religious conversion (1847) and the impact

SPAIN AND CATHOLIC EUROPE 177

of the Revolutions of 1848 led to his ideas becoming more entrenched. There were practically no reasons to expect that Donoso would give a warm welcome to socialist doctrines, ranging from his interest in upholding the elitist social order of the *moderado* regime to his lifelong lack of sympathy for a concept such as popular sovereignty.

In 1848, however, Donoso did go a step further: he gave up liberalism altogether. He doubted the ability of contemporary European liberalism to maintain certain conditions, in that it was a movement that opposed privilege and claimed to represent the people but, at the same time, shunned democracy and restricted franchise to a minority of educated property-owners (Sperber 1994: 71). For Donoso, 1848 was a proof of what happened when liberal postulates, such as equal treatment under the law, were taken to their fullest expression. Hence, in the *Ensayo*, Donoso's rupture with liberalism appears to be more spectacular than it might because it is in contrast with his more predictable attacks on socialism. One of the most crucial objections that Donoso raised against liberalism and socialism is that they both assumed the innate goodness of man so that, according to these schools of thought, 'man is at the same time a universal reformer and non-reformable and is thus transformed from man into God' (Donoso 1851e: 155).

In Donoso's view, this fundamentally optimistic view of man contradicted the fact that human nature had been irretrievably tainted by original sin and, according to the postulates of the Church, man was therefore in need of redemption and moral reform. Despite his insistence upon the necessity of free will, understood as the ability to make the choice between one's perdition or one's salvation, Donoso overemphasised all the possibilities of a terrible fate into which men could fall. To the dreams of human fraternity envisaged by some revolutionaries, Donoso opposed the view of human nature held by Thomas Hobbes, according to whom 'the natural and primitive state of man is a universal, incessant and simultaneous state of war' (Donoso 1851e: 198) showing by this references that he was not working in a Hispanic vacuum. In one of the most dramatic passages of the *Ensayo*, Donoso depicted humanity as being caught in a never-ending chain of prevarications, a ship without a captain, and a sort of dance of death:

And they do not know where they are going, nor where they are coming from, nor the name of the ship that carries them, nor the wind that pushes them along. If now and then a mournfully prophetic voice says, 'Woe to the mariners! Woe to the ship!', while the hurricanes rage and the ship begins to creak, the lubricious dances and the splendid feasting, the frenzied laughter, and the senseless clamouring nevertheless go on; until in a most solemn moment everything ceases at once, the splendid feasts, the frenzied laughter, the lubricious dances, the senseless clamour, the creaking of the forest, and the roar of the hurricanes; the waters are over all, and silence is over the waters, and the wrath of God over the silent waters (Donoso 1851e: 88).

The idea that human life was bound to strict laws, applying to both the physical and the moral world, allowed Donoso to emphasise yet further the danger of rebelling against this divine order, and of believing one could escape these laws. This led him to question both the excellence of human reason when operating *alone* (i.e. without divine illumination), and to describe rationalism as a sin consisting of a sin of pride and self-sufficiency – in fact, a sin that was the closest to original sin (Donoso 1851e: 152). The desire to praise divine grace led Donoso to exaggerate the shortcomings of men. The most controversial passages of the *Ensayo* are those in which human reason is reviled, such as the following one: 'between human reason and absurdity there is a secret affinity, an intimate kinship' (Donoso 1851e: 46). Donoso made statements whose accuracy was even questionable from a theological perspective, such as the idea that Christ had won over the world *despite* his miracles and his doctrine, and merely thanks to God's forgiveness towards the vileness of men (Donoso 1851e: 45). These negative statements found their culmination in a famous and oft-quoted passage:

I know from myself that if my God had not become flesh within the womb of a woman, and if He had not died on a Cross for the entire human lineage, the reptile that I tread on would be more despicable than men themselves (Donoso 1851e: 241)

Instead of addressing the human condition, seen as the true locus of social evil, Donoso believed that the liberals wrongly supposed that society's problems were essentially a matter of politics, capable of being solved by making changes and reforms to government (Donoso 1851: 136, 141). The only standard against which governments were judged was their legitimacy and this, according to Donoso, obscured questions which were more important. In his view, liberalism neither questioned the social structure nor concerned itself with religious aspects. It also placed what Donoso believed to be excessive hopes in the power of human reason: everyday parliamentary politics rested upon the belief that truth and understanding could be reached through argument and debate. He believed that the liberal 'principle of discussion' presupposed the infallibility of human reason; moreover, it spoke for a society that had emancipated itself from the dictates of the Church, which had the exclusive right 'to affirm and to negate' (Donoso 1851e: 24–7).

SPAIN AND CATHOLIC EUROPE

More original and truly applicable to modern times, was the opposition that Donoso established between *discussion* and *decision*. The idea that expediency, understood as the capacity for quick and coherent action, was a characteristic of any efficient government and had already been developed in Donoso's *Lecciones* (1836–7). In that earlier piece of writing, Donoso plainly declared that liberal parliamentary regimes lacked the ability to act in an expedient way; or, to put it more boldly, that they were not strong enough to resist the dangers of an eventual socialist revolution. Liberalism was characterised by its 'radical impotence' because discussion delayed action and paved the way for catastrophe (Donoso 1851e: 141). Borrowing a style proper to the Church prophets, Donoso announced the imminent advent of a revolutionary apocalypse. If anything, liberalism was a fragile and brief parenthesis in the face of it:

This school dominates only when society is in decline: the period of its domination is that transitory and fleeting period when the world does not know whether to go with Barabbas or with Jesus, and is torn between a dogmatic affirmation and a supreme negation. Society then willingly allows itself to be governed by a school which never says I *affirm* or *deny*, and which to everything says I *distinguish*. [...] It propagates scepticism, knowing, as it does, that a people who perpetually hear from the mouths of their sophists the pros and cons of everything end up not knowing where they stand. [...] The peoples, urged on by all their instincts, will come to a day when they spill out into the squares and the streets asking resolutely either for Barabbas or for Jesus, and scattering dust over the chairs of the sophists (Donoso 1851e: 138).

Donoso would later refer to the origins of modern liberal regimes: they were to be found not in the Middle Ages, but in the nineteenth-century revolutions which had had the middle classes as protagonists (Donoso 1852b, *OC* II: 775–6). In doing so, Donoso clearly broke with the kind of historicist readings often favoured by Spanish liberals, keen to seek an antecedent of their own fight for liberties in the Middle Ages. In the 1820s, the young Donoso had not been an exception to this rule and thus wrote a play about Juan de Padilla, depicted as a freedom fighter because of his key role in the Revolt of the *Comuneros* (1520–1521) staged by citizens of Castile against the allegedly despotic rule of Carlos I (Schramm 1936: 33–4). By contrast, in the 1850s, Donoso viewed liberal regimes as stemming directly from 'modern civilisation', which he now regarded as a rupture with the past rather than a continuation of it, namely Spain's heritage and core values.

Liberal regimes in contemporary Europe, according to Donoso, were full of incoherence. In the first place, they affirmed the solidarity between peoples and yet affirmed individualism in a way that came close to being an 'pagan egotism and yet deprived of the virility of hatred' (Donoso 1851e: 190). Secondly, liberal regimes proclaimed in theory an egalitarian principle, the right of all men to participate in the tasks of government, but in practice this was contradicted in a variety of ways: they had dismantled absolutism's society of estates, but still regarded hereditary monarchy as a fundamental institution of the State; they spoke of the rights of all citizens, while consistently restricting the right to vote to a minority of well-to-do citizens. Thirdly, Donoso referred to the 'repugnant materialism' embraced by liberalism, as it made a political virtue out of wealth, positing that 'the leadership of the rich [is] more legitimate than that of the nobility' (Donoso 1851e: 190–1).

The masterstroke of the *Ensayo*, in terms of persuasion, went far beyond the assertion that liberalism was only a weak and temporary barrier against revolution. It lies in having presented socialism as *the logical outcome of liberalism*. As Donoso put it, liberal regimes had begun by expropriating the properties of the Church, setting an example to follow for communists and socialists who strove towards the suppression of individual property if they were to proclaim the State as a 'universal and absolute property owner' (Donoso 1851e: 192–3). This argument was hardly a novelty for contemporary readers, considering that conservative-minded commentators often referred to the sale of Church property as a first step towards more ambitious expropriations schemes by the State, so that individual property rights might soon be in peril too. But it does represent a clear rupture in Donoso's thought, especially if we compare it with his speeches of the mid-1840s. With subtle reasoning, Donoso thus presented the transition from liberalism to socialism: the liberals' belief in the right of every man to participate in the affairs of government had been carried to its logical extension by the socialists, who now advocated the equality of all men. The belief in equality would lead, as a logical consequence, to the suppression of monarchy and of every aristocratic distinction, and to the affirmation of universal suffrage (Donoso 1851e: 191).

Donoso insisted on the similarity of ideas between socialism and liberalism but stressed that the former was superior to the latter. Socialist superiority was a matter of 'bravery' and expediency, that is, of being able to move decisively into revolutionary action (Donoso 1851e: 195). It also had a fundamentally idealistic view of human nature, believing it to be intrinsically good, but its solutions were more radical than the liberal ones: believing that there was no evil except that which existed in society, socialism proposed the subversion of social institutions and the entire destruction of the present order – with the aim of restoring that primitive goodness. Another sign of its superiority, when compared to liberalism, was the use of religious language in order to persuade its followers: it put forward the promise that men could realise paradise on earth, and especially that it would be a 'bloodless paradise' (Donoso 1851e: 230). Donoso further described socialism as a new religion: as a 'Satanic theology' and even as a 'semi-Catholicism' (Donoso 1851e: 139, 217). And yet, despite everything, the sense of condemnation of socialism prevailed:

> Do you call yourselves the Apostles of a new Gospel, and speak to us of evil and sin, of Redemption and grace, all things of which the old one is full? Do you call yourselves the depositories of a new political, social and religious science, and speak to us of liberty, equality and fraternity, all things as old as Catholicism, which is as old as the world? [...] God condemns you to be nothing but clumsy commentators on his immortal Gospel, just as you aspire with heedless and mad ambition to promulgate a new law from a new Sinai, if not from a new Calvary (Donoso 1851e: 165).

Donoso also warned about the dangers of turning the State into the agent of these dreams of social justice, something which would lead towards the annihilation of the individual. In a similar fashion to the modern critiques of totalitarianism, Donoso also described communism as 'governmentalism raised to the utmost power' (Donoso 1851e: 203–5). This, he argued, was hardly a solution to the old problem of keeping a balance between the rights of the State and those of the individual, of reconciling order and freedom. By the time Donoso was writing the *Ensayo*, he had completely despaired of the ability of the 'balancing parties', ranging from the French *doctrinaires* to the Spanish *moderados*, to cope with change and continuity at the same time (Donoso 1851e: 187). He no longer believed that revolutionaries – or at least those advocating radical change – could be appeased by a policy of concessions. His dramatic example here was that of Pius IX who had been betrayed by same people he was trying to help; in Donoso's view, he had been crucified by the liberals in the same way that Jesus had been by the Jewish people (Donoso 1850c, *OC* II: 469). The lesson to be drawn, so the argument went, was that the crisis in the Papal States stemmed directly from Pius IX's efforts to find an accommodation with liberalism (Sánchez León 2020: 153).

The only foreseeable solution, according to Donoso, was the great synthesis offered by Catholicism, described as 'the science of balance' which was capable of reconciling 'all of the human theses and antitheses' (Donoso 1851e: 187, 218). Donoso's ideas on the social role played by religion crystallised were in the term 'Catholic civilisation'. This concept had already been developed by him in a letter sent to Montalembert from Berlin (Donoso 1849a, OC II: 324–8) and which, in hindsight, can be regarded as an anticipation of the *Ensayo*. Above all, the Catholic civilisation was a political ideal: sustained by two pillars, order and authority, which were kept in a perfect balance. Donoso would later stress that a Catholic society was necessarily free from both despotism and revolutions (Donoso 1851e: 187). It is important to stress that his concept of 'Catholic civilisation' was conceived of in opposition to that of a 'philosophical civilisation' according to which 'the solution to the great social problem lies in breaking all the bonds that constrict and restrain human reason and man's free will' (Donoso 1849a, *OC* II: 324–5). In doing so, Donoso undertook a 'semantic inversion' of the term civilisation: it lost its progressive connotation as bearer of the advances made in both science and culture, and acquired a defensive one, linked to an alleged need to protect both religion and its institutions from the onslaught of revolution and modern ideas (Fernández Sebastián 2014b: 211).

In affirming that Catholicism was the root of Europe's identity and its *raison d'être*, Donoso was in a sense returning to an old debate on the validity of Guizot's *Histoire de la civilisation en Europe [History of European Civilisation]* (1828), and his comments on Spain and the Catholic world in general. In the *Ensayo*, Donoso challenged Guizot's idea of Europe as based upon plurality – in terms of culture, classes and world-views – and proposed instead a monistic ideal, centred upon the ability of Catholicism to act as the ingredient that gave harmony, unity and coherence to the whole:

> European civilisation was not called Germanic, nor Roman, nor absolutist, nor feudal: it was and is called Catholic civilisation. [...] Catholicism is not, then, as Mr. Guizot supposes, only one of the various elements that came into the composition of that admirable civilisation: it is more than that, even much more than that: it is that civilisation itself (Donoso 1851e: 66–7)

Finally, through his rejection of Guizot, Donoso was able to coincide fully with Balmes in a crucial conviction, namely that European civilisation was necessarily Catholic in character. Donoso, in his *Ensayo sobre el catolicismo, el liberalismo y el socialismo [Essay on Catholicism, liberalism and socialism]* (1851) and Balmes, in his *El protestantismo comparado con el catolicismo en sus relaciones con la civilización europea [Protestantism compared to Catholicism in its Relation to European Civilisation]* (1844), shared a common refusal not only to endorse a secular interpretation of European history but also to envisage its future in non-religious terms. Nonetheless, a key difference remains between them: whereas Balmes – and the *first* Donoso – were still working towards the reconciliation between Catholicism and modern civilisation, the starting point of the *later* Donoso was precisely the impossibility of such a reconciliation (Fernández Sebastián 1997: 141–3). In this sense, Donoso's ideal of a Catholic civilisation was impaired insofar as it lacked a progressive character: rather than an ideal to strive forward, it supposed an interpretation of the past. It was not comparable, for instance, to Balmes' idea of civilisation, one which brought Catholicism together with a concern about redistributive justice – namely, as a rule to follow in present and future circumstances. The political ideal that Donoso thought was inseparable from Catholic civilisation consisted of the following elements: a hereditary monarchy and a hierarchical society, both taking their principles from the Church (Donoso 1852b, *OC* II: 769–70).

Often bordering on idealization, Donoso's descriptions of the Church were used to prove the (dubious) point that, in the restless nineteenth-century, it was still the only society that was free from revolutionary turmoil: 'at the present time, only the Church offers the spectacle of an orderly society' (Donoso 1852b, *OC* II: 765). Bypassing the need for reform and changes that would allow the Church to stand on a common footing with modern civilisation, Donoso expressed his ideal of the Church with reference to the Middle Ages, a period when its doctrinal intransigence had allegedly saved the world from chaos (Donoso 1851e: 26). Things had changed radically, so Donoso's argument went, with the advent of Protestantism. As Balmes had done before him, Donoso would refer to the sixteenth-century Reformation as *the* major turning point in European history, and posited a link between religious heresy and political revolution:

What has saved the world so far is that the Church was in ancient times powerful enough to extirpate heresies. [...] The real danger to human societies began on the day when the heresy of the sixteenth century obtained the right of citizenship in Europe. Since then there has been no revolution which does not suppose a mortal danger for society. This consists in the fact that all revolutions are founded on the Protestant heresy, and are therefore fundamentally heretical; see, if not, how they all come to justify and legitimise themselves with words and maxims taken from the Gospel (Donoso 1851e: 201).

One of the *Ensayo*'s most enduring legacies would be Donoso's powerful reformulation of the reactionary commonplace: the causal link that existed between 'religious error' and 'political error'; in other words, the idea that heresy, arising from the exercise of free judgement outside the guidance of

184   SPAIN AND CATHOLIC EUROPE

the Church, was the prelude to revolution (Urigüen 1986: 60). Eighteenth-century reactionaries had already been keen to emphasise the common spirit of rebellion – against the authority of the Church and the State – that ran from the Reformation to the Enlightenment and from the Enlightenment to the French Revolution. In a similar way, the idea that reformers often employed religious language in order to hide their 'impious' intentions, such as the desire expressed by sixteenth-century Protestants and eighteenth-century *ilustrados* to purify religious practices, was not new (Herrero 1971: 86–9, 92–4). Donoso updated and modernised this reactionary myth when, with long-lasting consequences, he added both socialists and communists to the list of those who invoked the Gospel in order to justify revolution. It might be wrong, however, to consider this chain of historical associations as *passé*, considering that a twentieth-century commentator of Balmes and Donoso still felt entitled to trace a line of causation between the sixteenth-century reformer Martin Luther and the 'diabolical rule' of Adolf Hitler four centuries later (Menczer 1952: 185).

Finally, in order to place Donoso's ideas into perspective, I will analyse the most significant responses given to the *Ensayo* within Spain. Despite his newly won European reputation, Donoso's fame was far from being indisputable in his home country. As Sánchez León documents, the progressive liberals' press staged a veritable witch hunt against Donoso, thus mocking his novel reputation as 'celebrity ideologue' and 'prophet of Extremadura' (2020: 194–195). Not surprisingly, the critique of Donoso's work was brought in relation to an issue that was crucial in Spain: the role of religion in public life. As a result, an immediate response to Donoso were the *Veinte y seis cartas al Señor Marqués de Valdegamas, en contestación a los veinte y seis capítulos de su Ensayo* [*Twenty-six letters to Mr. Marquis of Valdegamas, reply to the twenty-six chapters of his Essay*] (1851) by Nicomedes Mateos, spiritualist philosopher and admirer of René Descartes. This book began with a letter addressed to the *progresista* party, written with a tone of warning: 'today, my friends, ultramontanism and theocracy have once again joined forces against liberalism' (Mateos 1851: viii). Mateos opposed what he believed to be Donoso's idea of the Church, insofar it had a strong inclination towards Ultramontanism – a Catholic school of thought that, in matters of spirituality but also governance, upheld the supremacy of the Pope over that of the civil authorities (Perreau-Saussine 2011: 49). If anything, Mateos argued, this showed that Donoso had borrowed too heavily from the works of French traditionalist writers, such as *Du Pape [On the Pope]* by De Maistre (1819), proving that 'your doctrine is only new in Spain, where you want to disseminate it [...] it is taken from Mr. De-Maistre' (Mateos 1851: 42).

Despite his criticism of the institutional Church, Mateos did not intend to exclude religion from Spain's public life. He conceived of his ideas as a continuation of the spirit of the deputies of the Cortes of Cádiz (1810–1812) who had already insisted upon the need to *spiritualise* the Church by separating religious from political concerns (Mateos 1851: viii-ix). In addition, Mateos also drew his ideas from French sources, namely the ideal of social Catholicism espoused by Jean-Baptiste Bordas-Demoulin and François Huet (Jiménez 1992: 229–30). Theirs was an explicit attempt to reconcile Catholicism with modern civilisation; for example, Huet would write that striving towards the freedom and equality of all men was a genuinely Christian concern, comparable to the salvation of the soul, because Christianity ought to bring about the redemption of men in both heaven and earth (Bordas-Demoulin 1856: 1–17). Yet instead of entrusting this mission to the institutional Church, Bordas-Demoulin and Huet spoke highly of the role played by the 'intelligent laymen' and went as far as to recommend the separation of Church and State, justifying their views as follows: 'the tolerant and liberal law is not an atheistic law; it is only atheocratic, which is quite different. It excludes the priest and not God, and it excludes him, not from the Church, but from the State' (Bordas-Demoulin 1856: 8).

How did Mateos, as a progressive liberal, vindicate liberalism in the face of Donoso's attacks? Curiously, he did so by insisting upon the religious content of liberalism. Its theological foundation was to be found in a concept of natural rights: notions of liberty, fraternity and equality inscribed by God in every human understanding (Mateos 1851: 115). Contrary to Donoso who had questioned the efficacy of the political reforms carried out by liberal regimes, Mateos was convinced that institutions were more powerful than men, and that the common good did not depend solely upon the moral qualities of individuals. Moreover, Mateos not only thought that Donoso's choice of language was *démodé*, as his apocalyptic threats were unlikely to move a nineteenth-century audience, but that so too was his proposed remedy. Human passions would not be contained by cautionary sermons, but by the development of civil liberties capable of reconciling the common good with individual freedoms (Mateos 1851: 130–1). Finally, Mateos argued that Donoso had chosen too easy a target when discussing socialism: Proudhon's 'exaggerated doctrines' were far from being unanimously accepted among all socialists (Mateos 1851: 139). This remark was fully justified in the late 1840s by the actual disagreements between Proudhon and Karl Marx on how to avoid pauperism and inequality, but especially on how to bring about a profound transformation of the prevailing productive relations (Stedman Jones 2016: 194–196).

A second reply to Donoso appeared a year later, after the publication of his *Ensayo*. This was *El socialismo y la teocracia [Socialism and Theocracy]* (1852), written by the Catalan lawyer José Frexas, who described himself as 'semi-philosopher in the morning; very often a lyric artist in the evening' (Frexas 1852: I-II). Seeking to discredit Donoso, Frexas chose the corruption prevalent in the regime of the *moderados* as his main target. He believed that both the civil and religious authorities of Spain had forgotten their mission; as a result, he despaired about both the Church and the political elite. Close to radical liberalism, Frexas wrote nostalgically about the austere Christian spirit of the first centuries, which he saw as incompatible with ecclesiastical riches and superstitious practices (Frexas 1852: I, 3) In Spain, he argued, an oligarchic government had turned politics into a 'system of intrigues and passions', while religion had become nothing but a 'series of exploitative policies' in the hands of a materialistic clergy (Frexas 1852, I: vi). Corruption was, according to Frexas, Spain's main problem – and not that it had embraced liberalism, as Donoso had argued in his speeches and in the *Ensayo*. The problem was not that a deliberative Cortes existed, but that it was dominated by deputies of dubious moral and intellectual quality, at least in Frexas' opinion: 'the ailment, the rot, the deadly gangrene, I will repeat it incessantly, does not stem from discussion itself, but from the poor quality of those who engage in it' (Frexas 1842: I, 47–8). Frexas' disappointment extended to political parties, who he described as being 'sects' that claimed to stand for 'public opinion' or 'national thought'. Here he was directing a negative comment on *El Pensamiento de la Nación [The Thought of the Nation]* (1844–1846), and he further described Balmes more as a 'politician' than a 'philosopher' because he had acted and written interestedly for the benefit of the Church (Frexas 1852: I, vii-viii).

The last of the Spanish responses to the *Ensayo* must be read taking into account a special circumstance: the premature death of Donoso in May 1853, when he was forty-four, allegedly due to the painful complications of syphilis at a terminal stage (Graham 1974: 304). His successor in seat 'R' of the Real Academia Española was Rafael María Baralt who, in his inaugural speech, paid homage to Donoso. Born in Venezuela, Baralt was the first Hispanic American to occupy such position, having won a reputation as man of letters in Spain during the 1840s (Julián 2012: 64–65). It can be argued that Baralt, a liberal with progressive and democratic inclinations, chose a peculiar strategy to discredit Donoso's ideas in the *Ensayo*: he argued that Donoso could be regarded neither in terms of literature or philosophy as part of the Spanish tradition. In consequence, he strongly advised *against* furthering Donoso's political message, which he reduced to two words: 'absolutism' and 'theocracy' that were neither Spanish nor Christian, but rather a foreign doctrine (Baralt 1860, II: 15, 33). In his view, the turn that Donoso had taken at the end of his life, marked by the desire to maintain social order and religious dogma at all costs, could only be attributed to the influence of French traditionalists such as De Maistre and Bonald.

Baralt did, however, acknowledge the power of rhetoric in Donoso's work, sharing his first-hand impressions on the paradoxical results of Donoso's eloquence: on the one hand, it created awe-inspiring effects and captivated its listeners; on the other, this sense of awe obscured the actual content of his ideas. This is how Baralt described the reactions to Donoso's speeches in the Cortes:

There was a certain sweet sympathy which the speaker used to inspire in most of his listeners: from his former political comrades, because the ideas which they held in regard to religious reaction were wonderfully in accord with those which they professed, and still profess, in matters of State; to his ultra-liberal adversaries, because they rejoiced in the inflamed anathemas which he directed against mixed parties; to the champions of the divine right of kings, because he defended their doctrine with unusual vehemence. Those of us who loved him, without going into his meaning, saw the man in the orator, and people who were strangers to politics gave tribute only through their wit, making doctrines take second place to eloquence, and the solidity of proofs and judgement to the delicate and showy filigree of voices with which he dressed his thoughts (Baralt 1860, II: 27).

The extremism of Donoso's views, as Baralt concluded, ended up serving a variety of purposes: it justified the *moderados'* renewed alliance with the Church, it gave new arguments to the *progresistas'* criticism of the *moderado* party, and it even strengthened the monarchist convictions of the Carlists. The next section will analyse further the European projection of Donoso's ideas, taking into account the fact that his post as Spanish ambassador in Paris became a platform for spreading his ideas among those with similar clerical and conservative views. After his death, the controversial aspects of his thought remained controversial, with the only difference that they would be distorted not only by both apologies and attacks, but also by adaptation to new contexts. Despite equivocal interpretations, nevertheless, two features of Donoso's thought would loom large in successive adaptations: the justification of dictatorship in extreme circumstances, and the Church's active involvement in political affairs.

IV. The return to order & authority

In a letter addressed to an unknown person, written around 1850, Donoso made the following confession: 'I stand with one foot in the world, and with another in loneliness; with one in politics, with another in religion, my soul thus turning into a sea of confusion' (Donoso 1850e, *OC* II: 477). This confession illustrates the way in which Donoso found himself increasingly at odds with a world which he had characterised as being hopelessly corrupt. In the *Ensayo* (1851), he had spoken of breaking away from such a world and bringing about instead the return of the timeless Catholic values. Despite occasional mystical overtones and his own world-weariness, Donoso did not encourage his readers to seek refuge in an ascetic ideal. In his view, preserving Catholicism from the onslaught of revolution required the active commitment of both Church and believers – notwithstanding, as the above quoted letter suggests, the compromises and moral dilemmas involved.

A key consideration to make is that, at every stage of his intellectual development, Donoso's ideas were accompanied by a practical political project. His last political venture was facilitated by his position as Spanish ambassador in Paris (1851–1853). The publication of the *Ensayo* in 1851 – it appeared simultaneously in Madrid and Paris, in Spanish and French respectively – turned Donoso into a celebrity (Schramm 1936: 240). Even before this happened, and thanks to the European reputation that his speeches had afforded him, Donoso could boast: 'in Paris, there has never been a foreign diplomat received by all classes of society, and especially by the upper classes, as I have been' (Donoso 1851b, *OC*, II: 705). A few months later, Donoso wrote to his former pupil Gabino Tejado about the success of the *Ensayo*: 'my book [...] has caused an explosion' (Donoso 1851c, *OC* II: 716). In fact, the *Ensayo* became an international best-seller: in 1852, it was translated into Italian; in 1854, into German and again in Italian; in 1858–1859, it was translated again into French in an edition curated by Veuillot; and in 1862 and in 1874, it was translated into English in the US and Ireland, respectively (González Cuevas 2015: 155).

In France during the early 1850s, Donoso was soon able to enjoy the confidence of the monarchists, both Legitimists and Orleanists of the party of order, and of the clerical Catholic party. In addition, he attended salons and made contact with a variety of personalities including the historian and politician François Guizot, the statesman Victor de Broglie, the liberal Catholic publicist Charles de Montalembert, the scholar and journalist Frédéric Ozanam, the ultramontane journalist Louis Veuillot, the philosopher and historian Alexis de Tocqueville, the statesman Jean-Gilbert Fialin Duke of Persigny, the Jesuit preacher Gustave Delacroix de Ravignan, among others (Graham 1974: 192–3). Louis Napoleon Bonaparte, then president of the Second French Republic, preferred Donoso to other diplomats. Donoso, in turn, expected Louis Napoleon to overcome the revolutionary crisis and to create a new conservative social order that could serve as a model for the rest of Europe (Graham 1974: 188, 191). By the end of 1851, when Louis Napoleon decided to consolidate his position with a *coup d'état*, a move that made him emperor of the French with the title of Napoleon III, Donoso supported him, both ideologically and financially, advancing his own money to the cause (Graham 1974: 199). It might be added that, in supporting a political project that Wilson aptly described as a 'crowned dictatorship', Donoso mirrored the sympathies that Louis Napoleon had raised among moderate liberals in Spain. As Pro argues, Paris was an important location within the tight network of economic and political interests managed by the *moderado* party's leadership in conjunction with the Spanish royal family. Already in 1849, Narváez – then government premier – lent a very substantial sum to Louis Napoleon; in early 1851, when Narváez resigned from the post, partly due to the wave of wrath brought on by Donoso's famous speech on Spain in December 1850, he was nevertheless given a warm welcome in France (Pro 2007: 45).

Throughout 1851, Donoso's sympathies for the cause of Louis Napoleon were consistently expressed in his communications to Madrid: in October, he defended dictatorship as the necessary remedy for France's actual circumstances, adding that a dictator had the right to seek power from the masses. He explained that, in a private interview, he had recommended Louis Napoleon to take the following course of action: to base his authority on the strength afforded by universal suffrage, to then annul it, and then dissolve 'revolutionary institutions' such as the National Assembly (Graham 1974: 199–201). The *coup d'état* took place began on the night of the 1st of December and culminated on the day of the 2nd, when two anniversaries were celebrated: the battle of Austerlitz and the coronation of Napoleon I. These coincidences would give rise to Marx's famous remark on the similarities between the man he called the Uncle (Napoleon) and the Nephew (Louis Napoleon): 'Hegel says somewhere that great historic facts and personages recur twice. He forgot to add: "Once as a tragedy, and again as farce"' (Marx 1852: 15).

Yet Donoso was not alone in his support of Louis Napoleon, in considering him as an 'instrument of providence' (Donoso 1851d, *OC* II: 952–3). Most French Catholics, ranging from the ultramontane right to the moderate centre, preferred Louis Napoleon to the alternative, a government of the anticlerical left (Chadwick 1998: 97). A plebiscite confirmed the legitimacy of Louis Napoleon who, in that precise moment, seemed to be the answer to the anxiety of the middle classes. Despite the fact that his enthusiasm for Louis Napoleon was short-lived, Montalembert thus publicly proclaimed his support in early December: 'To vote for the prince is to arm the power to quell the army of crime, to defend your churches, your homes, your women' (Graham 1974: 207–8). Several bishops encouraged their flocks to vote 'yes'; after all, Pius IX had welcomed the news of the *coup d'état*, an attitude echoed by the French ecclesiastical hierarchy.

Despite the relatively smooth ascent of Louis Napoleon, a moral dilemma remained unsolved. As Chadwick notes, it would keep reappearing in the nineteenth and twentieth centuries: the question was, what should be the Church's attitude to a *coup d'état*? (1998: 98). It is possible to argue that Donoso believed that the Church could not remain aloof from political affairs and was actually responsible for finding the best way to protect its interests. It would therefore be the duty of both priests and believers to make a conscious choice between government and revolution, and between religion and other competing ideologies such as socialism. This aspect of Donoso's thought can be illustrated by his appraisal of what became known as the Falloux Law in France, approved in early 1850 after several months of controversy. It brought about a thorough reform of the education system, based upon two principles: freedom of private education, giving free rein to schools run by the Church, and influence by the Church on the education system of the State (Aubert 1981: 69).

The Falloux Law was a great victory for the French Church, as it put an end to the state monopoly of education which, for the past forty years, had been kept under the control of the University and of state-formed teachers, who were now under suspicion of spreading socialist, republican or anticlerical ideas. This law was mainly the result of the efforts of Catholic liberals such as the bishop Félix Dupanloup and the publicist Montalembert. Yet it failed to satisfy the most intransigent Catholics such as the ultramontane Veuillot, who argued that this law meant for the Church an official renunciation of its claims to the monopoly of education which it had had under the Old Regime (Aubert 1981: 70). As Aubert notes, the discussions among French Catholics were so intense that the Pope intervened and urged the episcopate to accept the law. Donoso followed the process closely and supported position of intransigents. He would eventually declare that freedom of teaching was a 'false principle', completely unacceptable to the Church (Donoso 1852a, OC II: 761). In a letter dated July 1850 and addressed to the Duke of Valmy, French statesman and diplomat, Donoso strongly encouraged the Church's involvement in political matters:

I will frankly confess to you that I am appalled to see the path that a certain part of the French clergy has taken. Under the pretext of not wishing to make the Church sympathetic to a political party or to a particular form of government, they are trying to throw it into an adventurous path. How can these wretches not see that this path will inevitably lead to a catastrophe? [...] Our Lord has threatened that those who are ashamed to confess Him on Earth will be disregarded in Heaven (Donoso 1850c, OC II: 469).

According to Donoso's ideal of a militant clergy, it made more sense for the Church to support Christian politicians than to maintain its independence at all costs. One year before his death, Donoso's political programme could be summed up thus: 'coexistence between Church and State' (Donoso 1852a, OC II: 759). The contrast here with Balmes is significant. As shown in Chapter 3, Balmes constantly made the point that a politically-engaged clergy would not only jeopardise the spiritual mission of the Church but would also affect its workings as an institution. But even if Balmes' death was still very recent, circumstances had changed dramatically: in the 1850s, the Church was no longer in danger and therefore had no need to make compromises. In the long run, Donoso's views would take precedent over those of Balmes, a shift facilitated by developments taking place both within Spain, as the Concordat of 1851 laid the foundation for the Church's restoration, and within the rest of Catholic Europe, as the short-lived liberalism of Pius IX gave way to an increasingly intransigent stance. It might be added that in 1857, thanks to the so called Moyano Law, the Church in Spain was able to establish its own education system, in parallel to that of the State (Suárez Cortina 2017: 70).

It has been claimed that in the early 1850s, the ideas of Donoso, who was then living in France, did not exercise any significant influence in Spain; in other words, that there was not a well-defined political group interested in adopting and promoting his ideas (Garrido Muro 2015: 56–57). But in reality, Donoso was a key source of inspiration behind the projected constitutional reform of the government of Juan Bravo Murillo (1851–1852). This reform envisaged a radical alteration of the Spanish political system, designed to curtail the influence of both Cortes and political parties while strengthening the executive power of the monarch (Burdiel 2010: 237–238). Its goals and motivation were publicised in a pro-government newspaper, *El Orden*, whose editor was Gabino Tejado, a disciple of Donoso (Urigüen 1981: 98–99). Bravo Murillo's projected reform bore a strongly authoritarian character, echoing features of Napoleon III, and was conceived of as a radical remedy against the perceived shortcomings of a parliamentary system. Convinced that political parties were responsible for fostering discord and unrest, Bravo Murillo sought to affirm the independence of the public administration from politics, famously arguing before the Cortes that 'if there is a sacrifice to be made, then politics must be sacrificed to the administration, but never the administration to politics' (Comellas 1970: 311–9). If approved, however, the reform would have granted total impunity to the royal family and its *moderado* allies, freeing their profitable businesses and corrupt deals from any accountability vis-à-vis the Cortes or the press (Pro 2007: 54–55).

Having failed to obtain the approval of the Cortes for his reform, Bravo Murillo resigned. His immediate successors, General Federico Roncali (December 1852 to April 1853) and General Francisco Lersundi (April to September 1853), persisted in these illiberal attempts to reform Spain's constitutional system. They were able to count on the sympathies of the royal family, as well as on the support of right-wing *moderados*, such as the Marquis of Viluma and his brother general Pezuela (Urigüen 1984: 88–9). The projects of Roncali and Lersundi, albeit milder than what was pursued by Bravo Murillo, had the paradoxical effect of uniting the opposition to their regimes. Claiming that they were defending the continued existence of constitutional government in Spain, the opposition was now composed of the majority of the *moderados*, as well as progressive and radical liberals, including members of the Democratic Party (Partido Demócrata) – a party founded in 1849 that carried on the unfinished agenda of the 1848 Revolutions in Spain (García de Paso 2016: 199–200). Although the unpopular General Lersundi was succeeded in late 1853 by the government of Luis José

Sartorius, who momentarily was able to quell the opposition, it became evident that the relationship between the monarchy and liberalism was as complicated as ever.

During the last years of the *moderado* decade of power, the political game seemed caught in the dilemma of choosing between what were seen as mutually exclusive options: that the revolution might tame the monarchy, or that the monarchy might be tamed by the revolution (Burdiel 2010: 245–246). It was clear that the royal family still felt uncomfortable with constitutional government, namely with the idea that sovereignty, the ultimate justification of their power to rule, was something to be shared with the Cortes. A perfect illustration of this is a letter that Donoso wrote to the Count Athanasius Raczyński, then ambassador of Prussia in France. Writing in December 1852, Donoso explained how the Queen Mother had always hoped for the 'death of parliamentarism' but had never trusted herself to carry out the required task (Letter from Donoso to Raczyński, 21-XII-1852, cit. by Urigüen 1981: 89). She had therefore given support to the project of Bravo Murillo, who could conveniently claim that he was acting out of pure necessity. However, as Donoso concluded, when Bravo Murillo fell from power, she did nothing to rescue him, fearful that she would share his fate and lose whatever influence she might have within the regime.

The revolution of 1854 would stem, according to Burdiel, from the widespread realization that the Crown had become a threat to liberalism in Spain (2010: 298). Amalgamating a variety of opposition forces, from left-wing moderates to progressive liberals, from democrats to republicans, this revolution opened the way to the Progressive Biennium (1854–1856). For those who shared the views of Donoso, the revolution of 1854 was the 'deluge' described by the *Ensayo* with reference to 1848, and which had – finally and fatally – arrived in Spain (Urigüen 1981: 100). In fact, it was during the Biennium that the followers of Donoso constituted a distinctive political grouping, the so-called *neocatólicos*, as it will be discussed in the last section of this chapter.

One year before his death in 1853, the influence of Donoso proved to be decisive in another realm: the doctrinal re-orientation of Pope Pius IX, whose increasing intransigence was an attempt at coming to terms with the experiences of 1848–1849. Since the early 1850s, within the most conservative sectors of the Curia, the project of issuing a condemnation of all modern ideas regarded as erroneous gained ground (Aubert 1981: 294–5). The first stage of the project consisted of a series of consultations among eminent Catholics, both ecclesiastics and laymen. In May 1852, Cardinal Fornari, papal nuncio at Paris, requested on behalf of Pius IX statements from both Donoso and Veuillot about erroneous modern ideas (Graham 1974: 296; Cárdenas 2015: 729). In his reply to Fornari, Donoso argued that all erroneous ideas stemmed from two *negations*: 'society denies that God cares for his creatures, and that man was conceived in sin' (Donoso 1852a, OC II: 747). He also blurred the lines between religious and political discourse, arguing that 'among contemporary errors there is not a single one that does not result from heresy' (Donoso 1852a, OC II: 744). The confusion, involuntary or not, between what were contingent circumstances – such as the form of government – and truths that were deemed to be absolute and eternal – on the nature of God and men – led Donoso to reject parliamentary monarchies, division of powers, freedom of press, republicanism, universal suffrage and socialist doctrines. As a rule of thumb, he considered every 'political mistake' to be the consequence of a 'religious mistake':

In recent times, the main religious error consists in affirming the independence and sovereignty of human reason; the expression of this religious error in the political order consists in asserting the sovereignty of the intelligence, seen as the universal foundation of public law in the societies who fell victims to the first revolutions. [...] The second error concerns the will, and consists, as far as the religious order is concerned, in affirming that free will is essentially right, and thus does not need to be led but can lead itself. This is the principle on which universal suffrage is founded, and it has also been the origin of the republican system. [...] The third error concerns the appetites, and consists in affirming, as regards the religious order, that men who were conceived immaculately are driven by essentially good impulses; to this error in the religious order corresponds in the political order the belief that governments must fulfil a single end: the satisfaction of all concupiscence; on this all the socialist and demagogic systems principle are founded, which today strive for domination and which, following their natural course, will necessarily lead us downhill (Donoso 1852a, OC II: 755–6).

The consultation made by Pius IX in 1852 with Donoso and others paved the way in 1860 for the first draft of the *Syllabus errorum in Europa vigentium*, one of the most famous documents ever issued by the Papacy. Two years later, Pius IX asked a number of bishops for their opinion – a third of the 159 who replied were against the project – which was now incorporated into a second draft consisting of 61 propositions. This draft was leaked and aroused a great deal of controversy in the press (Chadwick 1998: 169). The commission in charge nevertheless continued to work. In 1863 two events brought the problem to the forefront again: first, speaking to a a broad audience at an international congress of Catholics in Belgium, the French publicist Montalembert defended his ideal of a 'free Church in a free State' while exhorting his fellow-believers not to be afraid of democracy and freedom; second, the professor of Church history at Munich, Ignaz von Döllinger, asserted the independence of Catholic scholarship from the ecclesiastical magisterial office (Aubert 1981: 294–5; Chadwick 1998: 170–3). Despite these discordant opinions, a *Syllabus errorum* was published as an appendix to the encyclical *Quanta Cura* in 1864. It consisted of 80 unacceptable propositions, including: pantheism, naturalism, rationalism, indifferentism, socialism, communism, denial of the Church's right to exercise temporal power and to own property, the State's monopoly of education, separation of Church and State, the right to rebel against the government, and freedom of religion. For the *Syllabus*, modern civilisation was unacceptable insofar as it affirmed society's independence from the Church and declared the self-sufficiency of human reason, while upholding the primacy of material progress, political freedom and absolute liberty of conscience. In particular, it centred its attacks upon all revolutions, seen as one and the same, namely as the sum of all evils (Cárdenas 2015: 732).

It is open to speculation what the reaction of Jaime Balmes would have been to the path of doctrinal intransigence taken by his admired Pope Pius IX. As Fradera stresses, Balmes fought constantly for the independence of the Spanish Church, an independence that he understood mainly as freedom from governmental interference, but he was nonetheless convinced that the Church stood in a relation of both dependence and obedience to Rome (Fradera 1996: 289). If he had been alive between the 1850s and 1870s, Balmes possibly would have preferred accommodation to confrontation with Rome, while seizing the opportunities that the Concordat afforded the Spanish Catholic Church to rebuild itself. Yet the Romanization of the Catholic Church was a much more complex process than doctrinal intransigence, as later epitomized in the declaration of Papal infallibility in the First Vatican Council (1869–1870), suggests. There were two sides to the coin: Papal supremacy on the one hand, and the globalization of Catholicism on the other (Ramón Solans 2020: 157). During this period, the Papacy acquired a heightened role as the point of confluence of increasingly active transnational networks. Despite the eventual annexation of the Papal States to the Kingdom in Italy (1870), the Pope went from being 'the head of an old feudal state' to becoming a 'global soft power' (Ramón Solans 2020: 164). In fact, the second half of the nineteenth-century was the heyday of 'devotional activism' in Catholic Europe, of which Spain was of course no exception, a veritable revival that combined the militant efforts of both the clergy and the laity (Schaefer 2014: 274–275).

Yet regardless of what happened *after* his death, what is really remarkable about Balmes is that – writing in the tumultuous 1840s – he was still able to find ways to distance himself from the obsession of his contemporaries with ideas such as revolution, transition, crisis, progress and other 'colossal events' (Balmes 1880: 105). It is understandable that, as a Catholic priest, he could entertain no doubts about the ability of the Church to survive yet another crisis. What is less self-evident, in a context marked by the growing polarisation of opinions, is that Balmes could achieve a balance between doctrinal orthodoxy and rational insight. In his view, both the friends and enemies of historical change needed to acknowledge that instability was a permanent feature in human affairs. Yet Balmes, in sharp contrast with most conservative and traditionalist thinkers, neither expressed nostalgia for the past nor any fear regarding the future:

All the revolutions that may come, in the end, can bring about no other result than to alter the position and relations of individuals and classes. Suppose whatever changes you will, you will hardly imagine any in property, or in the organisation of labour, or in the distribution of its products, or in domestic condition, or in social rank, or in political influence, that are of greater importance and magnitude than those which have taken place in previous ages. Transition has existed as it exists now; European nations have passed incessantly through different states. [...] Where is the power of feudalism, of the nobility and of the clergy? What became of the prerogatives, the privileges, the honours they enjoyed? [...] We think differently, we feel differently, we act differently, we live differently. [...] I would like to infer from this that, when great changes in the organisation of peoples are announced to us, we should not be reluctant to believe them for the sole reason that they seem very strange to us, because, even if we look closely, the present society is no less different from previous ones that of the future would be from the present one, in the various combinations that can be conceived and tried out. is one of the distinguishing characters of human things; and little thought has been given to the nature of man, and the one who prognosticates too much duration to that which is of itself so weak and so contemptible shows he has profited little from the lessons of history and experience. Whether society is under a revolutionary or a conservative power, whether one tries to push it forward or to stop it, it is always changing, constantly passing from one state to another, sometimes better, sometimes worse (Balmes 1880: 105–8).

V. Afterlives

In 1854, a revolution brought the *progresistas* into power, thus putting an end to the decade in power of the *moderados*. During the Progressive Biennium (1854–1856), the possibility of introducing religious freedom in Spain was discussed for the first time in the country's history and in May 1855, new legislation allowed the sale of Church properties again, leading to a break in relations with the Holy See (Urigüen 1986: 106; Tomás y Valiente 1978: 28–9). A group known as the *neocatólicos* (neo-Catholics or new Catholics) emerged in reaction to these developments, which they saw as posing a threat to the country's Catholic unity, as well as being a violation of the 1851 Concordat (De la Cueva 2018: 279). This was the case of men such as Gabino Tejado, Juan Manuel Ortí y Lara, Antonio Aparisi y Guijarro, Francisco Navarro Villoslada and Cándido Nocedal (González Cuevas 2000: 127). Writing in newspapers such as *La Regeneración [The Regeneration]* (founded in 1855) and especially in *El Pensamiento Español [The Spanish Thought]* (founded in 1860), the *neocatólicos* spoke vehemently both against liberalism and in favour of Catholicism, which they presented as the very foundation of Spanish national identity (Romeo 2015: 139–140).

The *neos* saw themselves as the natural followers of Donoso. This was especially the case of his former disciple Tejado, who oversaw the first edition of Donoso's complete works in 1854–1855 (González Cuevas 2015: 154–155). In general terms, the *neocatólicos* were derivative rather than original in their thought, and often compensated for their lack of original ideas by an excess of aggressive zeal (López Morillas 2010: 41). They succeeded in adapting Donoso's legacy to serve their own ends, that of fighting what they regarded as being the latest incarnation of the revolutionary danger: democracy. Viewed as the culmination of the individualism associated with the liberal society of citizens, democracy appeared in the eyes of the *neocatólicos* as incompatible with their own idea of an organic and corporative society – which, in its turn, was far more an idealization of the past than a reflection of it. But we can take a good example of how the rhetoric deployed by *neocatólicos* was aimed deliberately at mixing the religious with the political, while playing all the variations in the theme of a revolution, in a speech that Moreno Nieto delivered in the Cortes in order to oppose the course taken by the *progresista* government:

Gentlemen, who is the doctor, the supreme teacher, the apostle of the February revolution [1848]? Proudhon, the man who said: God does not exist, or if he does exist, that God is Satan. And until now it can be said that democracy has almost accepted this ungodly phrase. That is to say that its tendency is to destroy all the principles proclaimed by Catholic civilisation. And in its turn, the school representing Catholic civilisation has declared: freedom is evil. Today they stand face to face, without a trace of thinking of deals or alliances. Will this confrontation and this struggle last forever, gentlemen? Some say yes: and if you do not, remember the gloomy words Mr. Donoso Cortés uttered in prophetic tones, saying: between these two civilisations [the Catholic and the philosophical] there is an unfathomable abyss, an antagonism that will be eternal (Assembly 1855: 279).

This attitude of all-or-nothing, as shown in the conviction that Catholicism could not and must not enter into any sort of transaction with modern ideas, was the key characteristic of the *neocatólicos* – who, it might be added, were at the same time often decidedly modern in matters of economics and administration (Romeo 2011: 154). The intransigence of the *neocatólicos* received, albeit indirectly, the blessing of the Pope on the publication of the *Syllabus* (1864). In the early 1860s, they then directed their efforts at fighting the allegedly erroneous doctrines of *krausismo*, a philosophical school popular among forward-looking Spaniards, especially those associated with progressive liberalism. The *krausistas* drew their inspiration from Carl Christian Friedrich Krause (1781–1832), whose ideas were considered to pave the way towards the gradual secularization and liberalization of Spanish society (González Cuevas 2000: 125–7). *Krausismo* did not exclude religious concerns, although had a pantheistic outlook, but was regarded as being essentially heterodox – something that Balmes had already indicated in his *Fundamental Philosophy* [*Filosofía fundamental*] (Balmes 1846e: IV, 234). The campaign orchestrated by the *neocatólicos* against the *krausistas*, which had the support of both Pius IX and the government of General Narváez, soon bore fruit. In 1864, the government forbade university professors from expressing ideas which ran against the Concordat and the monarchy. In 1868, a decree by the Minister of Education Marquis of Orovio announced the dismissal of those who taught 'anti-Catholic and anti-monarchic doctrines', as in the case of professors Julián Sanz del Río, Nicolás Salmerón and Francisco Giner de los Ríos (González Cuevas 2000: 134–6).

However vocal they were, the *neocatólicos* were not representative of all Spanish Catholics. In the following decades, Catholics in Spain could be roughly divided according to their loyalties, either to the Carlist pretenders or to the ruling monarchs, and also according to their differing degrees of willingness to engage with liberal institutions and parliamentary politics. In the case of the *neocatólicos*, they remained faithful to Isabel II until the Glorious Revolution (1868) forced her to abdicate. Then during the Democratic Sexennium (1868–1874), the *neocatólicos* attempted a rapprochement with the Carlists (González Cuevas 2015: 156). One of their first steps in this direction was the creation in 1868 of an Asociación de Católicos (Association of Catholics) by the now elderly Marquis of Viluma. This association, which combined the forces of *neo* and Carlist leaders, collected thousands of signatures throughout Spain with the aim of protesting, albeit unsuccessfully, against the introduction of freedom of worship, a freedom which was recognised as an individual right by the Constitution of 1869. Some twenty years later, Viluma finally succeeded in his project of bringing Carlists and non-Carlists together, but this time with a major difference: those who in the 1840s were still able to pass as moderate liberals, had by this time given up their liberalism (Castro 2011: 65, 69). During the 1860s and early 1870s, militant Catholics and most of the Spanish Catholic Church would adhere to a staunch anti-liberalism, which they believed to be a just reaction against what they saw as the increasingly unacceptable challenges coming from the liberal State. An example of such a challenge was the Constitution of 1873, drafted after the proclamation of the First Spanish Republic (1873–1874), which included the separation of Church and State, although it was never promulgated.

In the 1876 Constitution, after a *coup d'état* that led to the restoration of the monarchy and the end of the Sexennium, the Catholic character of the Spanish State was reaffirmed and religious tolerance was maintained, albeit only within the private sphere (Suárez Cortina 2017: 73–4). This inaugurated a long period known as the Restoration, during which the Spanish Church 'was able to undertake its own restoration' (De la Cueva 2018: 279). During this period, mirroring many of the developments of the 1840s, Church-State relations were built upon a *quid pro quo*: the State needed clerical support to protect the monarchy of Alfonso XII from onslaughts coming from both the right and left, that is, from Carlists and from left-wing revolutionaries; the Church needed to have an some sort of accommodating relation with a moderate liberal regime as its best safeguard against a much-feared revolution from the left. This accommodation anticipated, in turn, the conciliatory policies espoused by Pope Leo XIII towards liberal regimes and nation-state projects, and which encouraged Catholics to participate in politics (Villalonga 2014: 312). Catholicism was reaffirmed as the official religion of the

State by the Constitution of 1876 although it did accept the practice of other religions under certain conditions.

During the Restoration, Catholicism continued to be the common denominator of the Spanish right, from conservative liberals to traditionalists (De la Cueva 2018: 280). At the same time, however, its most vociferous and anti-liberal currents tended to be excluded from political power. This was the case of the Carlists and the Integrists, members of the Partido Integrista (Integrist Party) founded in 1888 by Ramón Nocedal, son of Cándido, the *neocatólico* leader. In 1871, during an argument in the Cortes with the liberal Práxedes Mateo Sagasta, Nocedal was prompted to reveal the inspiration of his thought: he referred admiringly to De Maistre, Donoso Cortés and Balmes (Urigüen 1986: 54–5). But many disagreed with Nocedal's idea that these authors had espoused identical doctrines and had thus fought for the same causes, as was the case of Alejandro Pidal y Mon, son of Pedro José Pidal and nephew of Alejandro Mon, both distinguished *moderados*. Pidal famously referred to the legacy of Donoso as being a calamity, insofar as it had propitiated, among its followers, an abuse of rhetoric to the detriment of content:

Calamity, because [Donoso] founded a school, or better than a school, a conservatory of music and declamation, where a mob of vain orators and forgers of glittering anathemas learned their trade, still trying to solve the most arduous problems of religion and politics with a bombastic and pessimistic metaphor that, set against the ruins of society, only allows to perceive the mysterious and olympic depth of the prophetic genius that formulates it (Pidal y Mon 1889: 39).

In 1881, Pidal y Mon founded the Unión Católica (Catholic Union), a short-lived political party that aimed to unite all Spanish Catholics, following in the steps of the German Centre Party (Deutsche Zentrumspartei) that had been created in the context of Bismarck's *Kulturkampf* against Catholicism (Botti 2008: 72–73). However unsuccessful it was in attracting Carlists, Pidal's party did bring about a rapprochement with the liberal State and eventually joined the Partido Liberal-Conservador presided over by Antonio Cánovas del Castillo, architect of the Restoration (Álvarez Junco 2006: 61–62). The inspiration behind Pidal's project had been Balmes who, in the past, was viewed as one who pursued Catholic interests in the context of a liberal regime and using liberal means (Castro 2011: 74). This admiration for Balmes was also shared by Marcelino Menéndez y Pelayo, the rising star of the Catholic intelligentsia. Following in the steps of Balmes, Menéndez brought the identification between Spain and Catholicism a step further, giving the name of heterodox to any Spaniard who deviated from the Catholic norm, while vindicating Spain's cultural and scientific production from any accusation of backwardness (Botti 2008: 79; Campomar 1984: 80). But that is another story.

Conclusions

To tame the ongoing liberal revolution by infusing liberalism with an ecclesiastical and monarchical agenda – this was the role played by Balmes and Donoso during their lives. However keen they were to reduce or even eliminate the liberal component in Spanish politics, seen as being conducive to individualism, democracy and secularisation, the fact remains that they were as much part of the liberal revolution as any other of their contemporaries. Balmes and Donoso mastered the tools of liberalism to achieve their own objectives, which included, although not invariably, anti-liberal – or even illiberal – outcomes. González Cuevas concludes that Balmes represents the 'evolutive' type of traditionalist, in contrast to the 'intransigent' type of Donoso (2015: 146). Álvarez Junco concurs by affirming that, whereas Donoso was caught in a 'war against the modern world', Balmes was able to advance a much more 'modern formula' (2006: 54). Balmes' formula, which establishes a clear link between Catholicism and Spanish national identity, is often regarded as having paved the way for the twentieth-century National Catholicism that, by uniting the notions of the nation, Catholicism and the State, culminated in the Franco regime (1939–1975). Yet to posit Balmes (or Donoso) as the ideological godfathers of Franquismo is not merely simplistic; it is also inaccurate. To adopt this argument would be to transform trends and traits into ineluctable prophecies, and would simultaneously overlook the agency and responsibility of those allegedly intent on putting the ideals of Balmes and Donoso into practice. It would also entail ignoring the main point of contention between them: the fact that, unlike Donoso, Balmes questioned the right of the State to represent the whole of the Spanish nation, as well as to pursue religious goals that he believed belonged to the Church alone.

Balmes and Donoso continue to be known less for their lives than for their afterlives, once their ideas had been appropriated and adapted to fit both stereotypes and political agendas. The readiness to interpret Spanish Catholicism according to a 'premise of backwardness' (Luengo and Dalmau 2018: 427) might explain the general lack of interest in Balmes outside the realms of Spanish- and Catalan-speaking scholarship, apart from a few notable exceptions (Koch 1993, Villalonga 2014). In Donoso's case, his posthumous fame continues to be tainted by its association with the German jurist, Carl Schmitt. With regard to the Weimar Republic (1919–1933), Schmitt despaired of what he saw as a liberal parliamentary regime incapable of ending the mounting conflict between fascists and communists (Bravo 2013: 17). Seeking to buttress his own anti-Bolshevist agenda, which later mutated into outright support for the Nazi regime, Schmitt conveniently reduced Donoso's oeuvre to the latter's views on dictatorship. By concealing the fact that Donoso remained an employee of a liberal State until his death, Schmitt created the image of a 'decisionist' Donoso, for whom a dictatorship was nothing more than a *decision* conscientiously taken against a revolutionary threat; a decision that liberalism, paralysed by endless *discussion*, was unable to meet (Mehring 2020: 39–40). Schmitt used Donoso's defence of General Narváez's suppression of an incipient revolutionary movement in 1848 Spain to legitimise Hitler's right to prevent the outbreak of socialistic revolution in Germany. Regardless of how arbitrary the parallel traced by Schmitt was, the fact is that he succeeded in creating an enduring image of Donoso as a forerunner of the right-wing dictatorships of the twentieth century, as illustrated by a recent novel by Manuel Rivas. The novel references the works of both Donoso and Schmitt – who had close links to the Francoist intelligentsia – in order to furnish the protagonist with a convenient excuse to pose the following question 'Can you be a Christian, a Catholic conservative, and approve of Fascism? Isn't tyranny the ultimate moral failure?' (Rivas 2010: 250).

The present book explicitly eschews an appropriation of the works of Balmes and Donoso that might posit them as explicit or implicit supporters of events that occurred after their deaths. Instead, it argues for a recovery of their historical personae. While the existing literature is overwhelmingly eager to reduce Donoso's thinking to a collection of illiberal diatribes, I have highlighted Donoso's contribution to adapting the Church to the liberal revolution in Spain, thus renegotiating the relationship – or, to be more precise, the subordination – of the ecclesiastical institution to the liberal State. For most of his life, well before earning a European reputation as an ideologue of the anti-revolution, Donoso was a *moderado* politician: that is, a moderate, conservative-leaning liberal, rather than a progressive or even radical one. In the 1830s, he made a name as a journalist and expert in constitutional law; in the 1840s, he helped to engineer the *moderados*' return to power. In so doing, Donoso displayed not only the sheer scope of his cultural awareness, but equally his remarkable talent as a politician. Capable of being ruthless when necessary, Donoso succeeded in cultivating a close relationship with the influential royal family. The year 1845 marked a high point in Donoso's career as a politician: entrusted with crafting a new constitution, he advanced a concept of shared sovereignty between the Crown and the Cortes that epitomised the way in which the *moderados* practised liberalism. They were determined to strengthen the Crown, confident that they could control Isabel II, and sought to build a mighty and centralised State, led by a powerful minority. Significantly, the *moderados* sought a *modus vivendi* with the Church, on the assumption, then prevalent among Spanish liberals, that Spain should be a confessional State. In the mid-1840s, much to Balmes' displeasure, Donoso publicly defended the view that the Church, after having been deprived of a substantial part of its wealth by liberal legislation, should now be dependent upon the State for its maintenance.

Compared with Donoso the lawyer, Balmes the priest took longer to earn a national reputation. A prolific writer, Balmes updated Spanish Catholicism, enhancing its relationship with broader contemporary debates so that it could once again be taken seriously in the marketplace of ideas (Wilson 2004: xiv). Balmes sought to revise the traditional field of Catholic apologetics by making a case for the superiority of Catholicism, albeit in historical rather than theological terms. By appealing to history, Balmes strove to argue in a scientific way, supporting his arguments with objective facts and tested correlations. His main argument was that Catholicism had been the single unifying element in European history, and that it was not necessarily opposed to intellectual progress and political freedom. Like Donoso, Balmes was very much aware of broader European debates, and equally concerned with the inferior role usually assigned to Spain within "civilised" Europe. Balmes thus put forward the idea of Spain as a *Catholic nation* as an affirmation of the country's exceptional – rather than anomalous – standing within Europe. Balmes' argument is novel because it seeks to build a bridge between traditional Catholicism and the liberal idea of the nation (Álvarez Junco 2007: 417; Villalonga 2012: 59–60). A truly representative government, Balmes suggested, would cater to the majority. He thus advanced his own notion of the Spanish people, characterised as being naturally conservative and traditionally religious. With enduring consequences for generations to come, Balmes affirmed that religious unity was Spain's greatest political asset: agreement in religious matters, he argued, would necessarily be translated into social order and political stability. As noted above, his views on Church-State relations differed from those of the *moderados*, including Donoso, as Balmes asserted that the Church should not only be financially independent from the State, but steer away from politics, too.

During the period 1847–1848, the differences between Balmes and Donoso became more evident, spurred on by the liberal reforms of Pope Pius IX and the outbreak of the 1848 Revolutions in Europe. As Fradera maintains, the two men were subsequently to embark on paths that were not merely divergent, but diametrically opposed (1996: 347). It can be argued that both projected a European perspective onto what had always been prominent features of their respective worldviews. Balmes did so through his ideal of conciliation between tradition and what he called the 'modern spirit'. The only means to avert revolution, Balmes concluded, was not repression but evolution – namely, a commitment on the part of governments to promote greater political freedom and address social inequalities. However, Balmes' early death in March 1848 prevented him from witnessing the full development of the 1848 Revolutions. By contrast, Donoso cemented his international reputation as an interpreter of these revolutions. He became famous throughout Europe thanks to a speech delivered in the Spanish Cortes in 1849, in which he affirmed that dictatorship was not only a necessary but a legal means of saving society from a revolutionary threat. Whereas Balmes and the *first* Donoso strove to reconcile Catholicism and modern civilization, the starting point of Donoso in the early 1850s was the impossibility of such reconciliation. With long-lasting consequences for the future development of right-wing thought, Donoso presented socialism as the logical outcome of liberalism, regarding both as a vain attempt to change the course of history solely through political and economic reforms. What remained of the first Donoso, however, was his conviction that the Church should be an instrument at the service of the State. He continued to believe that, in the long term, only the Church could put an end to the rampant moral corruption in Europe that, in his view, would soon lead to disaster in the shape of a socialist revolution.

The differences between Balmes and Donoso, the two most significant thinkers of nineteenth-century Spain, can be summed up in a simple fact: during their respective lifetimes, they were neither friends nor allies; instead they saw themselves as competitors of equal rank. They may have pursued similar outcomes, but applied different means in order to achieve them. Balmes and post-1848 Donoso can best be described as the extremes of a traditionalist continuum: one leaning towards evolution and accommodation, the other towards regression and confrontation. Yet much is gained by studying Balmes and Donoso side by side, regardless of their differences. An analysis of their careers as a cleric and a politician, respectively, confirms the view that neither Church or State were monolithic entities, nor were their interests self-evident, but rather the result of contingency and negotiation. What we observe in Balmes and Donoso is the complex interplay of a series of loyalties to State, monarch, Church, nation, region, patronage and family networks, and even to several languages – loyalties that were sometimes complementary, sometimes not. Recreating these intricate circumstances indicates that, in future, the most original research on Balmes and Donoso will be underpinned by extensive archival research, as in the case of Fradera (1996) and Burdiel (2010). This in turn suggests that there is reason to hope that we may see a departure from the normative approach, adopted in much of the literature to date, of inscribing Donoso into a specific tradition of thought – be it Spanish, conservative or anti-liberal. Because tradition, as I have sought to demonstrate in this book, is neither timeless nor static, but always contested and in the process of taking shape.

Bibliography

Primary / Nineteenth-century sources

Alcalá Galiano, Antonio (1848). *Breves reflexiones sobre la índole de la crisis que están pasando los gobiernos y los pueblos de Europa.* Madrid: Establecimiento Tipográfico de D. Ramón Rodríguez de Rivera.

Alcalá Galiano, Antonio (1843). *Lecciones de derecho político constitucional.* Madrid: Imprenta de D. I. Boix.

Alvarado, Francisco de (1825). *Cartas críticas que escribió el Rmo. Padre Maestro Fr. Francisco Alvarado del Orden de Predicadores, o sea el Filósofo Rancio, en las que con la mayor solidez, erudición y gracia se impugnan las doctrinas y máximas perniciosas de los nuevos reformadores, y se descubren sus designios contra la Religión y el Estado.* Madrid: Imprenta de E. Aguado, vol. III.

Balmes, Jaime (1948–50). *Obras completas.* Ed. Ignacio Casanovas. Madrid: Editorial Católica, Biblioteca de Autores Cristianos, 8 vols.

Balmes, Jaime (1837). 'Discurso inaugural de la cátedra de matemáticas de Vich, pronunciado en 1° de octubre de 1837'. *OC* VIII: 562–75.

Balmes, Jaime (1838 ca.). 'Discurso sobre los males causados por la ociosidad'. *OC* VIII: 576–82.

Balmes, Jaime (1839). 'Reflexiones sobre el celibato del clero católico en parangón con la facultad de contraer de los protestantes'. *OC* V: 655–74.

Balmes, Jaime (1840a). *Observaciones sociales, políticas y económicas sobre los bienes del clero.* OC V: 675–753.

Balmes, Jaime (1840b). *Consideraciones políticas sobre la situación de España.* OC VI: 17–93.

Balmes, Jaime (1841). 'La Civilización' [series of four articles published in *La Civilización* between August and November]. *OC* V: 457–502

Balmes, Jaime (1842a). 'Discurso sobre la originalidad [delivered at the Academia de las Bellas Artes de Barcelona]'. *OC*, VIII: 226–41.

Balmes, Jaime (1842b). 'Estudios sociales. Observaciones preliminares' [*La Civilización*]. *OC* V: 493–502.

Balmes, Jaime (1842c). 'La religiosidad de la nación española' [article published in *La Civilización*, May]. *OC* VI: 185–202.

210 BIBLIOGRAPHY

Balmes, Jaime (1843a). 'Situación del clero español y urgente necesidad de un concordato' [*La Sociedad*, 15 April & 1 May]. *OC* VI: 264–88.

Balmes, Jaime (1843b). 'Consideraciones filosófico-políticas' [*La Sociedad*, 15 August]. *OC* VI: 341–56.

Balmes, Jaime (1844a). 'Prospecto' [*El Pensamiento de la Nación*, 7 February].

Balmes, Jaime (1844b). 'La religión en España' [*El Pensamiento de la Nación*, 6 March]. *OC* VII: 439–46.

Balmes, Jaime (1844c). 'Origen, carácter y fuerzas de los partidos políticos en España' [series of four articles published in *El Pensamiento de la Nación*, 27 March & 3, 10, 17 April]. *OC* VI: 472–99.

Balmes, Jaime (1844d). 'Reforma de la constitución' [series of eight articles published in *El Pensamiento de la Nación*, 22 & 29 May; 5, 12, 19 & 26 June; 3 & 10 July]. *OC* VI: 602–70.

Balmes, Jaime (1844e). '¿Cómo estamos? ¿Qué conducta deben seguir los hombres amantes de su Patria? [*El Pensamiento de la Nación*, 24 July]'. *OC* VI: 695–708.

Balmes, Jaime (1844f). 'Sobre el dictamen de la comisión del Congreso relativo a la reforma de la constitución' [*El Pensamiento de la Nación*, 13 November]. *OC* VI: 941–954

Balmes, Jaime (1844 g). 'Dotación de culto y clero' [*El Pensamiento de la Nación*, 18 December). *OC* VI: 1017–1023.

Balmes, Jaime (1844h). 'Sesión del 21 de diciembre y renuncia de varios señores diputados' [*El Pensamiento de la Nación*, 25 December]. *OC* VI: 1036–50.

Balmes, Jaime (1844i). *El protestantismo comparado con el catolicismo en sus relaciones con la civilización europea*. Buenos Aires: Emecé (1945).

Balmes, Jaime (1845a). 'La enmienda al proyecto de ley sobre dotación de culto y clero' [*El Pensamiento de la Nación*, 1 January). *OC* VII: 1043–50.

Balmes, Jaime (1845b). 'Renuncia de algunos diputados' [*El Pensamiento de la Nación*, 1 January], 1051–61.

Balmes, Jaime (1845c). 'Más sobre las discusiones del Congreso relativas a la devolución de los bienes del clero' [*El Pensamiento de la Nación*, 2 April]. *OC* VII, 117–127.

Balmes, Jaime (1845d). 'Negocios de Roma' [*El Pensamiento de la Nación*, 9 April]. *OC* VII: 128–135.

Balmes, Jaime (1845e). 'Dos escollos' [*El Pensamiento de la Nación*, 4 June]. *EP*: 493–8.

Balmes, Jaime (1845f). 'Documentos de Bourges' [series of four articles published in *El Pensamiento de la Nación*, 11, 18, 25 July & 1 August]. *OC* VII: 217–52.

Balmes, Jaime (1845g). *El criterio*. Mexico: Editorial Porrúa (2005).

Balmes, Jaime (1846a). 'La preponderancia militar' [*El Pensamiento de la Nación*, 18 March]. *OC* VII: 567–75.

Balmes, Jaime (1846b). 'El general Narváez' [*El Pensamiento de la Nación*, 15 April]. *OC* VII: 609–14.

Balmes, Jaime (1846c). 'Vindicación personal' [*El Pensamiento de la Nación*, 19 August]. *EP*: 725–34.

Balmes, Jaime (1846b). 'El partido carlista' [*El Pensamiento de la Nación*, 14 September). *EP*: 752–5.

BIBLIOGRAPHY

Balmes, Jaime (1846c). 'El matrimonio Montpensier y la diplomacia europea' [*El Pensamiento de la Nación*, 19 November]. *EP*: 769–75.

Balmes, Jaime (1846d). '¿Por dónde se sale?' [*El Pensamiento de la Nación*, 31 December]. *EP*: 783–94.

Balmes, Jaime (1846e). *Filosofía fundamental*. Barcelona: Imprenta de A. Brusi, 4 vols.

Balmes, Jaime (1847a). *Escritos políticos. Colección completa, corregida y ordenada por el autor*. Madrid: Imprenta de la Sociedad de Operarios del mismo Arte, Calle del Factor núm. 8.

Balmes, Jaime (1847b). *Pío IX*. *OC* VII: 947–1003.

Balmes, Jaime (1848). 'República francesa'. *OC* VII: 1025–53.

Balmes, Jaime (1880). *Cartas a un escéptico en materia de religión* [1846]. Mexico: Librería de Ch. Bouret.

Balmes, Jaime (1889). *Curso de filosofía elemental*. Paris-Mexico: Librería de Ch. Bouret.

Balmes, Jaime (n.d.). 'Sinopsis de *El protestantismo*'. *OC* VIII: 480–7.

Baralt, Rafael María (1860). 'Discurso' in *Discursos leídos en las recepciones públicas que ha celebrado desde 1847 la Real Academia Española*. Madrid: Imprenta Nacional, vol. II, 7–70.

Barruel, Abbé (1799). *Memories Illustrating the History of Jacobinism. A Translation from the French of the Abbé Barruel*. New York: Hudson & Goodwin, vol. I

Blanche-Raffin, Albéric de (1850). *Vida y juicio crítico de los escritos de D. Jaime Balmes, obra recientemente publicada en francés por A. de Blanche-Raffin, y traducido al castellano por varios admiradores del eminente publicista español*. Madrid: Imprenta de D. Anselmo Santa Coloma y Compañía.

Borrego, Andrés (1855). *Estudios políticos. De la organización de los partidos en España, considerada como medio de adelantar la educación constitucional de la nación, y de realizar las condiciones del gobierno representativo*. Madrid: Anselmo Santa Coloma Editor.

Bordas-Demoulin, Jean-Baptiste and François Huet (1856). *Essais sur la réforme catholique*. Paris: Chamerot.

Díaz, Nicomedes Pastor (1867). *Los problemas del socialismo. Lecciones pronunciadas en el Ateneo de Madrid en el curso de 1848 a 1849*. Madrid: Imprenta de Manuel Tello (Obras, vol. IV).

Diario de las sesiones del Congreso de Diputados en la legislatura de 1844 a 1845 (1844). Madrid: Imprenta Nacional, v. I.

Donoso Cortés, Juan (1970). *Obras completas*. Ed. Juan Valverde. Madrid: Editorial Católica, Biblioteca de Autores Cristianos.

Donoso Cortés, Juan (1829a). 'Carta a Manuel Gallardo' [August]. *OC* I: 174–6.

Donoso Cortés, Juan (1829b). 'Discurso de apertura en el Colegio de Cáceres'. *OC* I: 182–205.

Donoso Cortés, Juan (1832). 'Memoria sobre la situación actual de la monarquía, dirigida a Fernando VII' [San Ildefonso, 13 October]. *OC* I: 213–223.

Donoso Cortés, Juan (1834). *Consideraciones sobre la diplomacia y su influencia en el estado político y social de Europa desde la revolución de julio hasta el tratado de la Cuádruple Alianza*. *OC* I: 226–81.

Donoso Cortés, Juan (1835). 'La ley electoral considerada en su base y en su relación con el espíritu de nuestras instituciones'. *OC* I: 302–22.

212 BIBLIOGRAPHY

Donoso Cortés, Juan (1836–1837). *Lecciones de Derecho Político Constitucional*. *OC* I: 327–445.

Donoso Cortés, Juan (1837a). 'La religión, la libertad, la inteligencia' [*El Porvenir*, 13 July]. *OC* I: 487–91

Donoso Cortés, Juan (1838a). 'Polémica con el Dr. Rossi y juicio crítico acerca de los doctrinarios' [articles published in *El Correo Nacional* in July 1838]. *OC* I: 492–510.

Donoso Cortés, Juan (1838b). 'Consideraciones sobre el cristianismo' [articles published in *El Correo Nacional* in October and November 1838]. *OC* I: 653–62.

Donoso Cortés, Juan (1843). 'Discurso sobre la declaración de la mayoría de edad de Doña Isabel II' [6 November]. *OC* II: 9–14.

Donoso Cortés, Juan (1844a). 'Dictamen sobre el proyecto de reforma de la Constitución de 1837'. *OC* II: 74–87.

Donoso Cortés, Juan (1844b). 'Discurso pronunciado en el Congreso a propósito de una enmienda al proyecto de constitución' [16 November]. *OC* II: 88–93.

Donoso Cortés, Juan (1845a). 'Discurso sobre la dotación de culto y clero' [15 January]. *OC* II: 94–105.

Donoso Cortés, Juan (1845b). 'Discurso sobre la restitución de los bienes de la Iglesia' [14 March]. *OC* II: 106–20.

Donoso Cortés, Juan (1846a). 'Carta al duque de Riánsares' [Madrid, 15 July]. *OC* II: 140–44.

Donoso Cortés, Juan (1846b). 'Discurso sobre los regios enlaces' [17 September]. *OC* II: 145–59.

Donoso Cortés, Juan (1847). *Pío IX*. *OC* II: 195–225.

Donoso Cortés, Juan (1847–1848). *Estudios sobre la historia*. *OC* II: 226–77.

Donoso Cortés, Juan (1848). 'Discurso académico sobre la Biblia'. *OC* II: 278–300.

Donoso Cortés, Juan (1849a). 'Carta al conde de Montalembert' [Berlin, 26 May]. *OC* II: 324–8.

Donoso Cortés, Juan (1849b). 'Carta al conde de Montalembert' [Berlin, 4 June]. *OC* II: 328–30.

Donoso Cortés, Juan (1849c). 'Carta a Alberic de Blanche, marqués de Raffin' [Berlin, 21 July]. *OC* II: 342–5.

Donoso Cortés, Juan (1849d). 'Discurso sobre la dictadura' [4 January]. *OC* II: 305–23.

Donoso Cortés, Juan (1850a). 'Discurso sobre la situación general de Europa' [30 January]. *OC* II: 449–67.

Donoso Cortés, Juan (1850b). 'Carta a Louis Veuillot' [Madrid, 22 March]. *OC* II: 472–3.

Donoso Cortés, Juan (1850c). 'Carta al Duque de Valmy' [Madrid, 20 July]. *OC* II: 468–70.

Donoso Cortés, Juan (1850d). 'Discurso sobre la situación de España' [30 December]. *OC* II: 479–95.

Donoso Cortés, Juan (1850e). 'Carta a persona desconocida' [1850 ca.]. *OC* II: 477–8.

Donoso Cortés, Juan (1851a). 'Carta a Louis Veuillot' [Madrid, 3 March]. *OC* II: 703–4.

Donoso Cortés, Juan (1851b). 'Carta a Gabino Tejado' [Paris, 27 March]. *OC* II: 708–9.

Donoso Cortés, Juan (1851c). 'Carta a Gabino Tejado' [Paris, 22 June]. *OC* II: 715–6.

Donoso Cortés, Juan (1851d). 'Carta al Conde Raczyński' [Paris, 7 December]. *OC* II: 952–3.

Donoso Cortés, Juan (1851e). *Ensayo sobre el catolicismo, el liberalismo y el socialismo*. Ed. José Luis Monereo Pérez. Granada: Editorial Comares (2006).

BIBLIOGRAPHY 213

Donoso Cortés, Juan (1852a). 'Carta al Cardenal Fornari' (Paris, 19 June). *OC* II: 744–62.

Donoso Cortés, Juan (1852b). 'Carta al director de la *Revue des Deux Mondes*' [Paris, 15 November]. *OC* II: 762–81.

Forner, Juan Pablo (1795). *Preservativo contra el atheismo por Don Juan Pablo Forner, del Consejo de S.M., su Fiscal en la Rl. Audiencia de Sevilla*. Sevilla: D. Félix de la Puerta Impresor.

Frexas, José (1852). *El socialismo y la teocracia, o sean observaciones sobre las principales controversias políticas y filosófico-sociales, dirigidas al Exmo. Sr. D. Juan Donoso Cortés, Marqués de Valdegamas, en refutación de las más notables ideas de sus escritos y de las bases de aquellos sistemas*. Barcelona: Imprenta de Narciso Ramírez, 2 vols.

Guizot, François (1828). *The History of civilisation in Europe*, ed. Larry Siedentop. London: Penguin (1997).

Herzen, Alexander (1851). 'Donoso-Cortes, Marqués de Valdegamas, and Julian, Roman Emperor' in *From the Other Shore. The Russian People and Socialism*. Oxford: University Press [1997], 152–62.

M. (1855). *La Asamblea española de 1854 y la cuestión religiosa. Colección de discursos pronunciados sobre este asunto por los señores diputados en las Cortes constituyentes*. Madrid: Imprenta de D. Anselmo Santa Coloma.

Mateo, Tomás (1848). *Reflexiones sobre los principios políticos emitidos por el presbítero D. Jaime Balmes, en sus escritos El protestantismo comparado con el catolicismo, periódico Pensamiento de la nación y folleto titulado Pío IX*. Madrid, Imprenta de T. Aguado.

Mateos, Nicomedes (1851). *Veinte y seis cartas al Señor Marqués de Valdegamas, en contestación a los veinte y seis capítulos de su Ensayo sobre el catolicismo, el liberalismo y el socialismo*. Valladolid: Imprenta de D. Gerónimo Marcos Gallego.

Morón, Fermín Gonzalo (1841). *Curso de historia de la civilización de España, lecciones pronunciadas en el Liceo de Valencia y en el Ateneo de Madrid en los cursos de 1840 y 1841 por el profesor de Historia en ambos establecimientos literarios*. Madrid: Establecimiento tipográfico calle del Sordo núm. 11.

Martínez de la Rosa, Francisco (1835). *Espíritu del siglo*, Madrid, Imprenta de D. Tomás Jordán, vol. I [of VIII].

Marx, Karl (1852). *The Eighteenth Brumaire of Louis Bonaparte*. Maryland: Wildside Press [2008].

Mateos, Nicomedes. *Veinte y seis cartas al Señor Marqués de Valdegamas, en contestación a los veinte y seis capítulos de su Ensayo sobre el catolicismo, el liberalismo y el socialismo por Don Nicomedes M. Mateos, juez cesante*. Valladolid: Imprenta de D. Gerónimo Marcos Gallego, 1851.

Olavide, Pablo de (1798). *El Evangelio en triunfo o historia de un filósofo desengañado*. Madrid: Imprenta de Don Joseph Doblado, 4 vols.

Pidal y Mon, Alejandro (1889). 'Balmes y Donoso Cortés, Orígenes y causas del Ultramontanismo. La historia y sus transformaciones. Relaciones de la Iglesia española con la Santa Sede'. *La España del siglo XIX*, 3, 1–60.

Quintana, Manuel José (1853). *Cartas a Lord Holland sobre los sucesos políticos de España en la segunda época constitucional*. Madrid: Imprenta y Estereotipía de M. Ribadeneyra.

214 BIBLIOGRAPHY

Rico y Amat, Juan (1855). *Diccionario de los políticos ó Verdadero sentido de las voces y frases más usuales entre los mismos: escrito para divertimiento de los que ya lo han sido y enseñanza de los que aún quieren serlo.* Madrid: Imprenta de F. Andrés y Compañía.

Roca y Cornet, Joaquín (1847). *Ensayo crítico sobre las lecturas de la época.* Barcelona: Imprenta de A. Brusi, 2 vols.

Sardá y Salvany, Félix (1884). *El liberalismo es pecado. Cuestiones candentes.* Barcelona: Librería y Tipografía Católica.

Urbina, Antonio, Marqués de Rozalejo (1939). *Cheste o Todo un siglo (1809–1906). El isabelino tradicionalista.* Madrid: Espasa Calpe.

Vélez, Rafael de (1812). *Preservativo contra la irreligión: o los planes de la falsa filosofía contra la religión y el Estado, realizados por la Francia para subyugar a la Europa, seguidos por Napoleón en la conquista de España y dados a la luz por algunos de nuestros sabios.* Cádiz: Imprenta de la Junta de la Provincia.

Zevallos, fray Fernando de (1774–1776). *La falsa filosofía, o el ateísmo, deísmo, materialismo y demás nuevas sectas convencidas de crimen de estado contra los Soberanos, y sus Regalías, contra los Magistrados, y Potestades legítimas. Se combaten sus máximas sediciosas y subversivas de toda Sociedad, y aun de la Humanidad.* Madrid: Imprenta de D. Antonio de Sancha, 6 vols.

Secondary sources

Abellán, José Luis (1984). *Historia crítica del pensamiento español.* Madrid: Espasa Calpe, vol. IV [Liberalismo y romanticismo].

Acle-Kreysing (*neé* Acle Aguirre), Andrea (2016). 'Revolución, contrarrevolución... evolución: catolicismo y nuevas formas de legitimidad política en la España del siglo XIX. Los casos de Jaime Balmes y Juan Donoso Cortés'. *Hispania Sacra*, 68(137), 573–609.

Acle Aguirre, Andrea (2012). 'La religión, en guerra contra las pasiones humanas: conservadurismo de Jaime Balmes (1810–1848) y Juan Donoso Cortés (1809–1853)' in *La furia de Marte*. *Ideología, pensamiento y representación: XIV Encuentro de la Ilustración al Romanticismo. España, Europa y América (1750–1850)*, ed. Juan Ramón Cirici Narváez and Alberto Ramos Santana. Cádiz: Universidad de Cádiz, 159–173.

Aldridge, Owen (1971). *The Concept of the Ibero-American Enlightenment.* Chicago: University of Illinois Press.

Alonso, Gregorio (2020). 'Introducción. Benditas banderas: nacionalismo y catolicismo en la modernidad hispanoamericana'. *Rubrica Contemporanea* 9(17), 1–9.

Alonso, Gregorio (2017a). 'A Transatlantic Loyalty in the Age of Independence: Catholicism and Nation Building in Spain and Latin America' in *Nationalism and Transnationalism in Spain and Latin America, 1808–1923*, ed. Paul Garner and Angel Smith. Cardiff: University of Wales Press, 45–67.

BIBLIOGRAPHY

Alonso, Gregorio (2017b). '¿Dar la vida por la contrarrevolución?' Voluntarios españoles en defensa del poder temporal de Pío IX en 1850' in *El desafío de la revolución*. *Reaccionarios, antiliberales y contrarrevolucionarios (siglos XVIII y XIX)*, ed. P. Rújula and J.R. Solans. Granada: Comares, 124–140.

Alonso, Gregorio (2014). *La nación en capilla. Ciudadanía católica y cuestión religiosa en España*. Granada: Comares Historia.

Álvarez Junco, José (2007). *Mater dolorosa. La idea de España en el siglo XIX*. Madrid: Taurus.

Álvarez Junco, José (2006). 'El conservadurismo español, entre religión y nación' in *Del territorio a la nación. Identidades territoriales y construcción nacional*, ed. Luis Castells. Madrid: Biblioteca Nueva, 39–64.

Álvarez Junco, José (2001). 'La difícil nacionalización de la derecha española en la primera mitad del siglo XIX'. *Hispania* 209(3), 831–58.

Arranz Notario, Luis (2015). 'El pensamiento de Juan Donoso Cortés: 'La libertad no es otra cosa que la facultad de obedecer' in *Donoso Cortés. El reto del liberalismo y la revolución*, ed. Carlos Dardé Morales. Madrid: Comunidad de Madrid, 59–86.

Aubert, Roger, Johannes Beckmann, Patrick J. Corish & Rudolf Lill (eds.) (1981). *The Church in the Age of Liberalism*. London: Burns & Oates, vol. VIII.

Barnosell, Genís (2012). 'God and Freedom: Radical Liberalism, Republicanism, and Religion in Spain, 1808–1847'. *IRSH* 57, 37–59.

Barrio Alonso, Ángeles (2018). 'Social Movements' in *The History of Modern Spain. Chronologies, Themes, Individuals*, ed. José Álvarez Junco and Adrian Shubert. London/New York: Bloomsbury, 261–275.

Batllori, Miquel (1943). 'La inoriginalidad del discurso de Balmes sobre la originalidad'. *Revista de Ideas Estéticas*, 2, 1–12.

Batllori, Miquel (1946). 'Balmes en la historia de la filosofía cristiana'. *Razón y Fe*, 134 (II), 281–95.

Beneyto, José María (2018). 'Juan Donoso Cortés, Marquis of Valdegamas' in *Great Christian Jurists in Spanish History*, ed. Rafael Domingo and Javier Martínez Torrón, Cambridge: CUP, 294–312.

Bennett, Joshua (2019). *God and Progress. Religion and History in British Intellectual Culture, 1845–1914*. Oxford: University Press.

Botti, Alfonso (2008). *Cielo y dinero. El nacionalcatolicismo en España 1881–1975*. Madrid: Alianza Editorial.

Bravo Regidor, Carlos (2013). 'Carl Schmitt' in Carlos Bravo Regidor, Lorenzo Córdova Vianello and Enrique Serrano Gómez, *¿Por qué leer a Schmitt hoy?* Mexico: Fontamara.

Breña, Roberto (2021). 'Tensions and Challenges of Intellectual History in Contemporary Latin America'. *Contributions to the History of Concepts*, 16 (1), 89–115.

Burdiel Bueno, Isabel (2013). 'Monarquía y nación en la cultura política progresista. La encrucijada de 1854' in *Culturas políticas monárquicas en la España liberal. Discursos, representaciones y prácticas (1808-1902)*, ed. Encarna García Monerris, Mónica Moreno Seco and Juan Marcuello Benedicto. Valencia: Universitat de València, 213–232.

Burdiel Bueno, Isabel (2010). *Isabel II. No se puede reinar inocentemente*. Madrid: Espasa Calpe.

Burdiel Bueno, Isabel (1998). 'Myths of Failure, Myths of Success: New Perspectives on Nineteenth-Century Spanish Liberalism'. *The Journal of Modern History*, 70(4), 892–912.

Cabeza Sánchez-Albornoz, Sonsoles (1981). *Los sucesos de 1848 en España*. Madrid: Fundación Universitaria Española.

Callahan, William J. (1980). 'The Origins of the Conservative Church in Spain, 1793–1823', *European Studies Review* 10, 199–223.

Callahan, William J. (1984a). *Church, Politics and Society in Spain, 1750–1874*. Cambridge: Harvard University Press.

Callahan, William J. (1984b). 'Was Spain Catholic?' *Revista Canadiense de Estudios Hispánicos*, 8 (2), 159–182.

Campomar Fornieles, Marta M. (1984). *La cuestión religiosa en la Restauración. Historia de los heterodoxos españoles*. Santander: Sociedad Menéndez Pelayo.

Canal i Morell, Jordi (2000). *El carlismo. Dos siglos de contrarrevolución en España*. Madrid: Alianza.

Capellán de Miguel, Gonzalo (2006). '¿Mejora la humanidad? El concepto de progreso en la España liberal' in *La redención del pueblo: la cultura progresista en la España liberal*, ed. Manuel Suárez Cortina. Santander: Servicio de Publicaciones de la Universidad de Cantabria / Sociedad Menéndez Pelayo, 41–79.

Cárcel Orti, Vicente (1975). *Política eclesial de los gobiernos liberales españoles (1830–1840)*. Pamplona: Ediciones Universidad de Navarra.

Cárdenas Ayala, Elisa (2015). 'El fin de una era: Pío IX y el Syllabus', *Historia Mexicana* 65(2), 719–746.

Carr, Raymond (1966). *Spain 1808–1939*. Oxford: University Press.

Carr, Raymond (2001). 'Introduction' in *Spain: A History*, ed. R. Carr. Oxford: University Press, 1–9.

Casanovas, Ignacio (1948). *Balmes, su vida, sus obras y su tiempo* in Jaime Balmes, *Obras completas*. Madrid: Editorial Católica.

Castro, Demetrio (2011). 'Carlistas y conservadores en el siglo XIX. De Isabel II a la restauración' in *'Por Dios, por la patria y por el rey'. Las ideas del carlismo. IV Jornadas de Estudio del Carlismo*. Pamplona: Gobierno de Navarra, 37–79.

Chadwick, Owen (1998). *A History of the Popes, 1830–1914*. Oxford: Clarendon Press.

Clark, Christopher (2003). 'The New Catholicism and the European Culture Wars' in *Culture Wars: Secular-Catholic Conflict in Nineteenth-Century Europe*, ed. Christopher Clark and Wolfram Kaiser. Cambridge: CUP, 11–46.

Colom González, Francisco (2011). 'La imaginación política del tradicionalismo español' in *'Por Dios, por la patria y por el rey'. Las ideas del carlismo. IV Jornadas de Estudio del Carlismo*. Pamplona: Gobierno de Navarra, 179–198.

Colom González, Francisco (2006). *El altar y el trono: ensayos sobre catolicismo político iberoamericano*. Barcelona: Anthropos /Universidad Nacional de Colombia.

Comellas, José Luis (1970). *Los moderados en el poder. 1844–1854*. Madrid: Consejo Superior de Investigaciones Científicas.

BIBLIOGRAPHY

Connelly Ullman, Joan (1983). 'The Warp and Woof of Parliamentary Politics in Spain, 1808–1939: Anticlericalism versus 'Neo-Catholicism'. *European Studies Review* 13, 145–76.

Craiutu, Aurelian (2004). 'The method of the French doctrinaires'. *History of European Ideas* (30), 39–59.

Craiutu, Aurelian (2003). *Liberalism under Siege. The Political Thought of the French Doctrinaires*. Lanham: Lexington Books.

Cruz Valenciano, Jesús (2000). *Los notables de Madrid. Las bases sociales de la revolución liberal española*. Madrid: Alianza Editorial.

Cruz Valenciano, Jesús (1996). *Gentlemen, bourgeois and revolutionaries. Political change and cultural persistence among the Spanish dominant groups 1750–1850*. Cambridge: CUP.

De Mora Quirós, Enrique V. (2003). *La filosofía política de Jaime Balmes*. Cádiz: Universidad de Cádiz.

Dardé Morales, Carlos (2015). 'Donoso Cortés: un romántico católico en la era de las revoluciones' in *Donoso Cortés. El reto del liberalismo y la revolución*, ed. Carlos Dardé Morales. Madrid: Comunidad de Madrid, 1–30.

Dupont, Alexandre (2011). 'Louis Veuillot y el carlismo' in *'Por Dios, por la patria y por el rey'. Las ideas del carlismo. IV Jornadas de Estudio del Carlismo*. Pamplona: Gobierno de Navarra, 81–105.

De Felipe Redondo, Jesús and Josué J. González Rodríguez (2020). 'Los proyectos utópicos del movimiento obrero español, 1840–1870'. *Ayer* 117(1), 158–187.

De la Cueva Merino, Julio (2018). 'Religion' in *The History of Modern Spain. Chronologies, Themes, Individuals*, ed. José Álvarez Junco and Adrian Shubert. London/New York: Bloomsbury, 276–291.

Díez Álvarez, Luis Gonzalo (2003). *La soberanía de los deberes. Una interpretación histórica del pensamiento de Donoso Cortés*. Jaraíz de la Vera: Diputación Provincial de Cáceres / Institución Cultural 'El Brocense'.

Díez del Corral, Luis (1956). *El liberalismo doctrinario*. Madrid: Instituto de Estudios Políticos.

Evans, Richard and Hartmut Pogge von Strandmann (eds.) (2000). *The Revolutions in Europe, 1848–1849. From Reform to Reaction*. Oxford: University Press.

Escrig Rosa, Josep (2018). 'Pasión racional, razón apasionada. El primer antiliberalismo reaccionario en España'. *Ayer* 111(3), 135–61.

Estrada Sánchez, Manuel (1998). 'El enfrentamiento entre doceañistas y moderados por la cuestión electoral (1834–1836)'. *Revista de Estudios Políticos* 100, 241–272.

Fernández Sarasola, Ignacio (2005). 'La influencia de Francia en los orígenes del constitucionalismo español'. Available online at *Forum Historiae Juris* (https://forhistiur.net/2005-04-sarasola/)

Fernández Sebastián, Javier (2014a). 'Introducción. Tiempos de transición en el Atlántico Ibérico. Conceptos políticos en revolución' in *Civilización. Diccionario social y político del mundo iberoamericano. Conceptos políticos fundamentales, 1770–1870 [Iberconceptos II]*, ed. J. Fernández Sebastián. Madrid: Centro de Estudios Políticos y Constitucionales / Universidad del País Vasco, vol. 2, 25–72.

218 BIBLIOGRAPHY

Fernández Sebastián, Javier (2014b). 'España' in Civilización. Diccionario social y político del mundo iberoamericano. Conceptos políticos fundamentales, 1770–1870 [Iberconceptos II], ed. J. Fernández Sebastián. Madrid: Centro de Estudios Políticos y Constitucionales / Universidad del País Vasco, vol. 2, 201–216.

Fernández Sebastián, Javier (2008a). 'Debating Freedom of Thought and Expression during the Crisis of the Hispanic World: The Limits of Tolerance in a Catholic Society' in Columbia Faculty Seminar on 18th Century European Culture, New York, 21st February 2008.

Fernández Sebastián, Javier (2008b). 'The Concept of Civilisation in Spain, 1754–2005: From Progress to Identity.' Contributions to the History of Concepts (4), 81–105.

Fernández Sebastián, Javier & Juan Francisco Fuentes, eds. (2003). Diccionario político y social del siglo XIX español. Madrid: Alianza.

Fernández Sebastián, Javier (1997). 'La recepción en España de la Histoire de la civilisation de Guizot' in La imagen de Francia en España (1808–1850). ed. Jean-René Aymes and Javier Fernández Sebastián. Bilbao: Universidad del País Vasco, 127–149.

Flitter, Derek (2006). Spanish Romanticism and the Uses of History. Ideology and the Historical Imagination. London: Legenda, Modern Humanities Research Association and Maney Publishing.

Fradera, Josep Maria (2012).'The Empire, the Nation and the Homelands: Nineteenth-Century's Spain National Idea' in Region and State in Nineteenth-Century Europe. Nation-Building, Regional Identities and Separatism, ed. Joost Augusteijn and Eric Storm. Houndsmills: Palgrave Macmillan, 131–48.

Fradera, Josep Maria (1996). Jaume Balmes: els fonaments racionals d'una política catòlica. Barcelona: Eumo Editorial.

Fradera, Josep Maria (1992). Cultura nacional en una sociedad dividida. Cataluña, 1838–1868. Madrid: Marcial Pons.

Freeden, Michael and Fernández Sebastián (2019). 'Introduction. European Liberal Discourses. Conceptual Affinities and Disparities' in In Search of European Liberalisms. Concepts, Languages and Ideologies, ed. M. Freeden, J. Fernández Sebastián and Jörn Leonhard. New York: Bergahn Books, 1–35.

Fox, Inman (1998). La invención de España. Nacionalismo liberal e identidad nacional. Madrid: Cátedra.

Fuentes, Juan Francisco (2014). 'España' in Revolución. Diccionario social y político del mundo iberoamericano. Conceptos políticos fundamentales, 1770–1870 [Iberconceptos II], ed. Guillermo Zermeño Padilla. Madrid: Centro de Estudios Políticos y Constitucionales / Universidad del País Vasco.

Fuentes, Juan Francisco (2006). 'Progreso y clase media en la España liberal' in La redención del pueblo: la cultura progresista en la España liberal, ed. Manuel. Suárez Cortina. Santander: Servicio de Publicaciones de la Universidad de Cantabria / Sociedad Menéndez Pelayo, 291–313.

Gallego García, Elio (2013). Estado de disolución. Donoso Cortés y su destino en el pensamiento de Donoso Cortés. Madrid: Sekotia.

BIBLIOGRAPHY 219

García Cárcel, Ricardo (2013). *La herencia del pasado. Las memorias históricas de España.* Barcelona: Galaxia Gutenberg.

García de Paso, Ignacio (2016). 'El 1848 español. ¿Una excepción europea?'. *Ayer* 106(2), 185–206.

García Escudero, José María (1950). *Política española y política de Balmes* [Premio Nacional de Periodismo 'Francisco Franco' 1948]. Madrid: Ediciones Cultura Hispánica.

García Escudero, José María (1980). *Historia breve de las dos Españas.* Madrid: Fundación Vives de Estudios Sociales.

Garrido Muro, Luis (2015). '"Cómo organizar el caos": Donoso Cortés en la política española' in *Donoso Cortés. El reto del liberalismo y la revolución,* ed. Carlos Dardé Morales. Madrid: Comunidad de Madrid, 31–58.

Garrorena Morales, Ángel (1974). *El ateneo de Madrid y la teoría de la monarquía liberal (1836–1847).* Madrid: Instituto de Estudios Políticos.

González Cuevas, Pedro Carlos (2015). 'La proyección de Donoso Cortés en la política española de los siglos XIX y XX' in *Donoso Cortés. El reto del liberalismo y la revolución,* ed. Carlos Dardé Morales. Madrid: Comunidad de Madrid, 145–173.

González Cuevas, Pedro Carlos (2000). *Historia de las derechas españolas. De la Ilustración a nuestros días.* Madrid: Biblioteca Nueva.

Ginger, Andrew (2020). *Instead of modernity. The Western canon and the incorporation of the Hispanic (c. 1850–75).* Manchester: Manchester University Press.

Ginger, Andrew (2007). 'Spanish modernity revisited: revisions of the nineteenth century'. *Journal of Iberian and Latin American Studies* 13, 121–132.

Graham, John T. (1974). *Donoso Cortés: Utopian Romanticist and Political Realist.* Missouri: University Press.

Gunn, J.A.W. (2009). *When the French tried to be British: Party, Opposition, and the Quest for Civil Disagreement, 1814–1848.* Montreal: McGill-Queen's University Press.

Herr, Richard (1958). *The Eighteenth-Century Revolution in Spain.* Princeton: University Press.

Herrera, Robert (1995). *Donoso Cortés: Cassandra of the Age.* Grand Rapids: William B. Eerdmans Publishing Company.

Herrero Saura, Javier (1971). *Los orígenes del pensamiento reaccionario español.* Madrid: Cuadernos para el Diálogo.

Huerta de Soto, Jesús (2021). 'Reseña del libro *Cartas a un escéptico en materia de religión,* de Jaime Balmes. Colección Austral, Espasa Calpe, Madrid 1959'. *Procesos de Mercado: Revista Europea de Economía Política* 18(1), 551–553.

Iarocci, Michael (2006). *Properties of Modernity. Romantic Spain, Modern Europe, and the Legacies of Empire.* Nashville: Vanderbilt University Press.

Jiménez García, Antonio (1992). 'El espiritualismo de Nicomedes Martín Mateos (1806–1890)'. *Exilios filosóficos de España. Actas del VII Seminario de Historia de la Filosofía Española e Iberoamericana,* ed. Antonio Heredia Soriano. Salamanca, 229–44.

Jones Parry, E. (1936). *The Spanish Marriages 1841–1846. A Study of the Influence of Dynastic Ambition upon Foreign Policy.* London: Macmillan and Co.

Jover Zamora, José María (1976). *Política, diplomacia y humanismo popular: estudios sobre la vida española del siglo XIX.* Madrid: Turner.

Jover Zamora, José María (1991). La civilización española a mediados del siglo XIX. Madrid: Espasa Calpe.

Juliá, Santos (2004). *Historia de las dos Españas*. Madrid: Taurus.

Julián, Amadeo (2012). 'Rafael María Barat. Su vida, obras y servicios prestados a la República Dominicana'. *Clío* 81(183), 43–125.

Kamen, Henry (2008a). *The Disinherited. The Exiles Who Created Spanish Culture*. London: Penguin.

Kamen, Henry (2008b). *Imagining Spain. Historical Myth and National Identity*. Yale: University Press.

Kennedy, John J. (1952). 'Donoso Cortés as a Servant of the State'. *The Review of Politics* 14, 520–555.

Kirsch, Martin (2008). 'Los cambios constitucionales tras la revolución de 1848. El fortalecimiento de la democratización europea a largo plazo'. *Ayer* 70(2), 199–239.

Koch, Elena María (1993). *Die Katholische Soziologie in Spanien. Jaime Balmes und Juan Donoso Cortés (1840–1853)*. PhD dissertation (Rheinischen Friedrich-Wilhelms-Universität zu Bonn, Germany).

Kolar, Fabio and Ulrich Mücke (2019). 'Introducción' in *El pensamiento conservador y derechista en América Latina, España y Portugal, siglos XIX y XX*, ed. F. Kolar and U. Mücke. Madrid & Frankfurt am Main: Iberoamericana Vervuert, 7–36.

Labanyi, Jo (2005). 'Horror, Spectacle and Nation-formation: Historical Painting in Late-nineteenth-century Spain' in *Visualising Spanish Modernity*, ed. Susan Larson and Eva Woods. Oxford: Berg, 64–80.

Larios Mengotti, Gonzalo (2003). *Donoso Cortés: juventud, política y romanticismo*. Basauri: Grafite Ediciones.

Larraz, José (1948). *Balmes, conciliador de las fuerzas antirrevolucionarias. Discurso pronunciado en Vich, el 9 de julio de 1948 con ocasión del I Centenario de la muerte de Balmes*. Vic: Ayuntamiento.

Larraz, José (1965). *Balmes y Donoso Cortés*. Madrid: Ediciones Rialp.

Lawless, Geraldine (2018). 'How to tell time' in *Spain in the nineteenth century: New essays on experiences of culture and society*, ed. Andrew Ginger and Geraldine Lawless. Manchester: University Press, 63–88.

Lawrence, Mark (2014). *Spain's First Carlist War, 1833–40*. Houndmills / New York: Palgrave Macmillan.

Lida, Clara E. (2000). 'Los ecos de la República democrática y social en España. Trabajo y ciudadanía en 1848'. *SEMATA. Ciencias Sociais e Humanidades* 12, 323–338.

López Alós, Javier (2011a). *Entre el trono y el escaño. El pensamiento reaccionario español frente a la revolución liberal (1808–1823)*. Madrid: Congreso de los Diputados.

López Alós, Javier (2011b). 'El pensamiento reaccionario a través del principio de autoridad'. *Artificium: Revista Iberoamericana de Estudios Culturales y Análisis Conceptual* 2 (2), 21–41.

López Morillas, Juan (2010). *The Krausist Movement and Ideological Change in Spain, 1854–1874*. Cambridge: CUP.

BIBLIOGRAPHY

Louzao Villar, Joseba (2013). 'Nación y catolicismo en la España contemporánea. Revisitando una interrelación histórica'. *Ayer* 90(2), 65–89.

Luengo, Jorge and Pol Dalmau (2018). 'Writing Spanish history in the global age: connections and entanglements in the nineteenth century'. *Journal of Global History*, 13, 425–445.

Maier Allende, Jorge (2003). 'Los inicios de la prehistoria en España: ciencia versus religión', ed. José Beltrán Fortes and María Belén Deamos, *El clero y la arqueología española. II Reunión Andaluza de Historiografía Arqueológica*. Sevilla, 99–112.

Marcuello Benedicto, Juan Ignacio (2013). 'El discurso constituyente y la legitimación de la monarquía de Isabel II en la reforma política de 1845' in *Culturas políticas monárquicas en la España liberal. Discursos, representaciones y prácticas (1808–1902)*, ed. Encarna García Monerris, Mónica Moreno Seco and Juan Marcuello Benedicto. Valencia: Universitat de València, 51–176.

Marcuello Benedicto, Juan Ignacio (2005). 'Gobierno y <parlamentarización> en el proceso político de la monarquía constitucional de Isabel II'. *Revista de Estudios Políticos* 130, 5–32.

Marichal, Juan (1971). 'From Pistoia to Cádiz: A Generation's Itinerary 1786–1812' in *The Ibero-American Enlightenment*, ed. Owen Aldridge. Chicago: University Press.

Martín Artajo, Alberto (1962). *Los españoles según Balmes. Conferencia pronunciada en el Salón de la Columna de las Casas Consistoriales, el día 28 de octubre de 1962, en la solemne sesión anual que el Excmo. Ayuntamiento de Vich organiza, en conmemoración de la muerte de su preclaro hijo el Dr. Jaime Balmes y Urpiá, pbro.* Vich: Imprenta Anglada.

Martínez Albiach, Alfredo (1969). *Religiosidad hispana y sociedad borbónica*, Burgos: Publicaciones de la Facultad Teológica del norte de España.

Matsumoto-Best, Saho (2003). *Britain and the Papacy in the Age of Revolution. 1846–1851.* Woodbridge & Rochester: Royal Historical Society / The Boydell Press.

Mehring, Reinhard (2020). 'Carl Schmitt, Spanien und Donoso Cortés'. *Zeitschrift für Politik* 67(1), 33–48.

Menczer, Bela (1951). *Catholic Political Thought, 1789–1848.* Notre Dame: University of Notre Dame Press.

Menéndez y Pelayo, Marcelino (1910). *Dos palabras sobre el centenario de Balmes. Discurso de Marcelino Menéndez y Pelayo leído en la sesión de clausura del Congreso Internacional de Apologética el día 11 de septiembre de 1910.* Vich: Imprenta G. Portavella.

Menéndez y Pelayo, Marcelino (1948). *Historia de los heterodoxos españoles.* Madrid: Consejo Superior de Investigaciones Científicas, vol. VI [Heterodoxia en el siglo XIX].

Menéndez Pidal, Ramón (1991). *Los españoles en su historia.* Madrid: Espasa Calpe.

Millán, Jesús (2009). 'La retropía del carlismo. Referentes y márgenes ideológicos' in *Utopías, quimeras y desencantos. El universo utópico en la España liberal*, ed. Manuel Suárez Cortina. Santander: Universidad de Cantabria, 255–281.

Molina, Fernando and Miguel Cabo Villaverde (2012). 'An Inconvenient Nation: Nation-Building and National Identity in Modern Spain. The Historiographical Debate' in *Nationhood from Below. Europe in the Long Nineteenth Century*, ed. Maarten Van Ginderachter and Marnix Beyen. Houndmills / New York: Palgrave Macmillan, 47–72.

Bibliography

Moliner Prada, Antonio (1998). 'Anticlericalismo y revolución liberal (1833–1874)' in *El anticlericalismo español contemporáneo*, ed. Emilio La Parra López and Manuel Suárez Cortina. Madrid: Biblioteca Nueva, 69–125.

Mould, Michael (2011). *The Routledge Dictionary of Cultural References in Modern French*. London & New York: Routledge.

Mücke, Ulrich (2008). *Gegen Aufklärung und Revolution. Die Entstehung konservativen Denkens in der iberischen Welt (1770–1840)*. Cologne/Weimar/Vienna: Böhlau Verlag.

Nockles, Peter B. (1994). *The Oxford Movement in Context. Anglican High Churchmanship, 1760–1857*. Oxford: University Press.

Noel, Charles C. (1985). 'Missionary Preachers in Spain: Teaching Social Virtue in the Eighteenth Century'. *The American Historical Review*, 90, 866–892.

Núñez Florencio, Rafael (2018). 'Culture' in *The History of Modern Spain. Chronologies, Themes, Individuals*, ed. José Álvarez Junco and Adrian Shubert, London/New York: Bloomsbury, 229–245.

Núñez Seixas, Xosé Manoel (2018a). *Suspiros de España. El nacionalismo español, 1908–2018*. Barcelona: Crítica.

Núñez Seixas, Xosé Manoel (2018b). 'Nation and Nationalism' in *The History of Modern Spain. Chronologies, Themes, Individuals*, ed. José Álvarez Junco and Adrian Shubert, London/New York: Bloomsbury. 149–164.

Orozco, Teresa (2010). 'Die katholische Ordnungsgedanke und der Preis seiner Säkularisierung: Carl Schmitt als Leser Donoso Cortés' in *Rechtsstaat anstatt Revolution, Verrechtlichung statt Demokratie?*, ed. Detlef Georgia Schulze, Münster: Westfalisches Dampfboot, 302–311.

Palti, Elías José (2014). 'The 'Theoretical Revolution' in Intellectual History: From the History of Political Ideas to the History of Political Languages'. *History and Theory* 53, 387–405.

Palti, Elías José (2007). *El tiempo de la política. El siglo XIX reconsiderado*. Buenos Aires: Siglo XXI.

Palti, Elías José (2006). 'The Problem of 'Misplaced Ideas' Revisited: Beyond the 'History of Ideas' in Latin America'. *Journal of the History of Ideas* 67(1), 149–179.

Pan-Montojo, Juan (2006). 'El progresismo isabelino' in *La redención del pueblo: la cultura progresista en la España liberal*, ed. Manuel. Suárez Cortina. Santander: Servicio de Publicaciones de la Universidad de Cantabria / Sociedad Menéndez Pelayo, 183–208.

Payne, Stanley (1978). 'Spanish Conservatism, 1834–1923'. *Journal of Contemporary History*, 13 (4), 765–789.

Payne, Stanley (1984). *Spanish Catholicism. An Historical Overview*. Madison: University of Wisconsin Press.

Perreau-Saussine, Emile (2011). *Catholicism and Democracy. An Essay in the History of Political Thought*. Princeton & Oxford: Princeton University Press.

Peyrou, Florencia (2015). 'La amenaza revolucionaria en Europa, 1815–1848' in *Donoso Cortés. El reto del liberalismo y la revolución*, ed. Carlos Dardé Morales. Madrid: Comunidad de Madrid, 87–114.

BIBLIOGRAPHY 223

Portero Molina, José Antonio (1978). *Púlpito e ideología en la España del siglo XIX*. Zaragoza: Libros Pórtico.

Portillo Valdés, José María (2000). *Revolución de nación. Orígenes de la cultura constitucional en España, 1780–1812*. Madrid: Boletín Oficial del Estado / Centro de Estudios Políticos y Constitucionales.

Pro Ruiz, Juan (2019). *La construcción del Estado en España. Una historia del siglo XIX*. Madrid: Alianza Editorial.

Pro Ruiz, Juan (2017). 'Poder político y económico en el Madrid de los moderados (1844–1854)'. *Ayer* 66(2), 27–55.

Pro Ruiz, Juan (2016). 'El Estado grande de los moderados en la España del siglo XIX'. *Historia y política* 36, 19–48.

Pro Ruiz, Juan (2006). 'La mirada del otro: el progresismo desde el moderantismo' in *La redención del pueblo: la cultura progresista en la España liberal*, ed. Manuel Suárez Cortina. Santander: Servicio de Publicaciones de la Universidad de Cantabria / Sociedad Menéndez Pelayo, 271–289.

Revuelta González, Manuel (1996). 'El proceso de secularización en España y las reacciones eclesiásticas' in *Librepensamiento y secularización en la Europa contemporánea*, ed. Pedro F. Álvarez Lazo. Madrid: Universidad Pontificia Comillas, 321–72.

Revuelta González, Manuel (2002). 'El anticlericalismo español en el siglo XIX' in *Religión y sociedad en España (siglos XIX y XX)*, ed. Paul Aubert. Madrid: Casa de Velázquez, 155–178.

Rivas, Manuel (2010). *Books Burn Badly*. Trans. Jonathan Dunne. London: Harvil Secker.

Roig y Gironella, Juan (1971). *Balmes, ¿qué diría hoy?* Madrid, Speiro.

Romeo Mateo, María Cruz (2021). 'La nación de la Iglesia en la España del siglo XIX' in *Católicos, reaccionarios y nacionalistas. Política e identidad nacional en Europa y América Latina contemporáneas*, ed. María Cruz Romeo, María Pilar Salomón and Nuria Tabanera. Madrid: Comares, 13–30.

Romeo Mateo, María Cruz (2015). 'Escritores neocatólicos en el espacio público liberal: el filtro de la "modernidad"' in *Donoso Cortés. El reto del liberalismo y la revolución*, ed. Carlos Dardé Morales. Madrid: Comunidad de Madrid, 115–144.

Romeo Mateo, María Cruz (2012). 'Las guerras civiles del siglo XIX: ¿una ruta excepcional hacia la modernización' in *¿Es España diferente. Una mirada comparativa (siglos XIX y XX)*, ed. Nigel Townson, José Álvarez Junco, María Cruz Romeo Mateo, Edward Malefakis and Pamela Radcliffe. Madrid: Taurus, 65–110.

Romeo Mateo, María Cruz (2011). '¿Qué es ser neocatólico? La crítica antiliberal de Aparisi y Guijarro' in *Por Dios, por la patria y por el rey'. Las ideas del carlismo. IV Jornadas de Estudio del Carlismo*. Pamplona: Gobierno de Navarra, 129–163.

Romeo Mateo, María Cruz (2006), 'La tradición progresista: historia revolucionaria, historia nacional' in *La redención del pueblo: la cultura progresista en la España liberal*, ed. Manuel Suárez Cortina. Santander: Servicio de Publicaciones de la Universidad de Cantabria / Sociedad Menéndez Pelayo, 81–113.

Romeo Mateo, María Cruz (1998). 'Lenguaje y política del nuevo liberalismo: moderados y progresistas, 1834–1845'. *Ayer* 29, 38–62.

Bibliography

Rosenberg, Daniel (2020). 'Two Visions of Europe: Nietzsche and Guizot' in *European/Supra-European: Cultural Encounters in Nietzsche's Philosophy*, ed. Marco Brusotti, Michael McNeal, Corinna Schubert and Herman Siemens. Berlin: De Gruyter, 129–140.

Rosenblatt, Nancy A. (1976). 'Church and State in Spain: A Study of Moderate Liberal Politics in 1845'. *The Catholic Historical Review* 62 (4), 589–603.

Rueda, Germán and Luis E. da Silveira (1993). 'Dos experiencias. España y Portugal'. *Ayer* 9(2), 19–27.

Rújula, Pedro and Javier Ramón Solans (2017). 'Paradojas de la reacción. Continuidades, vías muertas y procesos de modernización en el universo reaccionario del XIX' in *El desafío de la revolución. Reaccionarios, antiliberales y contrarrevolucionarios (siglos XVIII y XIX)*, ed. P. Rújula and J.F. Ramón Solans. Granada: Comares, 1–12.

Sánchez Agesta, Luis (1978). *Historia del constitucionalismo español*. Madrid: Centro de Estudios Constitucionales.

Sánchez Agesta, Luis (1979). *El pensamiento político del despotismo ilustrado*. Sevilla: Universidad de Sevilla.

Sánchez León, Pablo (2006). 'Aristocracia fantástica: los moderados y la poética del gobierno representativo', *Ayer* 61(1), 77–103.

Sánchez León, Pablo (2020). *Popular Political Participation and the Democratic Imagination in Spain. From Crowd to People, 1766–1868*. Cham: Palgrave Macmillan.

Seco Serrano, Carlos (2000). *Historia del conservadurismo español. Una línea política integradora en el siglo XIX*. Madrid: Temas de hoy.

Schaefer, Richard (2014). 'Political Theology and Nineteenth-Century Catholicism'. *Nineteenth-Century Contexts* 36 (3), 269–285.

Schmitt, Carl (2009). *Donoso Cortés in gesamteuropäischer Interpretation. Vier Aufsätze*. Berlin: Duncker & Humblot.

Schmitt, Carl. (2006). *Interpretación europea de Donoso Cortés* [conferences and articles written in 1922, 1927, 1929 & 1944]. Trad. Francisco de Asís Caballero. Buenos Aires: Struhart & Cía.

Schramm, Edmund (1936). *Donoso Cortés: su vida y pensamiento*. Trad. Ramón de la Serna. Madrid: Espasa Calpe.

Shubert, Adrian (1990). *A Social History of Modern Spain*. London: Unwin Hyman.

Silver, Philip W. (1997). *Ruin and Restitution. Reinterpreting Romanticism in Spain*. Nashville: Vanderbilt University Press.

Smith, Angel and Paul Garner (2017), 'Hispanism, Nationalism and the Hispanic Corridor' in *Nationalism and Transnationalism in Spain and Latin America, 1808–1923*, ed. A. Smith and P. Garner. Cardiff: University of Wales Press, 1–17.

Smith, Angel (2014). *The Origins of Catalan Nationalism. 1770–1898*. Houndmills / New York: Palgrave Macmillan.

Sperber, Jonathan (1994). *The European Revolutions, 1848–1851*. Cambridge: CUP.

Stedman Jones, Gareth (2016). *Karl Marx: Greatness and Illusion*. London: Penguin Books.

Steinel, James (1971). 'Balmes's Ideas On Religious Toleration'. *Journal of Church and State* 13, 69–77.

BIBLIOGRAPHY 225

Suárez Cortina, Manuel (2017). 'Republicanism, the Nation State and the Religious Question in Mexico and Spain (1851–1917): A Comparative Perspective' in *Nationalism and Transnationalism in Spain and Latin America, 1808–1923*, ed. Paul Garner and Angel Smith. Cardiff: University of Wales Press, 68–92.

Suárez Cortina, Manuel (2006). 'Introducción: libertad, progreso y democracia en la España liberal' in *La redención del pueblo: la cultura progresista en la España liberal*, ed. M. Suárez Cortina. Santander: Servicio de Publicaciones de la Universidad de Cantabria / Sociedad Menéndez Pelayo, 7–39.

Suárez Verdeguer, Federico (1964). *Introducción a Donoso Cortés*. Madrid: Ediciones Rialp.

Thomson, Guy (2017). '"Democracia": Popular Liberalism in Sicily, Mexico, Spain and Colombia, 1848–1894' in *Nationalism and Transnationalism in Spain and Latin America, 1808–1923*, ed. A. Smith and P. Garner. Cardiff: University of Wales Press, 93–116.

Tomás y Valiente, Francisco (1978). 'El proceso de desamortización de la tierra en España'. *Agricultura y Sociedad* 7, 11–33.

Tully, Carol (2007). *Johann Nikolas Böhl von Faber (1770–1836). A German Romantic in Spain*. Cardiff: University of Wales Press.

Tuñón de Lara, Manuel (1973). *Estudios sobre el siglo XIX español*. Madrid: Siglo Veintiuno Editores.

Turner, Frank M. (1990). 'The Victorian Crisis of Faith and the Faith that was Lost' in *Victorian Faith in Crisis. Essays on Continuity and Change in Nineteenth-Century Religious Belief*, ed. Richard Helmstadter. London: Macmillan.

Urigüen, Begoña (1986). *Orígenes y evolución de la derecha española: el neo-catolicismo*. Madrid: Centro de Estudios Históricos.

Valverde, Carlos (1979). 'Los católicos y la cultura española' in *Historia de la Iglesia en España*, ed. Ricardo García Villoslada. Madrid: Editorial Católica, V, 475–573.

Varela Suanzes, Joaquín (1995). 'La doctrina de la constitución histórica: de Jovellanos a las Cortes de 1845'. *Revista de Derecho Político* 39, 45–70.

Vilar, Juan Bautista (1994). *Intolerancia y libertad en al España contemporánea. Los orígenes del protestantismo español actual*. Madrid: Fundamentos Maior.

Villalonga, Borja (2014). 'The Theoretical Origins of Catholic Nationalism in Nineteenth-Century Europe'. *Modern Intellectual History* 11 (2), 307–31.

Villalonga, Borja (2012). 'La nación católica: Balmes y la representación de España en el ochochientos'. *Historia Social* 72, 49–64.

Wilson, Francis Graham (2004). *Order and Legitimacy. Political Thought in National Spain*, ed. H. Lee Cheek Jr, M. Susan Power, Kathy B. Cheek and Thomas J. Metallo. New Brunswick & London: Transaction Publishers, vol. 9, 201–16.

Index

Alcalá Galiano, Antonio 48, 49, 95, 96, 98, 144
Alvarado, Francisco de 27, 29
Aparisi y Guijarro, Antonio 197
Aquinas, Thomas 70
Argüelles, Agustín 95
Augustine of Hippo 141

Baralt, Rafael María 186, 187
Barante, Prosper de 46
Barruel, Augustin 26
Bellarmino, Roberto 70
Bentham, Jeremy 38
Bismarck, Otto von 200
Blanche-Raffin, Albéric de 64
Böhl de Faber, Nicolás 40, 41
Bonald, Louis de 49, 187
Borbón y Borbón, Francisco de Paula de 87
Borbón y Borbón-Dos Sicilias, Enrique de 87
Borbón y Borbón-Dos Sicilias, Francisco de Asís Luis de (husband of Isabel II) 19, 87, 89, 97
Borbón y Borbón-Dos Sicilias, Luisa Fernanda (sister of Isabel II) 87, 91
Borrego, Andrés 82
Bossuet, Jacques-Bénigne 141
Bravo Murillo, Juan 39, 148, 192, 193
Brochetón y Muguruza, Luis 74
Broglie, Victor de 46, 189

Brusi, Antonio 85
Byron, Lord George Gordon 39, 42

Caballero, Fernán 40
Cabet, Étienne 166
Cádiz, Diego José de 27, 28, 130
Calatrava, José María 52, 115
Calderón de la Barca, Pedro 39
Campoamor, Ramón de 50
Cánovas del Castillo, Antonio 94, 200
Cantù, Cesare 69
Carlos I, King of Spain 39, 179
Chateaubriand, François-René de 39, 42, 49, 65
Cleonard, Count of (Serafín María de Sotto) 82
Condillac, Étienne de 39, 51, 132
Condorcet, Nicolas de 142
Constant, Benjamin 51
Cortés, Hernán 38
Cousin, Victor 46, 48, 51, 132

De Maistre, Joseph 49, 176, 184, 187, 200
Destutt de Tracy, Antoine 38, 39, 132
Díaz, Nicomedes Pastor 82, 92, 171
Don Carlos (Carlos María Isidro de Borbón), Pretender to the Spanish Throne 14, 16, 29, 42–44, 49, 76, 83, 84, 87–91, 94, 99, 103, 129
Donoso Cortés, Pedro 140
Donoso, Pedro (father) 38

Dupanloup, Félix 65, 69, 191
Durán, Agustín 41, 42

Espartero, Baldomero 15, 18, 65, 73, 77–79, 85, 90, 95, 100, 117, 118

Ferguson, Adam 39, 51
Fernández Canedo, María Elena 38
Fernando VII, King of Spain 14, 17, 28, 38, 42, 47, 75, 94
Ferrer i Subirana, Josep 85
Ferrer, Magí 108, 164
Ferretti, Gabriele (Cardinal) 163
Fichte, Johann Gottlieb 51
Fornari, Raffaele (Cardinal) 194
Forner, Juan Pablo 57, 67
Fourier, Charles 102, 166
Francis I, Austrian Emperor 165
Franco, Francisco 69, 131
Frederick William IV of Prussia 172
Frexas, José 186

Gallardo, Bartolomé José 52
García Carrasco, Teresa 45
Gibbon, Edward 51
Giner de los Ríos, Francisco 198
Gioberti, Vincenzo 153
González Bravo y López de Arjona, Luis 81
Gregory XVI, Pope 119, 128
Guéranger, Dom 65
Guizot, François 15, 37, 42, 46–48, 53–57, 59, 62–66, 80, 121, 182, 189
Gutiérrez de la Concha e Irigoyen, Manuel 78

Hegel, Georg Wilhelm Friedrich 51, 132, 190
Helvétius, Claude-Adrien 39
Hervás y Panduro, Lorenzo 26
Herzen, Alexander 174, 175
Hitler, Adolf 184, 204
Hobbes, Thomas 177

Isabel II, Queen of Spain 14, 16–19, 42, 43, 74–84, 86–94, 96, 97, 99, 103, 109, 115, 119, 122, 128, 129, 131, 137, 141, 150, 161, 167–169, 172, 199

Jordan, Camille 46
Jovellanos, Gaspar Melchor de 94

Kant, Immanuel 51, 132
Ketteler, Wilhelm Immanuel von 153
Krause, Carl Christian Friedrich 198

Lacordaire, Henri 65
Lamennais, Félicité de 89, 108, 163
Larra, Mariano José de 40
Laverde, Gumersindo 150
Leibniz, Gottfried Wilhelm 132
Leo XIII, Pope 17, 69, 199
Lersundi, Francisco 192
Lista, Alberto 41, 46, 47
Locke, John 39, 51, 132
López Soler, Ramón 41
López, Joaquín María 79
Louis Philippe, King of France 18, 46, 87, 146, 157, 165, 166, 169
Louis XV, King of France 165
Louis XVI, King of France 26
Luther, Martin 55

Machiavelli, Niccolò 39
María Cristina de Borbón-Dos Sicilias 14, 18, 42, 52, 65, 76–81, 88, 91, 144, 148
Martínez de la Rosa, Francisco 39, 46, 47, 65, 74, 114
Martínez Marina, Francisco 95
Marx, Karl 186, 190
Masdeu, Juan Francisco 57
Masson de Morvilliers, Nicolas 56
Mateo, Tomás 163
Mateos, Nicomedes 184
Mendizábal, Juan Álvarez de 53, 115, 144
Menéndez y Pelayo, Marcelino 54, 68, 124, 200

INDEX

Metternich, Clemens von 156, 161, 165, 172
Michelet, Jules 51
Milans del Bosch, Lorenzo 78
Mon, Alejandro 81, 86, 123, 200
Montaigne, Michel de 39
Montalembert, Charles de 189–191, 195
Montemolín, Count (Carlos Luis de Borbón
y Braganza) 16, 83, 88–90, 109, 122, 131
Montesquieu, Charles de 39, 51
Montpensier, Duke of (D'Orléans, Antoine)
87, 91
Mora, José Joaquín 65
Moreno Nieto, José 197
Morón, Fermín Gonzalo 57, 58
Mozzi, Luigi 26
Muñoz, Agustín (Duke of Riánsares) 77,
80, 81, 91, 97, 144, 145, 148

Napoleon I (Napoleon Bonaparte) 190
Napoleon III (Louis-Napoléon Bonaparte)
172, 189, 190
Narváez, Ramón María 78, 81, 89, 90, 98,
109, 129, 144, 145, 148, 155, 168, 169, 173,
189, 198
Navarro Villoslada, Francisco 197
Newman, John Henry 65, 174
Nicholas I of Russia 161, 172
Niebuhr, Barthold Georg 51
Nocedal, Cándido 150, 197, 200
Nocedal, Ramón 200
Nonotte, Claude 26

Olavide, Pablo de 58
Olózaga, Salustiano 79, 80
Orovio, Manuel Marquis of 198
Ortí y Lara, Juan Manuel 150, 197
Owen, Robert 102
Ozanam, Frédéric 65, 189

Pacheco, Joaquín Francisco 39, 48, 82, 97,
98
Padilla, Juan de 39, 179
Pauw, Cornelius de 39

Persigny, Duke of (Jean-Gilbert Fialin) 189
Pezuela, Juan de la (Count of Cheste) 78,
82, 192
Pidal y Mon, Alejandro 200
Pidal, Pedro José 81, 86, 90, 93, 200
Pius IX, Pope 16, 20, 33, 129, 149, 150,
153–161, 168, 169, 181, 190, 191, 193–195
Prim y Prats, Juan 78
Proudhon, Pierre-Joseph 166, 174, 185, 186,
198

Quadrado, José María 88
Quintana, Manuel José 38, 39, 42

Raczyński, Athanasius 193
Ravignan, Gustave Delacroix de 65, 189
Reid, Thomas 51
Rémusat, Charles de 46
Riego, Rafael de 44
Ríos Rosas, Antonio 82, 144
Rivas, Manuel 204
Rivera, Primo de 69, 131
Roca i Cornet, Joaquim 85, 171
Roncali, Federico 192
Rosmini, Antonio 153, 156
Rossi, Pellegrino 169
Rousseau, Jean-Jacques 39, 51
Royer-Collard, Pierre 46, 48, 51, 53

Sagasta, Práxedes Mateo 200
Saint-Simon, Henri de 51, 102, 166
Salmerón, Nicolás 198
Sanz del Río, Julián 198
Sartorius, Luis José 81, 144, 193
Saxe-Coburg and Gotha, Leopold of 87
Schelling, Friedrich Wilhelm 51, 132
Schlegel, August Wilhelm and Friedrich 40
Schmitt, Carl 11, 204
Serrano y Domínguez, Francisco 78, 97
Sorrondegui, Amparo 78, 79
Staël, Madame de (Anne-Louise Germaine
Necker) 39, 42, 51
Suárez, Francisco 70

Tejado, Gabino 188, 192, 197
Tocqueville, Alexis de 189
Toreno, Conde de (José María Queipo del Llano) 47, 114
Trápani, Count of (Francisco de Paula de las Dos Sicilias) 87, 91

Valmy, Duke of (François Christophe Edmond de Kellermann) 191
Vélez, Rafael de 28, 29, 67, 130
Veuillot, Louis 64, 153, 155, 167, 174, 176, 188, 189, 191, 194

Vico, Giambattista 51
Viluma, Marquis of (Manuel de la Pezuela) 76, 82, 83, 85–87, 90, 107, 108, 122, 123, 192, 199
Vitoria, Francisco de 70
Voltaire (François-Marie Arouet) 39, 67
von Döllinger, Ignaz 153, 195

Wiseman, Nicholas 174

Zevallos, Fernando de 26, 28
Zorrilla, José 40